The
WISD☀M
for CREATING
HAPPINESS
and PEACE

REVISED EDITION

The WISDOM for CREATING HAPPINESS and PEACE

DAISAKU IKEDA

PART 1: HAPPINESS

Published by World Tribune Press
A division of the SGI-USA
606 Wilshire Blvd.
Santa Monica, CA 90401

© 2021 Soka Gakkai

All rights reserved.
Printed in the United States of America.

Cover and interior design by Lightbourne, Inc.

25 24 23 22 21   1 2 3 4 5

ISBN: 978-1-944604-56-1

Library of Congress Control Number: 2021941574

CONTENTS

Translator's Note xi
Preface xiii

PART 1: HAPPINESS

Chapter 1: What Is True Happiness?

1.1	Leading the Happiest of Lives	1
1.2	Absolute Happiness and Relative Happiness	5
1.3	Happiness Is Forged Amid Life's Challenges	9
1.4	Happiness Lies Within Us	12
1.5	Creating a Life of Genuine Freedom	15
1.6	The Six Conditions for Happiness	19
1.7	Confronting Life's Fundamental Sufferings Head-On	25

Chapter 2: Developing a Life State of Happiness

2.1	Living With Optimism	29
2.2	The Key to Happiness Is Inner Transformation	31
2.3	The Life State of Practitioners of the Mystic Law	33
2.4	Our Happiness Is Determined by Our Inner Life Condition	35
2.5	Happiness Is Found Where We Are	37
2.6	Activating the Limitless Life Force of Buddhahood	40
2.7	Establishing Buddhahood as Our Basic Life Tendency	44
2.8	You Are All Noble Buddhas	50

Chapter 3: The Practice for Transforming Our State of Life

3.1	The Gohonzon—the Fundamental Object of Devotion	53
3.2	"Never Seek This Gohonzon Outside Yourself"	58
3.3	The Gohonzon Is Found in Faith Alone	62
3.4	The Real Aspect and Power of the Gohonzon	68
3.5	The Gohonzon Is the "Mirror" That Reflects Our Lives	74
3.6	The Profound Meaning of Nam-myoho-renge-kyo	82
3.7	Embracing the Gohonzon Is in Itself Attaining Enlightenment	91
3.8	The Mystic Law Exists Within Our Lives	93
3.9	A Practice Accessible to All	99
3.10	Chanting Nam-myoho-renge-kyo Is the Key to Victory in Life	101
3.11	The Lotus Sutra Is a Scripture of Cosmic Humanism	104
3.12	Gongyo Encompasses the Heart of the Lotus Sutra	107
3.13	Gongyo—A Ceremony in Which Our Lives Commune With the Universe	111
3.14	Polishing Our Lives Through Chanting Nam-myoho-renge-kyo	114
3.15	Change Starts From Prayer	117
3.16	Chanting Nam-myoho-renge-kyo Freely	122
3.17	Chanting With Unwavering Conviction	124
3.18	Developing a Strong Inner Core	126
3.19	Faith Is a Lifelong Pursuit	129
3.20	The Universal Language of Buddhas and Bodhisattvas	131

Chapter 4: "It Is the Heart That Is Important"

4.1	Living With an Awareness of the Importance of the Heart	135
4.2	Appreciation and Joy Multiply Our Good Fortune	138
4.3	Those Who Smile Are Strong	140
4.4	Polishing Our Hearts to Shine Like Diamonds	142
4.5	Mastering Our Minds	144
4.6	Remaining True to One's Commitment in Faith	148

4.7	When Our Life State Changes, the World Around Us Changes	153
4.8	Devoting Ourselves to Our Mission	156
4.9	Nothing Is Ever Wasted in Buddhism	159
4.10	Cultivating a Lofty Life State Imbued With the Four Virtues	161

Chapter 5: Transforming Suffering Into Joy

5.1	We Are the Protagonists of Our Own Lives	165
5.2	"Earthly Desires Lead to Enlightenment"	170
5.3	"Changing Poison Into Medicine"	172
5.4	Creating the Future With the Buddhism of True Cause	173
5.5	Living With Joy Throughout All	177
5.6	Both Suffering and Joy Are Parts of Life	180
5.7	Difficulties Are a Driving Force for Growth	182
5.8	Polishing Ourselves Through Adversity	184
5.9	Winter Always Turns to Spring	186
5.10	The Principle of Lessening Karmic Retribution	193

Chapter 6: The Principle of Cherry, Plum, Peach, and Damson

6.1	"Still I Will Bloom"	197
6.2	Bringing Out Our Positive Qualities	200
6.3	Live True to Yourself	203
6.4	Appreciating Your Uniqueness	206
6.5	Developing Your Own Individuality	208
6.6	Be a Shining Presence Like the Sun	212
6.7	Advancing Freely and Steadily	217
6.8	Everyone Has a Noble Mission	218
6.9	Building a Harmonious World of Brilliant Diversity	220
6.10	The Wisdom for Fostering the Positive Potential in All People	222

Chapter 7: Happiness for Both Ourselves and Others

7.1	"'Joy' Means That Oneself and Others Together Experience Joy"	227
7.2	The Bodhisattva Way Enables Us to Benefit Both Ourselves and Others	229
7.3	The Path of Mutual Respect and Growth	231
7.4	Treasuring the People Right in Front of Us	234
7.5	We Are Enriched by Helping Others	237
7.6	The Bodhisattva Practice of Respecting All People	239
7.7	Accumulating Treasures of the Heart	241
7.8	The Supreme Path of Benefiting Others	244

Chapter 8: Facing Illness

8.1	Struggling With Illness Can Forge Invincible Spiritual Strength	247
8.2	Transforming the Sufferings of Birth, Aging, Sickness, and Death	250
8.3	Chanting Nam-myoho-renge-kyo Is the Wellspring of Life Force	254
8.4	Turning Illness Into an Impetus for Growth	256
8.5	Falling Ill Is Not a Sign of Defeat	258
8.6	The Buddhist View of Illness	262
8.7	"Faith" Means to Continue to Believe Until the Very End	267
8.8	"Laugh Off the Devil of Illness"	271
8.9	Four Mottoes for Good Health	276

Chapter 9: Creating a Brilliant Final Chapter in Life

9.1	Enjoying a Rewarding and Fulfilling "Third Stage of Life"	283
9.2	Striving to the End With a Spirit of Ceaseless Challenge	291
9.3	The Secret to a Vigorous Old Age	294
9.4	A Source of Hope and Inspiration for a Happy Aging Society	297
9.5	Building an "Eternal Palace" in Our Lives	300

9.6	There Is No Retirement From Faith	303
9.7	Changing Our Attitude Toward Aging	305
9.8	Making an Art of Life	311

Chapter 10: Joy in Both Life and Death

10.1	Consolidating the State of Buddhahood in This Lifetime	315
10.2	Death Gives Greater Meaning to Life	320
10.3	The Buddhist View of Life That Transcends the Suffering of Death	322
10.4	The Oneness of Life and Death	325
10.5	Savoring Joy in Both Life and Death	327
10.6	Advancing on the Path of Buddhahood in Both Life and Death	334
10.7	The Death of Someone Close to Us	338
10.8	Our Own Attainment of Buddhahood Enables the Deceased to Attain Buddhahood	341
10.9	Ties Based on the Mystic Law Are Eternal	343
10.10	Sudden and Untimely Deaths	346
10.11	Clear Proof of Attaining Buddhahood	350
10.12	Transforming the Sufferings of Birth and Death	353

Glossary   357

Notes   365

Index   373

About the Author   387

TRANSLATOR'S NOTE

The excerpts from SGI President Ikeda's writings contained in this volume have been selected from a huge variety of original sources covering many decades and including speeches, essays, lectures, and dialogues. Many of these writings have previously been published in English, but as part of the process of preparing this volume the translations have been checked and, where necessary, revised to ensure accuracy and consistency. The source information provided for each excerpt refers to the original Japanese text (the date and location a speech or lecture was delivered, the date and publication data for books, essays, dialogues, etc.).

The excerpts include in-text citations for the core texts of the Buddhism practiced by Soka Gakkai members. These consist of *The Lotus Sutra and Its Opening and Closing Sutras*, translated by Burton Watson (Tokyo: Soka Gakkai, 2009) (LSOC); *The Record of the Orally Transmitted Teachings*, translated by Burton Watson (Tokyo: Soka Gakkai, 2004) (OTT); and *The Writings of Nichiren Daishonin* vol. 1 (Tokyo: Soka Gakkai, 1999) (WND-1) and vol. 2 (Tokyo: Soka Gakkai, 2006) (WND-2). The sources for other works cited are to be found in the endnotes, along with a brief explanation of some Buddhist terminology. For further reference, please visit www.sokaglobal.org.

PREFACE

"Let Us Encourage Each Other and Advance Together"

The conversation I had with my mentor, Josei Toda, on the day we first met is still vivid in my mind today:

"Sensei, I would like to ask you a question."
"What would you like to know? Go ahead, ask whatever you wish."
"What is the correct way to live?"

It was the summer of 1947, two years after the end of World War II. In response to this earnest question from a nineteen-year-old youth seeking direction in life in the troubled postwar period, Mr. Toda was warm and embracing, like a compassionate father. He was a mentor who prized above all young people's desire to learn.

With powerful conviction, he introduced me to the life philosophy of Nichiren Daishonin and encouraged me to study and practice it with youthful energy and idealism. From that moment on, I steadfastly pursued the path of mentor and disciple, eagerly seeking instruction from Mr. Toda, whom I had taken as my mentor in life and in the eternal endeavor for kosen-rufu.

Ninety-eight percent of what I am today I learned from my mentor, at what I refer to as "Toda University." I once shared this point in a lecture I delivered at Columbia University Teachers College.

For Mr. Toda, a peerless humanistic educator and a leader of the people, the essence of both education and guidance in faith was encouragement. He inherited this spirit, which has today become a proud tradition of Soka, from his own mentor, Tsunesaburo Makiguchi, the Soka Gakkai's founder, who died in prison for his beliefs.

Nichiren Daishonin affirms that "The Lotus Sutra is the teaching that enables all living beings to attain the Buddha way" (WND-1, 59). The Daishonin's Buddhism of the Sun, revealing the essence of the Lotus Sutra, is a source of compassion and wisdom that can illuminate the hearts of all people. In *The Record of the Orally Transmitted Teaching*s, he states: "Great joy [is what] one experiences when one understands for the first time that one's mind [or life] from the very beginning has been a Buddha. Nam-myoho-renge-kyo is the greatest of all joys" (OTT, 211–12).

Encouragement in the realm of Soka means shining the light of the Mystic Law on each person, awakening their inherent Buddhahood, and revitalizing their lives at the most fundamental level.

As members of the Soka family, we have always reached out to support those around us, no matter how deep their sorrow, how great their despair, or how challenging their karma. We have stood together with them, encouraging them to be confident that they can surmount any hardship, find a way forward, and become happy without fail.

This great grassroots movement, undaunted by any manner of oppression, has spread throughout the world, unleashing life's innate power, fostering diverse individuals, each as unique as "the cherry, the plum, the peach, the damson" (OTT, 200), and enabling people everywhere to triumph in their own human revolution.

It is no exaggeration to say that this movement of, by, and for the people—built upon unshakable principles and beautiful unity that seeks to empower all—is the hope of global society.

Natural disasters, pandemics, and other ongoing trials afflict people in every corner of the world, and words of encouragement play a crucial role in strengthening community ties and fortifying the resilience to rise to the challenge of various crises.

In Buddhism, the ideal of leadership is symbolized by the wheel-turning sage king, a monarch who governs with what is called a wheel treasure. Nichiren Daishonin offers the following observation:

> To go round and round unendingly in the cycle of birth and death, birth and death, throughout

the three existences of past, present, and future, is what is called being a wheel-turning sage king. The wheels that the wheel-turning sage kings possess when they make their appearance in the world, their "wheel treasures" are the words and sounds that we ourselves utter. And these sounds, our "wheel treasures," are Nam-myoho-renge-kyo. This is what is called "the great wisdom of equality." (OTT, 76)

While steadfastly chanting Nam-myoho-renge-kyo and grappling with our own and others' sufferings of birth, aging, sickness, and death, our words of conviction and earnest encouragement that triumph over all malicious slurs and lies are like our very own "wheel treasures" that we are turning around the globe. Inheriting this great humanistic spirit, our youthful global citizens of Soka are currently dynamically engaged in the shared endeavor to achieve the United Nations Sustainable Development Goals, which are based on the fundamental wish that no one be left behind.

My mentor has been a constant presence in the depths of my heart in my ongoing efforts to speak and write about kosen-rufu and the meaning of life, Buddhism and society, peace and the dignity of life, youth and the future, and many other topics.

The writings, speeches, lectures, dialogues, and poetry from my lifelong struggle of words, one in spirit with my mentor, have been compiled into 150 volumes of collected works. As the compilation process was nearing completion, some of our enterprising members, brimming with youthful spirit, proposed the idea of compiling a selection of excerpts from that collection for the new era of worldwide kosen-rufu. Motivating this project was their enthusiasm to produce a common study resource for our members around the world. Adopting the title "The Wisdom for Creating Happiness and Peace," they set about choosing excerpts covering a range of themes and coordinating the translation of these selections.

I am delighted by their noble spirit of voluntarily taking on this time-consuming and challenging task. They have exerted themselves tirelessly to respond to the ardent seeking spirit of their fellow members, to promote the united progress of worldwide kosen-rufu, and to support the efforts of future generations of members to study Nichiren Buddhism and the Soka Gakkai spirit.

The results of their dedicated work were published in monthly installments in the Soka Gakkai's study magazine, *Daibyakurenge*. As I reviewed the page proofs, I felt as if I were engaging in a fresh dialogue with my beloved disciples.

Over the four years during which those installments were published in Japanese, painstaking efforts were made to translate them and ensure that readers around the world could access them. I am pleased they, along with additional excerpts, are now being published in book form, and I would like to express my boundless gratitude to all those involved in this task.

I would like to dedicate this book, a collection of words of encouragement that embody the oneness of mentor and disciple, to Presidents Makiguchi and Toda and entrust it to our precious successors.

Nichiren Daishonin states:

> When teacher and disciples have fully responded to one another and the disciples have received the teaching, so that they gain the awakening referred to where the sutra says, "I took a vow, hoping to make all persons equal to me, without any distinction between us," this is what the sutra calls "causing living beings to awaken to the Buddha wisdom." (OTT, 30)

As mentors and disciples committed to fulfilling the vow of the Bodhisattvas of the Earth, let us demonstrate at all times and in all places the "wisdom of the truth that functions in accordance with changing circumstances" (OTT, 10). President Toda calls to us in one of his poems that I treasure:

> The journey to propagate
> the Mystic Law
> is long;
> let us encourage each other
> and advance together.

PREFACE

Let us, therefore, "encourage each other and advance together" as we continue on our journey to propagate the Mystic Law into the eternal future of the Latter Day of the Law!

Nothing would give me greater pleasure than if this book provides encouragement and sustenance to Soka Gakkai members everywhere as they proceed along that path.

—On August 14, 2020, the seventy-third anniversary of the start of my journey of kosen-rufu alongside my mentor.

Daisaku Ikeda

WHAT IS TRUE HAPPINESS?

1.1 Leading the Happiest of Lives

President Ikeda's conception of happiness is an inspiring teaching for all, imparting courage to those overwhelmed by suffering and hope to those shrouded in despair. This first chapter introduces this all-embracing concept of happiness.

In this selection, President Ikeda responds to questions from members in Thailand about the purpose of life and how we should live our lives.

"How do I live my life?" "How can I live the very best life?"—these are fundamental questions. How to live is an inescapable issue that confronts all who are born in this world, one that has been pursued by countless philosophies, ideologies, and religions. At the most basic level, politics, economics, and science, too, are inseparable from this issue. Their original purpose is to help people live the happiest of lives. None of these areas of human endeavor, however, can provide an answer to the question "What constitutes the best life?" They have no clear or conclusive answer that is rationally convincing.

Buddhism supplies a coherent answer to this question. Shakyamuni Buddha, the Great Teacher T'ien-t'ai, and Nichiren Daishonin each set forth a clear response. In particular, the conclusions of Shakyamuni and the Daishonin are exactly the same.

Moreover, based on his conclusion, Nichiren Daishonin left behind a concrete "tool" that all people can use to become happy. He bestowed the Gohonzon—which second Soka Gakkai president Josei Toda referred to as a "happiness-producing device"—upon all humankind.

What is the definition of *human happiness*? There is a Thai saying: "False happiness makes people become haughty and arrogant. Real happiness makes people joyful and fills them with wisdom and compassion."

Is one happy just because one is wealthy? All too many people have allowed money to ruin their lives.

President Toda stressed the importance of absolute happiness over relative happiness. Absolute happiness is not how one stands compared with others, nor is it a transitory, illusory happiness that fades with the passing of time. Mr. Toda taught that we practice Nichiren Buddhism to attain a state of life in which, no matter what circumstances we may encounter, we can feel that life itself is a joy. When we attain that state of life, our lives overflow with unsurpassed joy, wisdom, and compassion—just as the Thai proverb says, "Real happiness makes people joyful and fills them with wisdom and compassion."[1]

The Daishonin states, "Both oneself and others together will take joy in their possession of wisdom and compassion" (OTT, 146). Our practice of Nichiren Buddhism and our organization for kosen-rufu exist so that we, and also others, may attain absolute happiness.

All kinds of things happen in life. There is sorrow, there is suffering. Every day, there are things we may find unpleasant or annoying. Married couples may sometimes quarrel. Even if a couple does get on well, they may have a sick child, or one of them may suffer illness. We face all kinds of sufferings and problems. How formidable are the challenges of living!

Faith is the engine that enables us to persevere in life to the very end. Our Buddhist practice serves as the propulsive force for piercing through the clouds of suffering like a rocket and powerfully ascending higher and higher, without limit, to fly serenely through the skies of happiness.

When we chant Nam-myoho-renge-kyo, hope and the strength to always live positively surge within us. Buddhism teaches that earthly desires—deluded impulses that are a cause of suffering—can be a springboard to enlightenment. Through faith in the Mystic Law, we can develop the ability to change all that is negative in our lives into something positive. We can transform all problems into happiness, sufferings into joy, anxiety into hope, and worry into peace of mind. We will always be able to find a way forward.

The Daishonin writes, "*Myo* [of *myoho*, the Mystic Law] means to revive, that is, to return to life" (WND-1, 149). It is the immense power of the Mystic Law that gives vitality to and breathes fresh life into all things, including individuals, organizations, societies, and nations.

As human beings, we also possess our own unique karma. You may wish you could have been born into a wealthier family, but the reality is that you weren't. There are many areas in life where karma comes into play. Essentially, the concept of karma can be understood only when viewed from the perspective of life's eternity over the three existences of past, present, and future. There are past existences and the law of cause and effect to take into account.

And these past existences may not necessarily all have been on this planet. Many in astronomy and related fields today think that, given the enormously vast numbers of stars and planets in the known universe, other intelligent life forms similar to human beings must exist.

In any case, our present reality is that we have been born here on Earth. This is an inalterable fact. How can we discover our true path? How can we change our karma and build a truly wonderful and meaningful existence? The answer is, in short, by embracing faith in the Mystic Law. Through our practice of Nichiren Buddhism, we can change any negative karma and transform the place where we are into the Land of Tranquil Light, a place overflowing with happiness.

Moreover, Nichiren Buddhism focuses on the present and the future. By always moving forward from this moment on, we can develop our lives boundlessly. We can also open up infinite possibilities for our next life and lifetimes after that. We can reveal the immeasurable treasures within us and make our lives shine with the full brilliance of those treasures. Such is the power of practicing Nichiren Buddhism.

From a speech at a Soka Gakkai Thailand general meeting, Bangkok, Thailand, February 6, 1994.

1.2 Absolute Happiness and Relative Happiness

How, in the face of the sufferings of birth, aging, sickness, and death, can we lead positive and fulfilling lives? In this selection, President Ikeda describes a life of limitless value creation in pursuit of absolute happiness by cultivating a strong life force and bounteous wisdom.

What is the purpose of life? It is happiness. The goal of Buddhism and of faith, too, is to become happy.

Nichiren Daishonin writes: "There is no true happiness for human beings other than chanting Nam-myoho-renge-kyo. The [Lotus Sutra] reads, '. . . where living beings enjoy themselves at ease'" (WND-1, 681). "Enjoy themselves at ease" here means being freely able to live the kind of life one desires and wholeheartedly enjoying that life.

If you possess strong life force and abundant wisdom, it is possible to enjoy the challenge of overcoming life's hardships in much the same way that waves make surfing exhilarating and steep mountains give mountaineering its appeal.

Because the Mystic Law is the source of the life force and wisdom for overcoming life's difficulties, the Daishonin states that there is no greater happiness than chanting Nam-myoho-renge-kyo.

Reality is harsh. Please courageously challenge the stern realities of life and win, and win again, in everything—in daily life, work, school, and family relations. The teachings of Buddhism and our practice of faith are the driving force for unlimited improvement.

Where people possess wisdom and life force derived from their Buddhist practice, they can move everything in a brighter, more positive, and more encouraging direction. Wise, genuine practitioners of Nichiren Buddhism are able to enter into a winning rhythm in actuality, not just in theory.

Second Soka Gakkai president Josei Toda gave the following guidance on happiness:

> I would like to say a few words about happiness. There are two kinds of happiness: absolute happiness and relative happiness. Absolute happiness is attaining Buddhahood. . . . Relative happiness means that your everyday wishes are fulfilled one by one—for

instance, to have a million yen, a wonderful spouse, fine children, a nice house or clothes, and so on. . . . Such happiness is not of great consequence. Yet everyone is convinced that this is what being happy is all about.

What, then, is absolute happiness? Absolute happiness means that being alive and here itself is a joy. . . . It also implies a state where one is free of financial worries and enjoys adequate good health, where there is peace and harmony in one's family and one's business prospers, and where all that one sees and hears brings one a wonderful sense of pleasure and joy. When we achieve such a state of life, this world, this strife-ridden saha world, will itself become a pure land. This is what we call attaining the state of Buddhahood. . . .

How can we achieve this? We must shift from the pursuit of relative happiness to that of absolute happiness. Only our practice of Nichiren Buddhism can make this happen. I'm working furiously to share this truth with others; so I hope you will have utter confidence in my words and lead such lives [of absolute happiness].[2]

Founding Soka Gakkai president Tsunesaburo Makiguchi once said: "There are some people who go around saying, 'I saved the money I wanted, bought the house I wanted, so now I can sit back, enjoy a drink, and indulge in a few luxuries. What more can I want in life than that?' This kind of person has no understanding of the true purpose of life." On this point, Mr. Makiguchi clearly stated, "The purpose of life is to create supreme value and to attain the greatest happiness."

The name Soka Gakkai (literally, "Value-Creating Society") means an organization whose members are committed to creating supreme value and attaining the greatest happiness.

The purpose of life is to realize this kind of happiness, in other words, absolute happiness. Absolute happiness is something that doesn't change with time; it is eternal and unaffected by external factors, welling forth from the depths of one's life. It is not a transitory thing like worldly status and fortune or some other fleeting satisfaction.

What matters is living in accord with the Law and attaining an elevated state of life based on the Law. The state of life we attain, like the Law itself, is eternal. As practitioners of Nichiren Buddhism, we can make our way as champions of life throughout eternity.

Some people say that happiness is just a state of mind and that if you think you're happy you will be, even if you're suffering from illness or poverty. But if it's just something you're telling yourself without actually feeling any real sense of happiness in the depths of your being, then it's ultimately meaningless.

The "treasures of the heart" that we accumulate through our practice of Nichiren Buddhism will manifest in our lives over time as "treasures of the body" and "treasures of the storehouse" (see WND-1, 851).

Every day, I am earnestly praying that you may enjoy comfortable lives, good health, and longevity. And I will continue to pray wholeheartedly for this as long as I live. It is my ardent wish that you each fulfill all of your heart's desires, so that you can declare in your closing days: "My life has been a happy one. I have no regrets. It has been a satisfying life."

From a speech at a Rio de Janeiro general meeting,
Brazil, February 13, 1993.

1.3 Happiness Is Forged Amid Life's Challenges

True happiness is not a matter of chance. It is forged through our earnest efforts to grapple with life's many challenges.

I would like to talk a little about the subject of happiness. Happiness is the fundamental goal of life. It is also the goal of faith. And it is the goal of Buddhism. It is extremely important, then, to understand just what happiness is. I think it is fair to say that people in all ages and places have earnestly sought the answer to the question "What is happiness?" and that, for all too many today, it still remains unanswered.

The WISDOM for CREATING HAPPINESS and PEACE, Part 1

Some possess great material wealth but are unhappy, perhaps becoming mean spirited or doing nothing but fighting and quarreling with others. On the other hand, it is quite possible to be materially poor yet enjoy great happiness, being purehearted and seeing the beauty in all things like a poet.

Happiness is something very personal. Of two people in similar circumstances, one may be unhappy and the other happy. People are all different and perceive things differently. The reality of people's lives is infinitely diverse.

For instance, there are many women who, though they seem to have good fortune when they are single—possessing youth, beauty, and wealth—end up extremely sad and unhappy when they get married. Living like a princess in a palace, eating food from gold plates, and wearing stylish, immaculate clothing is not happiness. It is in fact stifling and boring, illusory and empty. Though people in such circumstances may seem to be very happy, it is all a show; in reality, their happiness is very fragile and fleeting.

Some, on the other hand, may appear to be suffering misfortune but are, with strong determination and dignity, forging a life state of happiness that is like a magnificent painting.

By surviving the tragic misfortunes of youth and experiencing many times the hardship of others, we can lead lives that are many times richer, filled with tremendous vitality and inner strength in our final chapter.

If our lives are always smooth sailing, we'll never be able to savor real happiness. It goes without saying that the treasure of happiness cannot be found in a life of ease and idleness. The diamond of happiness can be found only by making our way into the deep mountain recesses of life with great effort and exertion. It is not to be found in idly seeking fun and pleasure amid the bustle and bright lights of the city or in leading an easy existence.

The renowned Scottish poet Robert Burns had this to say about happiness in one of his verses [that in Standard English translation reads]:

> If happiness have not her seat
> And center in the breast,
> We may be wise, or rich, or great,
> But never can be blessed!
> No treasures nor pleasures
> Could make us happy long:
> The heart always is the part always
> That makes us right or wrong.³

In other words, happiness and unhappiness, ultimately, are found within us. As Nichiren Daishonin says, "It is the heart that is important" (WND-1, 1000).

From a message to a nationwide young women's division leaders meeting, Japan, June 16, 1999.

1.4 Happiness Lies Within Us

In this selection, President Ikeda outlines the Buddhist way of life—opening the palace of happiness within our lives instead of seeking it outside, and helping others do the same.

Where is the palace of happiness, the indestructible bastion of happiness, that so many are eagerly seeking? And how is it to be acquired?

In *The Record of the Orally Transmitted Teachings*, Nichiren Daishonin states, "Chanting Nam-myoho-renge-kyo is what is meant by entering the palace of oneself" (OTT, 209).

The indestructible life state of Buddhahood exists within us all. It could be described as an everlasting palace of happiness, adorned with countless glittering treasures. By embracing faith in the Mystic Law and chanting Nam-myoho-renge-kyo, we can enter this palace within our lives. In other words, the Daishonin teaches that we have the capacity to make the "palace of oneself" shine with supreme brilliance.

People seek all kinds of worldly "palaces of happiness." Some seek wealth or social standing, while others wish for fame, celebrity, or popularity. But none of those things have the permanence of a steadfast mountain peak. In our ever-changing existences, they are like the light of fireflies, flickering beautifully but destined to fade and disappear all too soon.

A life spent in pursuit of the ephemeral, transitory glories of the world is also ephemeral and transitory. Chasing eagerly after forms of happiness that are insubstantial and impermanent is a sad and empty way to live.

As the Daishonin says, one's own highest state of life is an eternal and indestructible palace, a true bastion of happiness.

People may live in fine houses or possess great wealth, but if their hearts are mean and their life conditions are low, they will not be truly happy; they will be dwelling in palaces of misery. In contrast, people who have beautiful, generous hearts and a high life condition, irrespective of their present circumstances, are certain to attain both material and spiritual happiness. This accords with the Buddhist principle of the oneness of life and its environment—that our lives and our surroundings are one and inseparable.

When we open the palace of our own lives, it will eventually lead to the "palace of happiness" opening in others' lives and the "palace of prosperity" opening in society. There is an underlying continuity between the process of opening one's own palace and others doing likewise. This is a wonderful principle of Buddhism.

In today's complex society, where it is all too easy to succumb to negative influences, the wisdom to live mindfully and meaningfully is crucial. Our Buddhist practice enables us to open up our lives and become happy. By continuing to develop and deepen our faith and wisdom, we can become true champions as human beings and ongoing victors in the journey of life.

Supreme happiness is savored by those who, through practicing Nichiren Buddhism, make the palace of their lives shine eternally throughout the three existences of past, present, and future.

You are each building and opening your own palace of happiness day by day through your activities for kosen-rufu. You are certain, as a result, to attain Buddhahood in this lifetime and to become noble champions of happiness dwelling in a great palace of life as vast as the universe itself. I hope you will continue forging ahead on the great path of faith with confidence and optimism, filled with strong conviction and pride.

From a speech at a Nagano Prefecture general meeting, Karuizawa, Japan, August 12, 1990.

1.5 Creating a Life of Genuine Freedom

At the First Nationwide Women's Division Leaders Meeting in April 1988, President Ikeda proposed designating May 3 as Soka Gakkai Mother's Day. In his speech at this historic meeting, he discussed what it means to live with true freedom.

What is freedom? How can we fully enjoy freedom? Countless sages and philosophers over the centuries have pondered this. In fact, quite apart from this intellectual quest, all people long for freedom. People wish to live freely, without constraints or limitations. This is an innate human desire. Even if we can't clearly define it, we all know that freedom is a vital condition for happiness.

And though all seek freedom, very few attain it in the truest sense.

How can human beings themselves change, and how can we gain an understanding of the real nature of life? These are the most fundamental challenges facing humanity. In this respect, the religious revolution we of the Soka Gakkai are carrying out based on the principles of Nichiren Buddhism is key. You are all noble trailblazers in this endeavor.

Our environment is important, but it is not everything, nor is it absolute. Mr. Toda attained a life state of eternal freedom in a prison cell, the most constrained of environments.

Some of you may feel as if you're "fettered" by your mother-in-law, or "tied down" by your children! Or your husband, your household chores, or your job may at times all seem like heavy iron chains!

In your activities for kosen-rufu, too, things may happen that weigh you down so much that you feel bound and tied.

You might exclaim to yourself: "Ah, I'm just a prisoner!" "I'm a servant to my husband and children!"

You may envy some people for the apparent ease of their lives, but if you look closely, you will find that they have no real freedom either.

We must develop inner freedom—a true freedom that exists on a deeper level than what we can achieve by simply changing our intellectual outlook or point of view.

In *The Record of the Orally Transmitted Teachings*, the Daishonin states: "Outside of each instant of thought of our deluded minds there is no Buddha mind. The births and deaths of [us living beings of] the nine worlds are the true reality. . . . , and hence we can 'freely choose.' Chanting Nam-myoho-renge-kyo is being 'free to choose'" (OTT, 212). In other words, the world of Buddhahood does not exist apart from our deluded lives as ordinary people in the nine worlds [the life states of hell through bodhisattva]. Throughout the cycle of birth and death, we have been fettered by earthly desires, karma, and suffering, but when illuminated by the Mystic Law, our lives reveal their true inherent nature and become utterly free. By chanting Nam-myoho-renge-kyo, the Daishonin tells us, we can live with absolute freedom.

Freedom is not found somewhere apart from the seeming constraints of the nine worlds, of life's realities. Nor is true freedom found in escaping reality. Where is there to escape to? We can't escape from the universe. And more important, we can't escape from our own lives.

As long as we are fettered by karma, afflicted by weakness, defeated by suffering, and held back by misguided ways of thinking, we'll never find freedom anywhere.

The Daishonin says, "Now is the time to break free from the bonds of this realm of birth and death" (WND-2, 333). The practice of the Mystic Law—chanting Nam-myoho-renge-kyo—is the sword that severs the chains of delusion that shackle us.

The life state of Buddhahood brings us true freedom. It is a state of supreme freedom spanning the three existences—past, present, and future—that brims with the power and wisdom to develop our lives as we wish in accord with our determination in faith. The Mystic Law is the ultimate principle for attaining genuine freedom in the real world.

As the Daishonin states in *The Record of the Orally Transmitted Teachings*, "The Thus Come One eternally endowed with the three bodies [the Dharma body, reward body, and manifested body], his [eternal] life span, the distinctions of benefits, the benefits of responding with joy [on hearing the Mystic Law]—all these are matters that pertain to one's own person. Hence the six sense organs that one received at the time of birth from one's father and mother are all clean and pure and operate freely and without obstruction" (OTT, 235).

The Daishonin tells us that all these qualities and benefits he enumerates apply to us. They are taught in the "Life Span" (sixteenth), "Distinctions in Benefits" (seventeenth), "The Benefits of Responding with Joy" (eighteenth), and "Benefits of the Teacher of the Law" (nineteenth) chapters of the Lotus Sutra.

Each word and phrase of the Lotus Sutra has direct relevance to our lives. The teachings of Nichiren Buddhism are not abstract ideals.

In particular, the Daishonin states that the six sense organs—namely, sight, hearing, smell, taste, touch, and consciousness, which we are born with and constitute our physical and mental awareness—are originally pure, free, and unobstructed.

The purpose of our Buddhist faith and practice is to achieve such a state of untrammeled personal freedom. True and eternal freedom is attained by living aligned and in rhythm with the Mystic Law, by chanting Nam-myoho-renge-kyo and sharing it with others.

This is the way to become an awakened, liberated person, to achieve a free, expansive, unobstructed state of being, and lead a truly unencumbered life in which we can savor the utmost happiness and joy to our heart's content. That's why no matter what happens, we must never stop practicing.

The religious revolution the Soka Gakkai is carrying out is a struggle to liberate humanity, to liberate all people, so that they can enjoy eternal inner freedom.

Such inner freedom doesn't come by sitting around and

waiting for it; it must be fought for and won. To that end, I ask that each of you strive to gain mastery over yourself. A commitment to self-mastery is the foundation from which everything will follow in accord with the Buddhist principle of consistency from beginning to end, enabling you to create a life of genuine happiness and freedom.

From a speech at a nationwide women's division leaders meeting, Tokyo, Japan, April 27, 1988.

1.6 The Six Conditions for Happiness

President Ikeda presents six points for attaining happiness in this speech at an SGI general meeting in the United States and stresses that all of them are included in the practice of Nichiren Buddhism.

In his writings, Nichiren Daishonin states, "You must not spend your lives in vain and regret it for ten thousand years to come" (WND-1, 622).

How should we live our lives? What is the most valuable and worthwhile way to live? A well-known Japanese poem goes: "The life of a flower is short / Sufferings only are there many."[4] The meaning of these lines is that flowers suddenly come into bloom and then, just as suddenly, their petals fall and scatter; ultimately, the only thing that lasts for a long time is suffering. Life, indeed, may be like that in some ways.

A philosopher once remarked that perhaps the only way to determine happiness or unhappiness in life is by adding up, at the end of one's days, all the joys and all the sorrows one had experienced and basing one's final evaluation on whichever figure was larger.

Despite having illustrious positions in society or great material wealth, there are many people who fail to become happy. Despite enjoying wonderfully happy marriages or relationships, people must ultimately be parted from the person they love through death. Being separated from loved ones is one of the unavoidable sufferings inherent in the human condition. There are many who, despite gaining great fame and popularity, die after long, agonizing illnesses. Despite being born with exceptional beauty, not a few have been brought to misery by this seeming advantage.

Where is happiness to be found? How can we become happy? These are fundamental questions of life, and human beings are no doubt destined to pursue them eternally. The teachings of Nichiren Buddhism and faith in the Mystic Law provide fundamental answers to these questions.

Ultimately, happiness rests on our establishing a solid sense of self. Happiness based on such externals as possessing a fine house or a good reputation is "relative happiness." It is not a firm, unchanging "absolute happiness." Some might seem to be in the most fortunate circumstances, but

WHAT IS TRUE HAPPINESS?

if they feel only emptiness and pain, then they cannot be considered happy.

Some people live in truly splendid houses yet do nothing but fight in them. Some people work for famous companies and enjoy a prestige that many envy yet are always being shouted at by their superiors, are left exhausted from heavy workloads, and feel no sense of joy or fulfillment in life.

Happiness does not lie in outward appearances or in vanity. It is a matter of what we feel inside; it is a deep resonance in our lives. I would venture, therefore, that the first condition for happiness is fulfillment.

To be filled each day with a rewarding sense of exhilaration and purpose, a sense of tasks accomplished and deep fulfillment—people who feel this way are happy. Those who have this sense of satisfaction even if they are extremely busy are much happier than those who have free time on their hands but feel empty inside.

As practitioners of Nichiren Buddhism, we get up in the morning and do gongyo. Some perhaps may do so rather reluctantly! Nevertheless, doing gongyo is itself a truly great and noble thing. Gongyo is a solemn ceremony in which we are, in a manner of speaking, gazing out across the universe; it is a dialogue with the universe.

Doing gongyo and chanting daimoku before the Gohonzon represent the dawn, the start of a new day, in our lives; it is the sun rising; it gives us a profound sense of contentment in the depths of our being that nothing can surpass. Even on this point alone, we are truly fortunate.

Some people appear to be happy but actually start off the day feeling depressed. A husband might be admonished by his wife in the morning and begin his day dejected, wondering, "How on earth did I get into such a marriage?" He will savor neither happiness nor contentment. Just by looking at our mornings, it is clear that we in the SGI lead lives of profound worth and satisfaction.

In addition, each of you is striving to do your best in your job or other responsibilities and to win in all areas of life while using your spare time to work for Buddhism, kosen-rufu, people's happiness, and the welfare of society. In this Latter Day of the Law teeming with perverse individuals, you are exerting yourselves energetically, often amid many hardships and obstacles, chanting daimoku for others' happiness, traveling long distances to talk with friends and show them warm concern and understanding. You are truly bodhisattvas. There is no nobler life, no life based on a loftier philosophy. Each of you is translating this unsurpassed philosophy into action and spreading its message far and wide. To possess a philosophy of such profound value is itself the greatest fortune. Accordingly, the second condition for happiness is to possess a profound philosophy.

The third condition for happiness is to possess conviction. We live in an age in which people can no longer clearly distinguish what is right or wrong, good or evil. This is a global trend. If things continue in this way, humanity is destined for chaos and moral decay. In the midst of such times, you are upholding and earnestly practicing Nichiren Buddhism, a teaching of the highest good.

In "The Opening of the Eyes," the Daishonin writes: "This I will state. Let the gods forsake me. Let all persecutions assail me. Still I will give my life for the sake of the Law" (WND-1, 280). In this same letter, he instructs his believers not to be swayed by temptations or threats, however great—such as being offered the rulership of Japan or being told that one's parents will be beheaded (see WND-1, 280).

The important thing is holding on resolutely to one's convictions, come what may, just as the Daishonin teaches. People who possess such unwavering conviction will definitely become happy. Each of you is such an individual.

The fourth condition is living cheerfully and vibrantly. Those who are always complaining and grumbling make not only themselves but everyone else around them miserable and unhappy. By contrast, those who always live positively and filled with enthusiasm—those who possess a cheerful and sunny disposition that lifts the spirits and brightens the hearts of everyone they meet—are not only happy themselves but are a source of hope and inspiration for others.

Those who are always wearing long, gloomy expressions whenever you meet them and who have lost the ability to rejoice and feel genuine delight or wonder lead dark, cheerless existences.

On the other hand, those who possess good cheer can view even a scolding by a loved one, such as a spouse or partner, as sweet music to their ears, or can greet a child's poor report card as a sign of great potential for improvement! Viewing events and situations in this kind of positive light is important. The strength, wisdom, and cheerfulness that accompany such an attitude lead to happiness.

To regard everything in a positive light or with a spirit of goodwill, however, does not mean being foolishly gullible and allowing people to take advantage of our good nature. It means having the wisdom and perception to actually move things in a positive direction by seeing things in their best light, while all the time keeping our eyes firmly focused on reality.

Faith and the teachings of Buddhism enable us to develop that kind of character. The acquisition of such character is a more priceless treasure than any other possession in life.

The fifth condition for happiness is courage. Courageous people can overcome anything. The cowardly, on the other hand, because of their lack of courage, fail to savor the true, profound joys of life. This is most unfortunate.

The sixth condition for happiness is tolerance. Those who are tolerant and broad minded make people feel comfortable and at ease. Narrow and intolerant people who berate others for the slightest thing or who make a great commotion each time some problem arises just exhaust and intimidate everyone. Leaders must be tolerant and have a warm approachability that makes people feel relaxed and comfortable. Not only are those who possess a heart as wide as the ocean happy themselves, but all those around them are happy too.

The six conditions I have just mentioned are all ultimately encompassed in the single word *faith*. A life based on faith in the Mystic Law is a life of unsurpassed happiness.

The Daishonin declares, "Nam-myoho-renge-kyo is the greatest of all joys" (OTT, 212). I hope all of you will savor the truth of these words deep in your lives and show vibrant actual proof of that joy.

*From a speech at an SGI general meeting,
Weston, Florida, June 23, 1996.*

1.7 Confronting Life's Fundamental Sufferings Head-On

In this selection, President Ikeda stresses that the Soka Gakkai and Nichiren Buddhism directly tackle the universal and inescapable issues of birth, aging, sickness, and death, and he clarifies that the path to true happiness is to be found in that pursuit.

What is the purpose of life? It is to become happy. What, then, is true happiness? Can fame, wealth, or social status, no matter how immense, bring us true happiness?

Such things alone do not create lasting happiness at life's deepest level. Nor can they solve the most fundamental sufferings of existence—birth, aging, sickness, and death. It is for this very reason that Nichiren Daishonin expounded his teaching.

Birth—the pain of being born and of living. There are innumerable sufferings in life. And there is also our karma to deal with. There are accidents that we cannot anticipate. There are such problems as divorce, difficulties with our children, and frustrations at work. The question is how do we overcome all of these and other sufferings?

Aging—the suffering of growing older. Right now, you are all young; you are all healthy and possess the beauty of youth. But you will invariably age and grow old. There's no inoculation against this, and the most expensive medicine will not cure you of old age.

Sickness—the suffering of illness. Some suffer from cancer. Others suffer from mental or spiritual illnesses. Life is a battle against myriad diseases and disorders. Second Soka Gakkai president Josei Toda often said that there is an illness called poverty, just as there is an illness called meanness of spirit. He also asserted that the karma of being hated by others and ending life in defeat can also be termed a kind of illness. It is the power of the Mystic Law that cures these kinds of illnesses that afflict the body and mind at a fundamental level.

Death—this is the most uncompromising of the four sufferings. None of us here today will be alive in a hundred years. As the French literary giant Victor Hugo declared, "We are all under sentence of death but with a sort of indefinite reprieve."[5]

WHAT IS TRUE HAPPINESS?

There are many ways of dying as well. Some die by their own hand, others are murdered. Some suffer unspeakable agony before they die. How should we view our inexorable fate of death? How can we overcome the suffering it causes? These are crucial questions. And what happens after death? Do we still exist? Or is there nothing? If we do exist, in what state do we exist? Such things are beyond ordinary human understanding.

The sufferings of birth, aging, sickness, and death are universal to humankind. They are the basic issues we face in our unending search for happiness. Yet almost all of society's leaders sidestep them. They furtively avert their eyes from the very issues that any leader who feels a sense of responsibility for the welfare of the people cannot possibly neglect. This is a great misfortune for the people.

The Soka Gakkai confronts these fundamental problems head-on. And Nichiren Daishonin reveals the means for resolving them completely.

He elucidates the Mystic Law, which enables us to serenely overcome the four sufferings and all other kinds of hardships and obstacles and in fact even use our sufferings as an impetus to propel us forward as we lead lives pervaded by the four virtues of eternity, happiness, true self, and purity.

Life is a struggle. Reality is a struggle. Nichiren Daishonin teaches that Buddhism is about winning. He exhorts us to be victorious. So we must win in life. To embrace the Mystic Law is to grasp the sword of victory. We can triumph over all. We can triumph and enjoy our lives. A "person of faith" is synonymous with "a person of victory."

Therefore, I hope all of you will be victorious in your lives. Live your lives so that you can declare: "I have no regrets. I enjoyed my life. I encouraged many others and gave them hope. It was a good life."

From a speech at an SGI-USA youth division general meeting, San Francisco, California, March 14, 1993.

DEVELOPING A LIFE STATE OF HAPPINESS

2.1 Living With Optimism

Nichiren Buddhism teaches that inherent in the lives of all people is the life state of Buddhahood, which is worthy of supreme respect and is replete with the highest wisdom, courage, and compassion. When we reveal that life state, our perspective is transformed and we can build a state of unimpeded, absolute happiness. This chapter presents President Ikeda's teachings concerning that inner transformation.

In this selection, he explains how those who embrace the Mystic Law can lead lives of optimism, in which life is in itself a joyous experience.

Let's lead vibrant, enjoyable lives. We have the Gohonzon. We have the Mystic Law. That means that each of us is an embodiment of the Mystic Law, an embodiment of infinite good fortune, and a majestic treasure tower. As a result, we will not be defeated; we have nothing to fear.

When we firmly believe that our life is the treasure tower and that we each embody Buddhahood, we come to find life itself enjoyable and pleasant. Attaining and savoring such a wonderful state of mind is the purpose of our Buddhist faith and practice.

Those who live their lives in the realm of the Soka Gakkai, in the realm of kosen-rufu, will enjoy such a joy-filled state of life eternally, throughout the three existences of past, present, and future.

Do we live our lives as optimists or pessimists?

Pessimists focus on the sad, painful, gloomy side of things. "What will I do if my husband dies?" "What will I do if my wife falls ill?" "What if I can't achieve my goals?" "What if my daughter falls in love with someone who is no good for her?"

If you're always thinking pessimistic thoughts, pessimism will taint your mind. You will never be able to be happy. If you're always seeing things in a negative, gloomy light, bemoaning your situation and worrying—"I never have any money," "Oh, no, another meeting!" or "What if I'm scolded again today?"—then life will be nothing but a painful austerity!

On the other hand, you can look at the bright side of everything. You can take what happens and view it in a positive, hopeful, and cheerful light. This is optimism, the ultimate form of which is faith in the Mystic Law. For example, if you get sick, you can say: "Now I can get some rest! It'll give me a chance to ponder the three existences!"

And with hope in your heart you can declare that you won't let this sickness defeat you, that you will survive it, and thus vanquish the "devil of illness."

Optimists are strong. They see the positive in everything and decide to make it a reality for all to see.

I hope you will live with optimism, remaining undefeated by whatever happens in life, transforming hardship into joy, and laughing off adversity like the famous comic actor Charlie Chaplin.

From a speech at an SGI-Canada Vancouver general meeting, Vancouver, British Columbia, October 1, 1993.

2.2 The Key to Happiness Is Inner Transformation

Happiness is a function of our state of mind. This is why the Soka Gakkai movement, which embraces the philosophy that "it is the heart that is important" and seeks to transform our lives, is the fundamental path to happiness.

We may encounter all kinds of problems in the course of life. There will also undoubtedly be times when we are faced with circumstances beyond our control. But why is it that, in the same situation, one person advances vibrantly, while another sorrows and laments? It is because happiness is an internal condition, something we feel in our hearts.

If we can live our lives with joy, if we enjoy living, then we are winners. That's why transforming our hearts and minds is so important. This is the essence of Nichiren Buddhism.

External appearances are not what matters. There are many people whose circumstances are the envy of others but who are actually very unhappy. Those with strong, wise, resilient, and generous hearts remain upbeat and positive, no matter what happens.

"It is the heart that is important" (WND-1, 1000), writes the Daishonin. This is the foundation for happiness—a foundation we establish through the Mystic Law.

The Daishonin declares, "The wonderful means of truly putting an end to the physical and spiritual obstacles of all living beings is none other than Nam-myoho-renge-kyo" (WND-1, 842).

Happiness is not just a word. It is not found in objects, nor is it determined by wealth, social status, or celebrity.

The key, first of all, is to chant Nam-myoho-renge-kyo. When we do so, we will feel an upsurge of life force.

To feel joy in the depths of our lives, no matter what happens, to take delight in each moment of each day as we converse with friends and chant to our heart's content—these are examples of genuine happiness.

Our Soka Gakkai movement teaches the fundamental way to achieve such happiness.

If we live out our lives based on faith in the Mystic Law, we will experience joy in both life and death. Let us serenely surmount every obstacle and keep moving forward with joy and high spirits.

From a speech at a joint training session, Nagano, Japan, August 6, 2005.

2.3 The Life State of Practitioners of the Mystic Law

Describing three characteristics or qualities of practitioners of Nichiren Buddhism, President Ikeda calls on us to be courageous and filled with hope as we build a self that can savor joy at all times.

What characterizes the life state of genuine practitioners of Nichiren Buddhism?

First of all, it is having no fear—not being disturbed or daunted by anything.

Lies and deceit abound in society. It is foolish to allow ourselves to be swayed by such things; it only leads to unhappiness. The Mystic Law and Nichiren Daishonin are absolutely free of any falsehood. The wisest possible course, therefore, is to dedicate our lives to the widespread propagation of the Law—to kosen-rufu.

On account of our faith in Nichiren Buddhism, we may from time to time encounter unpleasantness from others. We may also find ourselves working much harder than many around us. But that is all part of our Buddhist practice.

The Daishonin teaches that we can attain enlightenment in this lifetime. This entails weathering the trials of the three obstacles and four devils. But if we can do that, we can attain enlightenment in this lifetime and enjoy the boundless life state of Buddhahood throughout eternity. That's why we need to forge ahead fearlessly, positively, and courageously, come what may.

The second characteristic is living with vibrant hope. Nothing is stronger than hope. The Mystic Law is a source of eternal hope. People who never lose hope, no matter what happens, are truly happy.

The third characteristic is a state of life in which we savor joy at all times. It is to have such joy that, even at the time of death, one can say with a heartfelt smile: "What a wonderful life that was! Now where shall I go next?" That is the life state of a genuine practitioner of Nichiren Buddhism.

Our Buddhist practice enables us to achieve an expansive state of being in which we can enjoy everything in life. As the Daishonin says, faith in the Mystic Law is "the greatest of all joys" (OTT, 212).

From a speech at a Chubu region representatives conference, Aichi, Japan, May 26, 1997.

2.4 Our Happiness Is Determined by Our Inner Life Condition

Happiness is not determined by our circumstances but is something each of us creates for ourselves through our inner life condition. Nichiren Buddhism teaches the way to elevate that life condition.

The English poet John Milton wrote, "The mind is its own place, and in itself Can make a Heav'n of Hell, a Hell of Heav'n."[1] This statement, a product of the poet's profound insight, resonates with the Buddhist teaching of "three thousand realms in a single moment of life."

How we see the world and feel about our lives is determined solely by our inner life condition. Nichiren Daishonin writes: "Hungry spirits perceive the Ganges River as fire, human beings perceive it as water, and heavenly beings perceive it as amrita. Though the water is the same, it appears differently according to one's karmic reward from the past" (WND-1, 486).

"Karmic reward from the past" refers to our present life state, which is the result of past actions or causes created through our own words, thoughts, and deeds. That state of life determines our view of and feelings toward the external world.

The same circumstances may be perceived as utter bliss by one person and unbearable misfortune by another.

And while some people may love the place where they live, thinking it's the best place ever, others may hate it and constantly seek to find happiness somewhere else.

Nichiren Buddhism is a teaching that enables us to elevate our inner state of life, realizing genuinely happy lives for ourselves as well as prosperity for society. It is the great teaching of the "actual three thousand realms in a single moment of life," making it possible for us to transform the place where we dwell into the Land of Eternally Tranquil Light.

Moreover, the good fortune, benefit, and joy we gain through living in accord with the eternal Law [of Nam-myoho-renge-kyo] are not temporary. In the same way that trees steadily add growth rings with each passing year, our lives accumulate good fortune that will endure throughout the three existences of past, present, and future. In contrast, worldly wealth and fame as well as various amusements and pleasures—no matter how glamorous or exciting they may seem for a time—are fleeting and insubstantial.

From a speech at a Wakayama Prefecture general meeting, Wakayama, Japan, March 24, 1988.

2.5 Happiness Is Found Where We Are

The writings of Nichiren Daishonin show us we can build a state of unshakable happiness in our own lives here and now.

In *The Record of the Orally Transmitted Teachings*, Nichiren Daishonin explains the following passage from the "Encouragements of the Bodhisattva Universal Worthy" chapter of the Lotus Sutra, "Before long this person will proceed to the place of enlightenment" (LSOC, 364), stating:

> The words "this person" refer to the practitioner of the Lotus Sutra. The place where the person upholds and honors the Lotus Sutra is the "place of enlightenment" to which the person proceeds. It is not that he leaves his present place and goes to some other place. The "place of enlightenment" is the place where the living beings of the Ten Worlds reside. And now the place where Nichiren and his followers chant Nam-myoho-renge-kyo, "whether . . . in mountain valleys or the wide wilderness," these places are all the Land of Eternally Tranquil Light. This is what is meant by the "place of enlightenment." (see OTT, 192)[2]

"This person" refers to the practitioner, or votary, of the Lotus Sutra. In the specific sense, it indicates Nichiren Daishonin himself, while in the more general sense, it refers to all people who embrace and practice Nam-myoho-renge-kyo of the Three Great Secret Laws. The place where people embrace and practice the correct teaching of Buddhism is the "'place of enlightenment' to which the person proceeds," in other words, the place where we strive to attain Buddhahood in this lifetime.

There is no need to leave this trouble-filled saha world for some otherworldly pure land or ideal paradise. The "place of enlightenment" is none other than the dwelling place of living beings of the Ten Worlds. Now, the place where Nichiren Daishonin and his disciples who chant Nam-myoho-renge-kyo reside is the land of Eternally Tranquil Light, or the Buddha land, whether it be "in mountain valleys or the wide wilderness" (LSOC, 316). It is the "place of enlightenment," the Daishonin asserts. The place where each practitioner lives becomes the Land of Tranquil Light. This passage alludes to the profound transformative power inherent in a single life moment.

People often tend to think of happiness as something abstract and removed from their present realities. They imagine, for example, that they would be happier if they could move to another place, or that they would enjoy more comfortable and pleasant lives if they could change jobs. They always feel that the grass is greener on the other side and place their hopes on a change of external circumstances. Young people are particularly susceptible to this tendency.

However, we all have different missions to fulfill in life and different places where we need to live to fulfill them. Those who decide to put down solid roots where they are and continue to live their lives with perseverance and hope while struggling with reality will be victors in life. It's important not to live aimlessly, lacking any clear purpose. I therefore say to you: "Dig beneath your feet, there you will find a spring" and "Live in a way that is true to yourself."

In short, a real sense of happiness and deep satisfaction in life can be found only within us. The Mystic Law is the fundamental Law of life. Through our Buddhist practice, we can tap the power of the Mystic Law to propel our lives forward. This is why the place where we carry out our Buddhist practice and society, too, become the Buddha land. We are able to transform where we live right now into a place of victory and happiness.

From a speech at a university groups and Toshima Ward joint training session, Tokyo, Japan, December 7, 1986.

2.6 Activating the Limitless Life Force of Buddhahood

President Ikeda explains the nature of the world of Buddhahood, the highest life state of the Buddhist analysis of life articulated in the principle of the mutual possession of the Ten Worlds, and how we can manifest it.

Life, which is constantly changing from moment to moment, can be broadly categorized into ten states, which Buddhism articulates as the Ten Worlds. These consist of the six paths—the worlds of hell, hungry spirits, animals, *asuras*, human beings, and heavenly beings—and the four noble worlds—the worlds of voice-hearers, cause-awakened ones, bodhisattvas, and Buddhas. The true reality of life is that it always possesses all ten of these potential states.

None of the Ten Worlds that appear in our lives at any given moment remain fixed or constant. They change instant by instant. Buddhism's deep insight into this dynamic nature of life is expressed as the principle of the mutual possession of the Ten Worlds.

In his treatise "The Object of Devotion for Observing the Mind," Nichiren Daishonin illustrates clearly and simply how the world of human beings, or life state of humanity, contains within it the other nine worlds:

> When we look from time to time at a person's face, we find him or her sometimes joyful, sometimes enraged, and sometimes calm. At times greed

appears in the person's face, at times foolishness, and at times perversity. Rage is the world of hell, greed is that of hungry spirits, foolishness is that of animals, perversity is that of asuras, joy is that of heaven [heavenly beings], and calmness is that of human beings. (WND-1, 358)

The nine worlds are continually emerging and becoming dormant within us. This is something that we can see, sense, and recognize in our own daily lives.

It is important to note here that the teachings of Buddhism from the very beginning were always concerned with enabling people to manifest the noble and infinitely powerful life state of Buddhahood. And, indeed, that should always be the purpose of Buddhist practice. Focusing on this point, the great teaching of Nichiren Daishonin, by establishing the correct object of devotion [the Gohonzon of Nam-myoho-renge-kyo], sets forth a practical means for revealing our inner Buddhahood. As such, Nichiren Buddhism is a practice open to all people.

A look at history to this day shows that humanity is still trapped in the cycle of the six paths, or lower six worlds. The character for "earth" (*ji*) is contained in the Japanese word for "hell" (*jigoku;* literally, "earth prison"), imparting the meaning of being bound or shackled to something of the lowest or basest level. Humanity and society can never achieve substantial revitalization unless people give serious thought to casting off the shackles of these lower worlds and elevating their state of life. Even in the midst of this troubled and corrupt world, Buddhism discovers in human life the highest and most dignified potential of Buddhahood.

Though our lives may constantly move through the six paths, we can activate the limitless life force of Buddhahood by focusing our minds on the correct object of devotion and achieving the "fusion of reality and wisdom."

Buddhahood is difficult to describe in words. Unlike the other nine worlds, it has no concrete expression. It is the ultimate function of life that moves the nine worlds in the direction of boundless value.

Even on cloudy or rainy days, by the time a plane reaches an altitude of about thirty-five thousand feet, it is flying high above the clouds amid bright sunshine and can proceed smoothly on its course. In the same way, no matter how painful or difficult our daily existence may be, if we make the sun in our hearts shine brightly, we can overcome all adversity with calm composure. That inner sun is the life state of Buddhahood.

In one sense, as the Daishonin states in *The Record of the Orally Transmitted Teachings*, "'Bodhisattva' is a preliminary step toward the attainment of the effect of Buddhahood" (OTT, 87). The world of bodhisattvas is characterized by taking action for the sake of the Law, people, and society. Without such bodhisattva practice as our foundation, we cannot attain Buddhahood. Buddhahood is not something realized simply through conceptual understanding. Even reading countless Buddhist scriptures or books on Buddhism will not lead one to true enlightenment.

In addition, attaining Buddhahood doesn't mean that we become someone different. We remain who we are, living out our lives in the reality of society, where the nine worlds—especially the six paths—prevail. A genuine Buddhist philosophy does not present enlightenment or Buddhas as something mysterious or otherworldly.

What is important for us as human beings is to elevate our lives from a lower to a higher state, to expand our lives from a closed, narrow state of life to one that is infinitely vast and encompassing. Buddhahood represents the supreme state of life.

From On Life and Buddhism,
published in Japanese in November 1986.

2.7 Establishing Buddhahood as Our Basic Life Tendency

In this selection, President Ikeda explains that in Nichiren Buddhism, Buddhahood is not something we hope to achieve after death but is instead an open and manifest life state that we can achieve within our lives as we are.

One way to view the principle that each of us is an entity of the mutual possession of the Ten Worlds is to look at it from the perspective of our basic life tendency. While we all possess the Ten Worlds, our lives often lean toward one particular life state more than others—for instance, some people's lives are basically inclined toward the life state of hell, while others tend naturally toward the state of bodhisattva. This could be called the "habit pattern" of one's life, a predisposition formed through karmic causes that a person has accumulated from the past.

Just as a spring returns to its original shape after being stretched, people tend to revert to their own basic tendency. But even if one's basic life tendency is the life state of hell, it doesn't mean that one will remain in that state twenty-four hours a day. That person will still move from one life state to another—for instance, sometimes manifesting that of humanity, sometimes that of anger, and so on. Likewise, those whose basic life tendency is anger—driven by the desire to always be better than others—will also sometimes manifest higher life states such as heaven or bodhisattva. However, even if they momentarily manifest the state of bodhisattva, they will quickly revert to their basic life tendency of anger.

Changing our basic life tendency means carrying out our human revolution and fundamentally transforming our state of life. It means changing our mindset or resolve on the deepest level. The kind of life we live is decided by our basic life tendency. For example, those whose basic life tendency is hunger are as though on board a ship called *Hunger*. While sailing ahead in the state of hunger, they will sometimes experience joy and sometimes suffering. Though there are various ups and downs, the ship unerringly proceeds on its set course. Consequently, for those on board this ship, everything they see will be colored by the hues of hunger. And even after they die, their lives will merge with the realm of hunger inherent in the universe.

Establishing the state of Buddhahood as our basic life tendency is what it means to "attain Buddhahood." Of course, even with Buddhahood as our basic life tendency, we won't be free of problems or suffering because we will still possess the other nine worlds. But the foundation of our lives will become one of hope, and we will increasingly experience a condition of security and joy.

My mentor, Josei Toda, once explained this as follows:

> Even if you fall ill, simply have the attitude, "I'm all right. I know that if I chant to the Gohonzon, I will get well." Isn't the world of Buddhahood a state of life in which we can live with total peace

of mind? That said, however, given that the nine worlds are inherent in the world of Buddhahood, we might still occasionally become angry or have to deal with problems. Therefore, enjoying total peace of mind doesn't mean that we have to renounce anger or some such thing. When something worrying happens, it's only natural to be worried. But in the innermost depths of our lives, we will have a profound sense of security. This is what it means to be a Buddha. . . .

If we can regard life itself as an absolute joy, isn't that being a Buddha? Doesn't that mean attaining the same life state as the Daishonin? Even when faced with the threat of being beheaded, the Daishonin remained calm and composed. If it had been us in that situation, we'd have been in a state of complete panic! When the Daishonin was exiled to the hostile environment of Sado Island, he continued instructing his disciples on various matters and produced such important writings as "The Opening of the Eyes" and "The Object of Devotion for Observing the Mind." If he didn't have unshakable peace of mind, he would never have been able to compose such great treatises [under such difficult circumstances].[3]

Our daily practice of gongyo—reciting portions of the Lotus Sutra and chanting Nam-myoho-renge-kyo—is a solemn ceremony in which our lives become one with the life of the Buddha. By applying ourselves steadfastly and persistently to this practice for manifesting our inherent Buddhahood, we firmly establish the life state of Buddhahood in our lives so that it is solid and unshakable like the earth. On this foundation, this solid stage, we can freely enact at each moment the drama of the nine worlds.

Moreover, kosen-rufu is the challenge to transform the fundamental life state of society into that of Buddhahood. The key to this lies in increasing the number of those who share our noble aspirations.

When we base ourselves on faith in Nichiren Buddhism, absolutely no effort we make is ever wasted. When we establish Buddhahood as our basic life tendency, we can move toward a future of hope while creating positive value from all our activities in the nine worlds, both past and present. In fact, all of our hardships and struggles in the nine worlds become the nourishment that strengthens the world of Buddhahood in our lives.

In accord with the Buddhist principle that earthly desires lead to enlightenment, sufferings (earthly desires, or the deluded impulses of the nine worlds) all become the "firewood" or fuel for gaining happiness (enlightenment, or the world of Buddhahood). This is similar to how our bodies digest food and turn it into energy.

A Buddha who has no connection to the actual sufferings

of the nine worlds is not a genuine Buddha—namely, one who embodies the mutual possession of the Ten Worlds. This is the essential message of the "Life Span" (sixteenth) chapter of the Lotus Sutra.

The world of Buddhahood can also be described as a state of life where one willingly takes on even hellish suffering. This is the world of hell contained in the world of Buddhahood. It is characterized by empathy and hardships deliberately taken on for the happiness and welfare of others, and it arises from a sense of responsibility and compassion. Courageously taking on problems and sufferings for the sake of others strengthens the world of Buddhahood in our lives.

Because of the principle of the mutual possession of the Ten Worlds, our Buddhist practice enables us to live true to ourselves. Buddhist teachings that lack this principle reject the nine worlds, seeking to reach the state of Buddhahood by breaking free of these lower states. But this approach actually detracts from one's humanity. It means a life of prohibitions and proscriptions, of constant fault-finding and self-negation, and leads ultimately to "reducing the body to ashes and annihilating consciousness." Of course, self-reflection and self-control are important, but taken to the extreme they can turn one into a rigid, narrow-minded person who barely knows what it means to be alive.

This may be a case of the remedy being worse than the disease. A better approach more often is to overlook people's minor shortcomings and instead give them hope and purpose so they can move forward positively. By living in this way with vibrant self-confidence, a person's faults will naturally recede and transform. For instance, the fault of impatience might turn into the virtue of energetic action.

This is true of our own lives and applies to fostering others as well. The key is to be true to oneself, without trying to impress others or to be something we're not. We're all human; at times we laugh, at times we cry. We get angry, and we become confused.

As ordinary people, just as we are, when we commit ourselves on the deepest level to kosen-rufu, the state of Buddhahood becomes our basic life tendency.

We should allow ourselves to be angry when anger is called for, to worry when there is something we need to worry about, to laugh when something is funny, and to enjoy what is enjoyable. The Daishonin says, "Suffer what there is to suffer, enjoy what there is to enjoy" (WND-1, 681). Living this way each day, with vitality and joy, we move dynamically toward the goal of absolute happiness for ourselves and others.

From The Wisdom of the Lotus Sutra, *vol. 4,*
published in Japanese in December 1998.

2.8 You Are All Noble Buddhas

President Ikeda's novels The Human Revolution *and* The New Human Revolution *depict the true history of the Soka Gakkai spirit, their protagonist Shin'ichi Yamamoto representing President Ikeda himself. In this excerpt from* The New Human Revolution, *Shin'ichi as Soka Gakkai president gives guidance at an informal meeting with members during a visit to Mie Prefecture in April 1978. He stresses that each individual is a noble Buddha with an incredibly precious mission.*

The Soka Gakkai is a realm of faith. It starts and ends with faith. The key is to look at everything through the eyes of faith.

What is faith? It is having absolute conviction that all things are part of your own life and being, that you embody the Mystic Law and are a Buddha. Nichiren Daishonin writes, "You must never think that any of the eighty thousand sacred teachings of Shakyamuni Buddha's lifetime or any of the Buddhas and bodhisattvas of the ten directions and three existences are outside yourself" (WND-1, 3).

Believe that the boundless life state of Buddhahood resides within you, earnestly chant Nam-myoho-renge-kyo, and polish your life—this, the Daishonin teaches, is the only way to free ourselves from suffering and delusion. You are all originally Buddhas. Believe in yourself. There's no need to compare yourself to others and let that determine your happiness.

DEVELOPING A LIFE STATE OF HAPPINESS

The path to establishing an indestructible state of absolute happiness exists nowhere but in polishing your own life and bringing forth the Buddha nature inside you.

If you can't believe you embody the Mystic Law, you'll never have self-confidence in the truest sense of the word, and you'll always be searching for the path to happiness outside yourself.

What happens then? You'll end up being swayed by people's opinions and other external circumstances, happy one minute and sad the next. You'll compare yourself to others in all areas—social status or position, economic standing, personality, looks, and so on. When you think you're a bit better than someone, you'll feel superior. You'll become conceited, unable to see yourself objectively. But the moment you think you're lacking, you'll feel depressed, worthless, and powerless.

Moreover, if you're too concerned about what others think of you, you'll be hurt and offended by even the most inconsequential words or actions. You'll hate and resent these people for saying something "terrible" about you, not appreciating you, or showing no compassion.

Some people worry so much about others' opinions that they'll go to any lengths to win their favor.

The fundamental cause of resentment is being deluded about the true nature of your life. Unable, though you practice Nichiren Buddhism, to really believe you are a treasure tower and a Buddha, you seek happiness outside. This provides an opening for devilish influences.

You are all magnificent, noble Buddhas. You are people with an incredibly precious mission. Don't compare yourselves to others. Value and accept yourselves for who you are and always strive to develop your own unique potential.

And just as each one of you is a Buddha, so is everyone else around you. That's why it's important to respect and treasure your fellow members to the utmost. That is the key to the unity of the Soka Gakkai.

From The New Human Revolution, *volume 29,*
"Rikiso" (Sprinting forward) chapter.

THE PRACTICE FOR TRANSFORMING OUR STATE OF LIFE

3.1 The Gohonzon—the Fundamental Object of Devotion

Nichiren Buddhism teaches the importance of chanting Nam-myoho-renge-kyo with faith in the Gohonzon in order to transform our lives and manifest the life state of Buddhahood. Here, President Ikeda explains the meaning of the Gohonzon as the fundamental object of devotion.

The Japanese word *honzon* means "object of fundamental respect or devotion"—in other words, the object that we respect and devote ourselves to as the basis of our lives. It is only natural, therefore, that what we take as our object of devotion will have a decisive impact on the direction of our lives.

Traditionally, objects of devotion in Buddhism were often statues of the Buddha. In some cases, paintings of the Buddha were used. While statues of the Buddha did not exist in early Buddhism, they later began to appear in the Gandhara region of northwest India, due to the influence of Hellenic culture. They were, if you like, a product of cultural exchange on the ancient Silk Road. Through statues and paintings, people became familiar with the image of the Buddha, leading them to arouse faith in the Buddha and revere him.

The object of devotion in Nichiren Buddhism, however, is the Gohonzon,[1] which consists of written characters. In that sense, rather than simply a visual or graphic depiction, I would call it the highest and noblest expression of the world of the intellect, of the great wisdom of the Buddha of the Latter Day of the Law. In this respect alone, Nichiren Daishonin's object of devotion is fundamentally different from those traditionally worshipped in Buddhism.

Written words are wondrous; they have tremendous power. Take people's names, for example. When people sign their names, it embodies everything about them—their character, social position, power, emotional and physical condition, personal history, and karma.

Similarly, the daimoku of Nam-myoho-renge-kyo [which is inscribed down the center of the Gohonzon] encompasses all things in the universe. All phenomena are expressions of the Mystic Law, as the Great Teacher T'ien-t'ai indicates when he states [in *Great Concentration and Insight*], "Arising

THE PRACTICE FOR TRANSFORMING OUR STATE OF LIFE

is the arising of the essential nature of the Law [Dharma nature], and extinction is the extinction of that nature" (WND-1, 216).

The true aspect of the ever-changing universe (all phenomena) is perfectly expressed, just as it is, in the Gohonzon. The true aspect of the macrocosm of the universe is exactly the same for the microcosm of each of our lives. This is what the Daishonin tells us in his writings. In addition, the Gohonzon expresses the enlightened life state of Nichiren Daishonin, the Buddha of the Latter Day of the Law.

In that sense, the Gohonzon inscribed by the Daishonin is an embodiment of the fundamental Law of the universe that should be revered by all people; it is the true object of fundamental devotion.

The universe contains both positive and negative workings or functions. Representatives of the Ten Worlds are all depicted on the Gohonzon—from the Buddhas Shakyamuni and Many Treasures, who represent the world of Buddhahood, to Devadatta, who represents the world of hell. The Daishonin teaches that such representatives of the positive and negative workings of the universe are all without exception illuminated by the light of Nam-myoho-renge-kyo, enabling them to display "the dignified attributes that they inherently possess," and that this is the function of the Gohonzon (see WND-1, 832).

When we do gongyo and chant Nam-myoho-renge-kyo before the Gohonzon, both the positive and negative tendencies in our lives begin to manifest "the dignified attributes that they inherently possess." The world of hell with its painful suffering, the world of hungry spirits with its insatiable cravings, the world of *asuras* with its perverse rage—all come to function to contribute to our happiness and to the creation of value. When we base our lives on the Mystic Law, the life states that drag us toward suffering and unhappiness move in the opposite, positive direction. It is as if sufferings become the "firewood" that fuels the flames of joy, wisdom, and compassion. The Mystic Law and faith are what ignite those flames.

In addition, when we chant Nam-myoho-renge-kyo, the positive forces of the universe—represented by all Buddhas, bodhisattvas, and heavenly deities such as Brahma and Shakra [the protective gods of Buddhism]—will shine even more brightly, their power and influence increasing and expanding endlessly. The gods of the sun and moon that exist in the microcosm of our lives will also shine brilliantly to illuminate the darkness within. All of the workings—both positive and negative—of the Ten Worlds and the three thousand realms function together at full power, propelling us toward a life of happiness, a life imbued with the four virtues of eternity, happiness, true self, and purity.

In life, it is only natural that we sometimes fall ill. Based on the teaching of the Mystic Law, however, we can look at illness as an inherent part of life. Seeing it this way, we will not be swayed by illness when it happens to us, or allow it to be a source of suffering and distress. Viewed from the perspective of the eternity of life, we are definitely on the way to

THE PRACTICE FOR TRANSFORMING OUR STATE OF LIFE

establishing a "greater self" overflowing with absolute happiness. In addition, we will be able to overcome any obstacle we encounter in life, using it as a springboard for developing a new, more expansive state of being. Life will be enjoyable, and death will be peaceful, marking the solemn departure for our next wonderful lifetime.

When winter arrives, trees are, for a while, bare of flowers and leaves. But they possess the life force to grow fresh green leaves when spring comes. Similar to this, but on an even more profound level, for us, as practitioners of the Mystic Law, death is the dynamic process by which our life itself transitions, without pain, to quickly begin its next mission-filled existence.

From a speech at an SGI-USA youth training session,
Malibu, California, February 20, 1990.

3.2 "Never Seek This Gohonzon Outside Yourself"

In this selection, President Ikeda explains the profound principle of tapping the power of the Gohonzon in our lives. The immeasurable life force and limitless wisdom expressed by the Gohonzon are also inherent in our lives, and our Buddhist faith and practice enable us to exercise them with unrestricted freedom.

In any religion, the object of worship or devotion holds a place of prime importance. What, then, is the true meaning of the object of devotion, or the Gohonzon, in Nichiren Buddhism?

In "The Real Aspect of the Gohonzon," the Daishonin states: "Never seek this Gohonzon outside yourself. The Gohonzon exists only within the mortal flesh of us ordinary people who embrace the Lotus Sutra and chant Nam-myoho-renge-kyo" (WND-1, 832). Discussing this passage in one of his lectures, Mr. Toda said:

> Although we may pray to this great Gohonzon thinking it exists outside us, the reality is that it resides directly within the lives of us who chant Nam-myoho-renge-kyo with faith in the Gohonzon of the Three Great Secret Laws. This passage from the Daishonin is truly inspiring.
>
> Those who do not yet have faith in the Mystic Law are people at the "stage of being a Buddha in theory" [the first of the six stages of practice], where

THE PRACTICE FOR TRANSFORMING OUR STATE OF LIFE

> the Buddha nature, while appearing vaguely to be present, does not function in the least. We [Soka Gakkai members], on the other hand, because we chant to the Gohonzon, are at the "stage of hearing the name and words of the truth" [the second of the six stages of practice]. At this stage, the Gohonzon already shines brilliantly within us.
>
> However, the degree to which it shines will differ depending upon the strength of each person's faith. It's like a light bulb. A high-watt light bulb shines brightly, and a low-watt light bulb shines faintly.
>
> To continue with the analogy of a light bulb, for those who haven't yet embraced the Mystic Law, the light bulb isn't connected to a power source. Whereas for us, practitioners of the Mystic Law, the light bulb that is the Gohonzon is turned on. Therefore, our lives shine brightly.[2]

Everything depends on the strength of our faith. When we have strong faith, our life itself becomes a "cluster of blessings" (WND-1, 832), which is how the Daishonin describes the Gohonzon. He further states, "This Gohonzon also is found only in the two characters for faith"[3] (WND-1, 832).

People of strong faith, therefore, never reach a deadlock. No matter what happens, they can transform everything into a source of benefit and happiness. Naturally, in the long course of our lives, we are bound to encounter various kinds of problems and suffering. But we will be able to turn all difficulties into nourishment for developing a higher state of life. In this respect, for practitioners of Nichiren Buddhism, everything is ultimately a source of benefit and happiness at the most profound level. The word *unhappiness* does not exist in the vocabulary of those who have strong faith.

Toward the end of his *Commentary on "The Object of Devotion for Observing the Mind,"* Nichikan Shonin [a great restorer of Nichiren Buddhism who began the task of systematizing the Daishonin's teachings] writes:

> When we embrace faith in this object of devotion [the Gohonzon] and chant Nam-myoho-renge-kyo, our lives immediately become the object of devotion of three thousand realms in a single moment of life; they become the life of Nichiren Daishonin. This is the true meaning of the phrase "he [the Buddha] then adorned the necks of the ignorant people of the latter age [with the five characters of Myoho-renge-kyo]"[4] (see WND-1, 376). Therefore, we must venerate the power of the Buddha and the power of the Law and strive to develop our own power of faith and power of practice. We must not spend our lives in vain and regret it for all eternity, as the Daishonin says.[5] (See WND-1, 622)

In this passage, Nichikan Shonin clearly states that, through faith in the Gohonzon, our lives can instantly

THE PRACTICE FOR TRANSFORMING OUR STATE OF LIFE

manifest the object of devotion and life state of Nichiren Daishonin. It was for this very purpose that the Daishonin inscribed the Gohonzon. Here, we find the supreme essence of Nichiren Buddhism.

Faith enables us to manifest the Gohonzon that exists within us; it allows us to bring forth the diamond-like state of the Buddha and make it shine brightly.

Within the depths of our lives, we each inherently possess boundless life force and a wellspring of infinite wisdom. Faith allows us to freely tap that inner life force and wisdom.

Mr. Toda often used to say: "What's inside you comes out. What's not there, won't." The strong and pure state of Buddhahood and the weak and base states of hell, hunger, and animality all exist within our lives and are manifested in response to causes and conditions in our environment.

Since life is eternal throughout the three existences of past, present, and future, our past karma may also assail us in the present in the form of some major problem or suffering. However, just as the cause of suffering lies within our lives, we also possess the power to transform our suffering into happiness. This is the power of the life state of Buddhahood.

As Mr. Toda declared, ultimately human beings are the product of what lies inside them, no more, no less.

It's vital, therefore, that we each cultivate the "earth" of our lives and put down deep and extensive "roots" of happiness. We must manifest the Gohonzon that exists within us and forge a self that is as unshakable as a mighty tree. In terms of our life state, this will be expressed as outstanding humanity and exemplary behavior, while in terms of our daily lives, it will manifest as benefit and good fortune.

The crucial point is whether we have faith. We must never make light of the Daishonin's assertion that "it is the heart that is important" (WND-1, 1000).

What matters is not form or a person's position or wealth. Those who have faith in their hearts are truly happy.

From a speech at a representatives gathering,
Tokyo, Japan, April 3, 1993.

3.3 The Gohonzon Is Found in Faith Alone

In a lecture on Nichiren Daishonin's writing "The Real Aspect of the Gohonzon," President Ikeda discusses the profound significance of the Gohonzon's layout, explaining that the object of devotion inscribed by the Daishonin marked a new epoch in the history of Buddhism. He further notes that the beneficial power of the Gohonzon can be tapped only through faith.

The Gohonzon exists for the enlightenment and genuine happiness of all people throughout the Latter Day of the Law and into the eternal future.

THE PRACTICE FOR TRANSFORMING OUR STATE OF LIFE

Enabling all living beings to attain the same enlightenment as Buddhas—that is Shakyamuni's vow and the wish of all Buddhas past, present, and future. Nichiren Daishonin was the first person to reveal the object of devotion, or the Gohonzon, for actualizing this wish, manifesting it in the form of a "great mandala" (WND-1, 831).

He states, "This mandala is in no way my invention" (WND-1, 831). The Gohonzon, he assures us, is not his arbitrary creation. It is the object of devotion that depicts the five characters of Myoho-renge-kyo to which Shakyamuni Buddha, seated in the treasure tower of Many Treasures, and all the Buddhas who were his emanations were awakened. In other words, the Gohonzon perfectly represents the "true aspect of all phenomena" and the foundational principles of the mutual possession of the Ten Worlds and three thousand realms in a single moment of life, all of which were elucidated during the Ceremony in the Air of the Lotus Sutra.

When we look at the layout of the Gohonzon, we see that Nam-myoho-renge-kyo—referred to in this letter as "the five characters of the Lotus Sutra's title" (WND-1, 831)—is written down the center, flanked by representatives of each of the Ten Worlds. This indicates that all living beings of the Ten Worlds, from the Buddhas and bodhisattvas on down, are without exception embodied in the Gohonzon. And it accords with the passage from the "Treasure Tower" chapter of the Lotus Sutra that the Daishonin cited in this letter, "[Shakyamuni Buddha used his transcendental powers to] lift all the members of the great assembly up into the air" (WND-1, 832). The Gohonzon, therefore, includes "without exception all of the various beings" of the Ten Worlds. It is a representation of the mutual possession of the Ten Worlds, the principle that all living beings, when illuminated by the light of the Mystic Law, can display the "dignified attributes that they inherently possess" (WND-1, 832).

When the light of the wisdom and compassion of Buddhahood illuminates the Ten Worlds within our lives, we can bring forth the power of supreme goodness and create enduring value. It also means that each individual comes to shine as an entity of the Mystic Law and to display their inherently dignified nature.

In such a realm, everyone—no matter their circumstances or whether they are still transforming their karma—shines with the "dignified attributes that they inherently possess." Those in the world of hell, for instance, manifest the world of hell contained within the world of Buddhahood. Though there may still be suffering, it is not the hopeless suffering of wandering lost in eternal darkness. They can bring forth the courage to face difficult realities head-on, the wisdom to surmount the obstacles arising from within and from without, and the powerful life force to make new strides forward. Sufferings become challenges that aid one's personal transformation and growth, a springboard to great development.

Illuminated by the light of the Mystic Law, the noble state of life that is one with the Mystic Law functions

THE PRACTICE FOR TRANSFORMING OUR STATE OF LIFE

vibrantly even in the world of hell. The meaning of the sufferings of hell is thereby turned around completely.

Every person's life inherently embodies the principles of the mutual possession of the Ten Worlds and three thousand realms in a single moment of life. In essence, every person's life is perfect and complete—there is nothing extraneous to be subtracted and nothing lacking to be added. No life is without its joys and sorrows, its ups and downs. And no matter how we might try, we cannot avoid the universal sufferings of birth, aging, sickness, and death.

The mutual possession of the Ten Worlds is the true aspect of life, and each of the mutually inclusive Ten Worlds is an expression of the Mystic Law. The Gohonzon and our faith enable us to activate the Mystic Law in our lives and firmly establish it as our foundation.

The layout of the Gohonzon is based on the true aspect of all phenomena elucidated in the Lotus Sutra; it clarifies that we as ordinary people, in our present form, can reveal the boundless life state of Buddhahood.

No such object of devotion ever existed in Buddhism before this. Though there were many magnificent depictions of Buddhas and bodhisattvas in paintings and sculptures, there was no mandala embodying the principle of the mutual possession of the Ten Worlds that enabled ordinary people to attain enlightenment. Nichiren Daishonin was the first to reveal the Gohonzon that illuminates the "dignified attributes that we inherently possess," that is, the object of devotion for the enlightenment of all humanity. This

Gohonzon is truly the "great mandala never before known" (WND-1, 832), depicting the realm of religion that includes and benefits all people.

In the Daishonin's day—and often even today—we find the deeply rooted view that we are but small, insignificant beings and that, in contrast, ultimate reality, or enduring value, is something that lies somewhere outside of us, somewhere far away. Such thinking is inextricably connected with a belief in some otherworldly supernatural power.

Nichiren Buddhism, however, rejects this idea. It teaches that the true reality of life, in which the eternal and ultimate Law is revealed, is to be found in ordinary people living right here and now.

The term Buddha, after all, means "enlightened one." To what did the Buddha become enlightened? It was to that which should form the true basis of our life—namely, the Law and the true essence of our being. He awakened to the universal Law permeating all phenomena, which had previously been obscured by fundamental ignorance. He awakened to the greatness of each individual's life that is one and indivisible with that Law.

The Daishonin refers to the Gohonzon as the "object of devotion for observing the mind" (WND-1, 354–76). The purpose of the Gohonzon is to enable us to "observe our mind," that is, to see and awaken to the Buddhahood within our own lives. But being able to see the true nature of the mind, or attain enlightenment, is not achieved through contemplation or meditative practice. Faith is the foundation.

THE PRACTICE FOR TRANSFORMING OUR STATE OF LIFE

The "object of devotion for observing the mind" is the "object of devotion of faith."

The Gohonzon (Buddhahood) is expressed in the lives of those who have strong faith. A person may possess the Gohonzon, but without faith, they will receive no benefit. Faith is what causes the "cluster of blessings" (WND-1, 832) that is the Gohonzon to reveal itself in our life.[6] Accordingly, as long as our faith stays alive, the "cluster of blessings" will never disappear. Even if we were to lose our material Gohonzon in an accident or natural disaster, as long as we retain our faith, the Gohonzon within our lives is eternal and ever abiding, and we can activate its beneficial power.

Only when we have faith does the beneficial power of the Gohonzon emerge. Truly, the Gohonzon is found in our faith alone.

From The Teachings for Victory,
published in Japanese in December 2014.

3.4 The Real Aspect and Power of the Gohonzon

President Ikeda discusses the significance and layout of the Gohonzon, citing passages from the writings of Nichiren Daishonin and the Lotus Sutra.

Nichiren Daishonin states that he inscribed the Gohonzon as the "banner of propagation of the Lotus Sutra" (WND-1, 831). In other words, it is the object of devotion for kosen-rufu—that is, for accomplishing the wide propagation of the Mystic Law. In "The Real Aspect of the Gohonzon," he says,

> How wondrous it is that, around two hundred years and more into the Latter Day of the Law, I was the first to reveal as the banner of propagation of the Lotus Sutra this great mandala [the Gohonzon of Nam-myoho-renge-kyo] that even those such as [the learned Indian Buddhist monks] Nagarjuna and Vasubandhu, [and the Great Teachers of China] T'ien-t'ai and Miao-lo were unable to express. (WND-1, 831)

Carrying on the Daishonin's spirit, the Soka Gakkai is propagating the "object of devotion for kosen-rufu" that the Daishonin, while enduring great persecution, inscribed for the happiness of the people of the Latter Day of the Law.

The Daishonin models the Gohonzon after the Ceremony in the Air as depicted in the Lotus Sutra when

THE PRACTICE FOR TRANSFORMING OUR STATE OF LIFE

the "Life Span" (sixteenth) chapter is being expounded. The "Life Span" chapter reveals the eternity of the Mystic Law on three levels: the eternity of the Buddha (true effect), the eternity of living beings (true cause), and the eternity of the land (true land). [The true effect, true cause, and true land are together referred to as the three mystic principles.]

The significance of the Ceremony in the Air becomes clear with the integration of the three mystic principles in the "Life Span" chapter. The Ceremony in the Air symbolically reveals that the Buddha, the living beings, and the land are all entities of the eternal Mystic Law. In other words, the eternal Mystic Law pervades the entire universe. Nichiren Daishonin expressed this Law as Nam-myoho-renge-kyo.

In "The Object of Devotion for Observing the Mind," the Daishonin discusses the aspect or layout of the Gohonzon in detail.

The true object of devotion is described as follows:

> The treasure tower sits in the air above the saha world that the Buddha of the essential teaching [identified as the pure and eternal land]; Myoho-renge-kyo appears in the center of the tower with the Buddhas Shakyamuni and Many Treasures seated to the right and left, and, flanking them, the four bodhisattvas, followers of Shakyamuni, led by Superior Practices. Manjushri, Maitreya, and the other bodhisattvas, who are all followers of the four bodhisattvas, are seated

below. All the other major and minor bodhisattvas, whether they are disciples of the Buddha in his transient status or of the Buddhas of the other worlds, are like commoners kneeling on the ground in the presence of nobles and high-ranking court officials. The Buddhas who gathered from the other worlds in the ten directions all remain on the ground, showing that they are only temporary manifestations of the eternal Buddha and that their lands are transient, not eternal and unchanging. (WND-1, 366–67)

In form, the Gohonzon depicts a multitiered structure, with the treasure tower of Nam-myoho-renge-kyo as its central axis. Nam-myoho-renge-kyo in the center indicates the fundamental truth. Since Nam-myoho-renge-kyo is the central axis of life and the universe, it is expressed by the treasure tower that soars up in the center of the Ceremony in the Air.

On either side are the Buddhas Shakyamuni and Many Treasures, who represent functions of Myoho-renge-kyo (see WND-1, 384). Many Treasures is the Buddha of the past, signifying eternal truth, and represents the Law as the object of wisdom, or that which wisdom perceives. Shakyamuni is the Buddha of the present and represents the wisdom to perceive the Law. Indeed, these are two aspects of Nam-myoho-renge-kyo. The two Buddhas seated together indicates the "fusion of reality and wisdom."

The important point is that we make neither Shakyamuni nor Many Treasures our object of devotion. Both Shakyamuni

THE PRACTICE FOR TRANSFORMING OUR STATE OF LIFE

and Many Treasures, too, became Buddhas through Nam-myoho-renge-kyo. It is always Nam-myoho-renge-kyo, the fundamental Law for attaining Buddhahood, that we make our object of devotion. In terms of the layout of the Gohonzon, this is clear from Nam-myoho-renge-kyo being written large in the center with Shakyamuni and Many Treasures positioned to either side.

Awakened to Nam-myoho-renge-kyo, Buddhas unfailingly carry out bodhisattva practice to lead all people to enlightenment. The four bodhisattvas—Superior Practices, Boundless Practices, Pure Practices, and Firmly Established Practices—represent such bodhisattva practice.

The reason these four bodhisattvas—the leaders of the Bodhisattvas of the Earth—all have "practices" in their names [as indicated by the Chinese character that means "practice" or "action"] is that they express their wisdom of enlightenment as action. That is to say, they exhibit actions that are "superior," "boundless," "pure," and "unwavering" based on infinite life force that is one with the Mystic Law.

They can be said to correspond to the four noble virtues of Buddhahood—a state of life that is forever (eternity) secure (true self), refreshed (purity), and joyful (happiness).

The Bodhisattvas of the Earth, displaying the power inherent in life, seek to protect and free from suffering all living beings and the entire world.

The Daishonin says that all the other major and minor bodhisattvas of the theoretical teaching and those from other lands are not elevated into the air but are "on the ground."

These bodhisattvas could be said to represent various altruistic practices, or concrete actions taken to further the enlightenment of all people according to their individual circumstances.

These bodhisattvas are innumerable, and therefore they cannot all be depicted in the Gohonzon. Nevertheless, the Gohonzon unmistakably includes all of their benefit.

Each of these beings of the Ten Worlds who have gathered before the treasure tower of the Mystic Law express a part of the functions of the Mystic Law. Illuminated by the light of the Mystic Law, they embody the Mystic Law and "display the dignified attributes that they inherently possess" (WND-1, 832). Displaying their unique character, they express the richness of the Mystic Law. This is the meaning of "illuminating and manifesting one's true nature" (see WND-1, 746).

When the light of the sun passes through a prism, it divides into a continuous spectrum of colors from red to violet. Sunlight is the totality of these individual colors, each being a component of that light. The light of the sun contains countless hues. Therefore, when it shines on something, some of its colors are absorbed and some are reflected back, producing the various shades we see.

The Mystic Law is the ultimate source of life. It gives birth to and encompasses all things. Illuminated by the sunlight of this all-inclusive Mystic Law, everything shines with rich individuality.

The Daishonin explains that *myo* (of *myoho* or Mystic Law) has three meanings: to open, to be fully endowed, and to revive (see WND-1, 146). The benefit of the Gohonzon

THE PRACTICE FOR TRANSFORMING OUR STATE OF LIFE

naturally includes these three functions. The Gohonzon (Nam-myoho-renge-kyo) has the power to unlock the Buddha nature in all people; it contains all benefit and embraces all capacities; and it has the revitalizing power to liberate people from any kind of negative karma and misery. In short, it has the power to enable everything to display its highest potential. It is a life-giving teaching.

The Ceremony in the Air is a "realm transcending time and space." It does not take place in some historically specific time or place. That is precisely why we are able to join in the Ceremony in the Air anytime and anywhere.

By chanting to the Gohonzon, which is modeled on the Ceremony in the Air, we become one with the eternal and universal life in the present, and we open a state of life in which we can survey the entire universe from right where we are. Through our daily practice of gongyo and chanting Nam-myoho-renge-kyo, we join the eternal Ceremony in the Air here and now. We cause the treasure tower to shine within us and in our daily lives and activities. That is the wonder of the Gohonzon. A magnificent "cosmos" of life opens to us, and reality presents itself as a world of value creation.

From The World of Nichiren Daishonin's Writings, *vol. 2, published in Japanese in January 2004.*

3.5 The Gohonzon Is the "Mirror" That Reflects Our Lives

Discussing one of Nichiren's writings in which he likens the Gohonzon to a mirror that reflects our mind, President Ikeda describes how chanting Nam-myoho-renge-kyo before the Gohonzon enables us to polish our lives.

I would like to speak about an important point with regard to our attitude in faith through the analogy of mirrors. In Buddhism, mirrors have a wide variety of meanings and are often used to explain and illustrate various doctrines. Here, I would like to briefly discuss an example related to our Buddhist practice.

Nichiren Daishonin writes:

> A bronze mirror will reflect the form of a person but it will not reflect that person's mind. The Lotus Sutra, however, reveals not only the person's form but that person's mind as well. And it reveals not only the mind; it reflects, without the least concealment, that person's past actions and future as well. (WND-2, 619)

Mirrors reflect our face and outward form. The mirror of Buddhism, however, reveals the intangible aspect of our lives. Mirrors, which function by virtue of the laws of light and reflection, are a product of human ingenuity.

THE PRACTICE FOR TRANSFORMING OUR STATE OF LIFE

On the other hand, the Gohonzon, based on the Law of the universe and life, is the ultimate expression of Buddha wisdom. It enables us to attain Buddhahood by providing us with a means to perceive the true reality of our lives. Just as a mirror is indispensable for grooming our face and hair, we need a mirror of life that allows us to look closely at ourselves and our lives if we are to lead a happier and more beautiful existence.

In "On Attaining Buddhahood in This Lifetime," the Daishonin writes:

> A tarnished mirror . . . will shine like a jewel when polished. A mind now clouded by the illusions of the innate darkness of life is like a tarnished mirror, but when polished, it is sure to become like a clear mirror, reflecting the essential nature of phenomena [Dharma nature] and the true aspect of reality. (WND-1, 4)

Originally, every person's life is a brilliantly shining mirror. Differences arise depending on whether one polishes this mirror. A polished mirror corresponds to the life state of the Buddha, whereas a tarnished mirror corresponds to that of an ordinary unenlightened being. Chanting Nam-myoho-renge-kyo is how we polish our lives. Not only do we undertake this practice ourselves, we also endeavor to teach others about the Mystic Law so that they can make the mirror of their lives shine brightly too. In this respect, we could be called master "mirror polishers" in the realm of life. Even though people work hard at polishing their appearance, they often tend to neglect polishing their lives. While they fret over blemishes on their faces, they remain unconcerned about blemishes in the depths of their lives!

In the famous novel *The Picture of Dorian Gray* by Oscar Wilde, the youthful protagonist, Dorian Gray, is so handsome that he is called a "young Adonis." An artist who wishes to immortalize Dorian's beauty paints his portrait. It is a brilliant work, an embodiment of Dorian's youthfulness and beauty. It is then that something mysterious begins to happen. Dorian's beauty does not fade, even as he is gradually tempted by a friend into a life of hedonism and immorality. Although the years go by, he remains as youthful and radiant as ever. Strangely, however, the portrait begins to turn ugly and lusterless, reflecting Dorian's dissolute life.

Then, one day, Dorian cruelly breaks a young woman's heart, driving her to commit suicide. At that time, the face in the portrait takes on an evil and savage expression that is frightening to behold. As Dorian's disreputable behavior continues, so does the hideous transformation of the portrait. Dorian is filled with horror. This picture would forever portray the face of his soul in all its ugliness. Even if he were to die, it would continue to eloquently convey the truth.

Though Dorian makes a token effort to be a better person, the picture does not change. He decides to destroy

THE PRACTICE FOR TRANSFORMING OUR STATE OF LIFE

the portrait, thinking that if it were gone, he would be able to break free from his past. So he plunges a knife into the painting. Hearing an agonized cry, members of his household staff go to investigate. They discover a portrait of the handsome, young Dorian and, collapsed before it, an aged, repulsive-looking man, Dorian, with a knife sticking in his chest. The painting had been a portrait of Dorian's soul, his inner face, into which the effects of his actions had been etched without the slightest omission.

Though we can cover imperfections on our face with cosmetics, we cannot conceal imperfections on the inner face of our lives. The law of cause and effect is strict and inexorable.

Buddhism teaches that unseen virtue brings about visible reward. In the world of Buddhism, everything counts. Being two faced or pretentious, therefore, serves us absolutely no purpose.

Our inner face that is engraved with the positive and negative causes we make is to an extent reflected in our appearance. There is also a saying "The face is the mirror of the mind."

Just as we look into a mirror when we groom our faces, we need a mirror that reflects the depths of our lives to beautifully polish our inner faces. This mirror is none other than the Gohonzon for "observing the mind."

In "The Object of Devotion for Observing the Mind," Nichiren Daishonin explains the meaning of "observing the mind": "Only when we look into a clear mirror do we see, for the first time, that we are endowed with all six sense organs [eyes, ears, nose, tongue, body, and mind]" (WND-1, 356).

Similarly, "observing the mind" means to perceive that one's mind, or life, contains the Ten Worlds, and in particular, the world of Buddhahood. It was to enable people to do this that Nichiren Daishonin bestowed the Gohonzon for "observing the mind" upon all humankind.

In his *Commentary on "The Object of Devotion for Observing the Mind,"* Nichikan Shonin [a great restorer of Nichiren Buddhism who began the task of systematizing the Daishonin's teachings] likens the Gohonzon to a mirror, stating, "The true object of devotion can be compared to a clear mirror."[7] And in *The Record of the Orally Transmitted Teachings,* Nichiren Daishonin says, "The five characters Myoho-renge-kyo [embodied in the Gohonzon] similarly reflect the ten thousand phenomena [i.e., all phenomena], not overlooking a single one of them" (OTT, 51). The Gohonzon is the clearest of all mirrors, reflecting the entire universe exactly as it is. When we chant before the Gohonzon, we can perceive the true nature of our lives and manifest the world of Buddhahood.

Our attitude or determination in faith is perfectly reflected in the mirror of the Gohonzon and mirrored in the universe. This accords with the principle of three thousand realms in a single moment of life.

In a letter to Abutsu-bo, one of his loyal disciples on Sado Island, the Daishonin writes: "You may think you offered gifts to the treasure tower of the Thus Come One Many

THE PRACTICE FOR TRANSFORMING OUR STATE OF LIFE

Treasures, but that is not so. You offered them to yourself" (WND-1, 299).

An attitude in faith that reveres and honors the Gohonzon dignifies and honors the treasure tower of our own lives. When we chant before the Gohonzon, all Buddhas and bodhisattvas throughout the universe will instantly lend their support and protection. On the other hand, if we slander the Gohonzon, the opposite will be true [i.e., such support and protection will not be forthcoming]. Accordingly, our attitude or mind is extremely important. Our deep-seated attitude or determination in faith has a subtle and far-reaching influence.

There may be times, for instance, when you feel reluctant to do gongyo or take part in Soka Gakkai activities. That state of mind will be unerringly reflected in the universe, as if on the surface of a clear mirror. The heavenly deities will then also feel reluctant to play their part, and they will naturally fail to exert their full protective powers.

On the other hand, when you joyfully do gongyo and carry out activities for kosen-rufu with the determination to accumulate even more good fortune in your life, the heavenly deities will be delighted and actively function to support you. If you are going to take some action anyway, it is to your advantage to do so willingly and joyfully.

If you carry out your Buddhist practice reluctantly with a sense that it's a waste of time, doubt and complaint will erase your benefits. Of course, if you continue in this way, you will fail to perceive any benefit from your practice, only further reconfirming your incorrect conviction that there's no point in practicing. This is a vicious circle. If you practice Nichiren Buddhism filled with doubt and skepticism, you will get results that are, at best, vague and unsatisfactory. This is the reflection of your own weak conviction in faith on the mirror of the universe. On the other hand, when you stand up with strong conviction in faith, you will accrue limitless good fortune and benefit.

It's important that we vibrantly open up and free our mind of faith, which is both extremely subtle and far reaching, while striving for self-mastery. When we do so, both our lives and state of mind will expand limitlessly, and every action we take will become a source of benefit. Deeply mastering the subtle and far-reaching workings of the mind is the key to faith and to attaining Buddhahood in this lifetime.

There is a Russian proverb that says, "Don't blame the mirror if your face is awry." The reflection in the mirror is our own. But some people get angry with the mirror!

In the same way, our happiness or unhappiness is entirely a reflection of the positive and negative causes accumulated in our lives. We cannot blame others for our misfortunes. This is even more so in the realm of faith.

There is a Japanese folk tale about a small village where no one had a mirror. In those days, mirrors were priceless. A man returning from a trip to the capital handed his wife a mirror as a souvenir. It was the first time for her to see one. Looking into the mirror, she exclaimed: "Who on earth is

THE PRACTICE FOR TRANSFORMING OUR STATE OF LIFE

this woman? You must've brought a girl back with you from the capital!" And so a big fight ensued.

Though this is an amusing anecdote, many people become angry or distraught over phenomena that are actually nothing but a reflection of their own lives—their state of mind and the causes that they have created. Like the wife in the story who exclaims "Who on earth is this woman?" they do not realize their own folly.

Ignorant of the mirror of life of Buddhism, such people cannot see themselves as they really are. And ignorant of their own true selves, they naturally cannot give proper guidance and direction to others, nor can they discern the true nature of occurrences in society.

From a speech at an SGI-USA women's meeting, Calabasas, California, February 27, 1990.

3.6 The Profound Meaning of Nam-myoho-renge-kyo

What is Nam-myoho-renge-kyo, and what is the significance of the practice of chanting it? In this selection, President Ikeda refers to passages of the Daishonin's writings to explain the fundamentals of Nichiren Buddhism.

The practice of chanting Nam-myoho-renge-kyo contains immeasurable benefit, for it enables us to summon forth in our own lives the limitless power of the Mystic Law, the fundamental Law of the universe.

Nichiren Daishonin stood up to actualize happiness for all humankind through the boundless beneficial power of Nam-myoho-renge-kyo. The doctrinal basis for this endeavor is set forth with great simplicity and conciseness in the opening passage of his writing "On Attaining Buddhahood in This Lifetime":

> If you wish to free yourself from the sufferings of birth and death you have endured since time without beginning and to attain without fail unsurpassed enlightenment in this lifetime, you must perceive the mystic truth that is originally inherent in all living beings. This truth is Myoho-renge-kyo. Chanting Myoho-renge-kyo will therefore enable you to grasp the mystic truth innate in all life. (WND-1, 3)

This passage encapsulates the profound principles of Buddhism and the history of the religious revolution to bring about the enlightenment of all people. Each word and phrase is infused with the sublime wisdom of Buddhism.

The Daishonin's reference to "the sufferings of birth and death endured since time without beginning" is premised on the concept of transmigration, according to which living beings undergo an unceasing, suffering-filled cycle of birth and death that continues from the infinite past into the infinite future. Buddhism holds that this never-ending round of suffering ultimately arises from earthly desires, and that a negative cycle of earthly desires, karma, and suffering is part and parcel of transmigration. In this sense, "the sufferings of birth and death endured since time without beginning" also represent an interminable succession of delusion and suffering.

Because the thought of such endless transmigration is ultimately unbearable, people naturally came to wish for a way to put an end to this painful cycle of birth and death and free themselves from the chains of delusion and suffering.

In Buddhism, there are two basic approaches to liberation from the suffering of this cycle. One view holds that people can free themselves from the endless karmic cycle of birth and death by eradicating earthly desires believed to cause it. The other is the Mahayana approach, in which the essence of life that undergoes transmigration is not viewed as a transient, impermanent phenomenon.

The Mahayana teachings, for example, espouse the concept of undergoing the cycle of birth and death in accordance with the bodhisattva vow to guide living beings to enlightenment; or they view the alternation between birth and death itself as a cycle of emerging from and returning to the fundamental, all-embracing life of the universe. The latter view can be easily understood using the metaphor of waves on the ocean: birth is like a wave appearing on the surface of the ocean—the life of the universe—while death is the wave submerging back into that ocean. Gaining such an understanding of the essence of our own lives, which repeat the cycle of birth and death, is to attain "unsurpassed enlightenment," the highest awakening of the Buddha.

In this passage, to "perceive the mystic truth that is originally inherent in all living beings" means to "attain unsurpassed enlightenment." The wisdom to apprehend this universally inherent truth represents the supreme enlightenment of the Buddha.

The point where Buddhism radically departs from the philosophies and religions that preceded it is that it uncovered within the individual's own life the Law, or limitless inner power, for resolving all suffering on the most essential level. A Buddha is one who, based on this Law, has attained the ultimate wisdom to fundamentally put an end to suffering and construct unshakable happiness.

Buddhism is a teaching of unparalleled humanism that stresses the boundless potential within human beings. That's why it is called the "internal way."

THE PRACTICE FOR TRANSFORMING OUR STATE OF LIFE

To "perceive the mystic truth that is originally inherent in all living beings" is to "attain unsurpassed enlightenment," and it is the sole means for freeing oneself from "the sufferings of birth and death endured since time without beginning." This is Shakyamuni's starting point and the ultimate conclusion of Buddhist thought. The scripture that gives highest expression to this philosophy of the internal way is the Lotus Sutra, which teaches that all people can attain enlightenment. The Lotus Sutra could be said to embody the ultimate principle of respect for human dignity.

In this writing ["On Attaining Buddhahood in This Lifetime"], the Daishonin says that the "mystic truth that is originally inherent in all living beings" is the "principle of the mutually inclusive relationship of a single moment of life and all phenomena" (WND-1, 3). This latter principle refers to the inscrutable relationship that exists between ourselves—our minds or each life moment—and the universe; its meaning is that all phenomena are contained in one's life and that one's life pervades all phenomena.

The life of the universe enfolds and pervades everything, and because it does so, it is also inherent in all things. The oneness of the life of the universe and our individual lives lies at the heart of the principle of the mutually inclusive relationship of a single moment of life and all phenomena. To awaken to this mystic truth is to attain the Buddha's "unsurpassed enlightenment."

The question is how to enable all people to perceive this "mystic truth that is originally inherent in all living beings."

A widely accessible Buddhism will not be possible if only a very limited number of people can follow the way set forth for apprehending the mystic truth.

The initial step the Daishonin took in opening the great path to enlightenment for all people was to name the mystic truth. The universally inherent mystic truth originally had no name, but as the Daishonin explains in "The Entity of the Mystic Law," a sage awakened to this truth in his own life was able to give it the most appropriate name (WND-1, 421).[8] Naming something is a creative process. Giving a name that accurately captures the essence of a thing has the important effect of making that essence available to all people; it enables all people to share in its value.

In "On Attaining Buddhahood in This Lifetime," as indicated by the passage "the mystic truth that is originally inherent in all living beings is Myoho-renge-kyo" (see WND-1, 3), the Daishonin clearly states that this mystic truth that constitutes the fundamental Law of the universe is none other than Myoho-renge-kyo. Strictly speaking, the term Myoho-renge-kyo existed before this as the title of the Lotus Sutra, but the Daishonin was the first to identify Myoho-renge-kyo as the name of the principle of the true aspect of all phenomena, which the Lotus Sutra teaches is the profound wisdom of all Buddhas. Also, although the "Life Span" chapter of the Lotus Sutra expounds the life of the eternal Buddha from the standpoint of Shakyamuni, it was the Daishonin who first revealed that the "heart of the 'Life Span' chapter" is Myoho-renge-kyo (see WND-1, 371).

THE PRACTICE FOR TRANSFORMING OUR STATE OF LIFE

The eternal Buddha, since attaining enlightenment in the remote past, repeatedly undergoes the cycle of birth and death as a Buddha while appearing in various forms within the Ten Worlds to free living beings from suffering. The "Life Span" chapter reveals that living beings of the Ten Worlds (including Buddhas) and both birth and death are all manifestations of the great eternal life of the universe. Because the Daishonin says that the "heart of the 'Life Span' chapter" is Myoho-renge-kyo, we can infer that Myoho-renge-kyo is the name of the great, eternal, universal life that is revealed in the "Life Span" chapter.

Living beings in the nine worlds repeatedly undergoing birth and death also follow the rhythm of birth and death of emerging from and submerging back into the great eternal life that is Myoho-renge-kyo. They are embraced by Myoho-renge-kyo and at the same time possess Myoho-renge-kyo within them. This is why Myoho-renge-kyo is the name of the "mystic truth that is originally inherent in all living beings."

It was the Daishonin who first declared that Myoho-renge-kyo is to be chanted and spread in the Latter Day of the Law.

The Daishonin's next step in opening this great path was to establish the practice of chanting Nam-myoho-renge-kyo. He appended the word *nam*—a transliteration of the Sanskrit word *namas*, meaning "devotion"—to the universal truth of Myoho-renge-kyo and established the practice of invoking this truth. *Nam* means "to dedicate one's life."

Chanting Nam-myoho-renge-kyo aloud represents a determination and vow to dedicate one's life to the realm of truth of Myoho-renge-kyo in thought, word, and deed.

At the same time, chanting Nam-myoho-renge-kyo enables each person to actualize a way of life based on the universal truth of Myoho-renge-kyo. The crucial point in chanting Nam-myoho-renge-kyo in Nichiren Buddhism is not simply intoning the name of an external truth. It constitutes a practice to actually summon forth the inner truth that pervades the universe and our own selves and live our lives in accord with that truth. This practice could be described as a process of establishing a self capable of activating and tapping from within the "mystic truth originally inherent in all living beings."

In order to enable all people to perceive and actualize the "mystic truth originally inherent in all living beings," the Daishonin gave it the name Myoho-renge-kyo and established the practice of reciting that name—the practice of chanting Nam-myoho-renge-kyo. By doing so, he opened the way for all people to dedicate their lives to and live based on the mystic truth.

The Daishonin thus established the means by which all people can awaken to the fact that the truth of life and the universe exists within their own lives, and actively manifest that truth. Moreover, this truth is the enlightened wisdom of all Buddhas and is fully revealed in the Lotus Sutra, which is the highest teaching of Buddhism. By basing ourselves on that truth, we can lead lives of supreme value. Nichiren

THE PRACTICE FOR TRANSFORMING OUR STATE OF LIFE

Buddhism made this realm of truth accessible to anyone, anywhere, anytime, no matter what their background. It would be no exaggeration to say that the practice of chanting Nam-myoho-renge-kyo in Nichiren Buddhism gave rise to a Buddhism of the people, open to all. This practice of chanting is indeed the supreme Buddhist practice, making it possible for us to fundamentally transform our lives.

To chant Nam-myoho-renge-kyo is to summon forth our own innate Buddhahood (see WND-1, 887).[9] It is the direct path to manifesting that highest state of life. The wisdom and compassion of the Buddha that emerge through chanting Nam-myoho-renge-kyo enrich our beings and bring happiness to ourselves and others. Further, as more and more people come to chant Nam-myoho-renge-kyo for the happiness of themselves and others, it will be possible to forge an alliance of people filled with the compassion of the Buddha and to ultimately transform even the destiny of humankind.

Another point we should bear in mind regarding the true meaning of Nam-myoho-renge-kyo is that it is also the name of the life of the Buddha of the Latter Day, Nichiren Daishonin. Nam-myoho-renge-kyo and the life of the Buddha of the Latter Day are indivisibly connected. We could say that the fundamental truth of Myoho-renge-kyo that pervades life and the universe was identified and established for the first time only through the Daishonin himself practicing it and manifesting it in his behavior. He gave concrete expression to the Law that people had not been able to perceive up to that point.

Nichiren Daishonin's life as the Buddha of the Latter Day is none other than a life dedicated to battling evil and vanquishing fundamental ignorance. The struggle to free people from all misfortune and misery in the world, from all karma and the sufferings of birth, aging, sickness, and death, ultimately entails battling the ignorance that gives rise to evil and suffering.

The chanting of Nam-myoho-renge-kyo, established by the Daishonin for the happiness of oneself and others and the realization of kosen-rufu, has the power to clear the clouds of ignorance (see WND-2, 85). When we chant Nam-myoho-renge-kyo, the sun of the world of Buddhahood rises in our hearts. The ignorance and delusion, like heavy clouds shrouding the sun, are swept away. When the sun of Buddhahood comes to shine within us, the darkness of ignorance vanishes.

Nichiren Buddhism is not a teaching in which the Daishonin alone shines like the sun. It is a teaching in which all of us can bring the sun of Buddhahood to rise in our lives just as he did. We are truly fortunate in that we can manifest the same brilliant life state of Buddhahood as Nichiren Daishonin.

From Lecture on "On Attaining Buddhahood in This Lifetime," *published in Japanese in January 2007.*

3.7 Embracing the Gohonzon Is in Itself Attaining Enlightenment

President Ikeda explains how Nichiren Buddhism views the concept of attaining enlightenment, or Buddhahood.

Nam-myoho-renge-kyo is the ultimate Law that gives rise to, or is the source of, all Buddhas. To put it another way, the fundamental cause for the enlightenment of all Buddhas is not countless kalpas of practice but rather awakening to the fundamental Law of Nam-myoho-renge-kyo. The Buddhist practice for the Latter Day of the Law is to directly embrace Nam-myoho-renge-kyo. This is why practice over countless kalpas is not necessary in Nichiren Buddhism.

In his writing "The Object of Devotion for Observing the Mind," Nichiren Daishonin states: "Shakyamuni's practices and the virtues he consequently attained are all contained within the five characters of Myoho-renge-kyo.[10] If we believe in these five characters, we will naturally be granted the same benefits as he was" (WND-1, 365).

The practices of Shakyamuni and the Buddhas of the ten directions and three existences to attain enlightenment and the virtues resulting from those practices are all included in Nam-myoho-renge-kyo. For that reason, by embracing the "five characters of Myoho-renge-kyo," we naturally obtain the full benefits enjoyed by Shakyamuni and all Buddhas, and we are able to attain Buddhahood.

This is the principle that "embracing the Gohonzon is in itself observing one's own mind," or attaining enlightenment. It is also articulated as "attainment of Buddhahood in one's present form" and "immediate attainment of enlightenment."

The Daishonin says that those who embrace the Mystic Law "can readily become as noble a Buddha as Shakyamuni" (WND-1, 1030). The Daishonin's teaching opens the way for all people to reach the same great state of Buddhahood as Shakyamuni. Buddhahood is not a fiction or a metaphor, nor is it restricted to the inconceivably distant future. Nichiren Buddhism enables all people to attain Buddhahood in this lifetime.

The principle of "embracing the Gohonzon is in itself observing one's own mind" represents a revolution in the concept of attaining Buddhahood. As Mr. Toda explained:

> Just by chanting the single phrase of Nam-myoho-renge-kyo with faith in the Gohonzon, we can carry out the practice for attaining Buddhahood far more easily than the Buddhas described in the "Expedient Means" chapter of the Lotus Sutra, who practiced for tens of millions of years [over countless lifetimes before attaining Buddhahood].[11]
>
> While the widely accepted view of attaining Buddhahood is that it is a long, strenuous uphill climb to reach the summit of enlightenment, Nichiren Buddhism teaches that all people can reach that summit instantly. We can immediately and

THE PRACTICE FOR TRANSFORMING OUR STATE OF LIFE

directly attain the expansive state of Buddhahood here and now, as though suddenly gazing from on high over the mountain peaks below and enjoying a magnificent, 360-degree panorama of the world. We can then go out among the challenging realities of living and share with others the joy of attaining this lofty state of being. This is what is so wonderful and exciting about the practice of Nichiren Buddhism.

From Lectures on the "Expedient Means" and
"Life Span" Chapters of the Lotus Sutra, *vol. 1*,
published in Japanese in September 1995.

3.8 The Mystic Law Exists Within Our Lives

President Ikeda explains that, by making Buddhism easily accessible to all, the Daishonin's teaching of Nam-myoho-renge-kyo represents a great religious revolution.

In "On Attaining Buddhahood in This Lifetime," Nichiren Daishonin sternly cautions, "Even though you chant and believe in Myoho-renge-kyo,[12] if you think the Law is outside yourself, you are embracing not the Mystic Law but an inferior teaching" (WND-1, 3). "Inferior" here means "incomplete." The Mystic Law is the ultimate truth that is perfect and complete; in contrast, an incomplete teaching sets forth only a partial truth.

The above passage contains a profound philosophy that overcomes one of the serious pitfalls to which religion tends to succumb. It also embodies a crucial philosophy of faith for attaining genuine happiness.

Religion is generally held to be a universal endeavor to connect the human being to the infinite, absolute, and sacred. While in a sense this may be true, it seems that many religions postulate from the outset a separation between the secular and the sacred, and between human beings and gods or Buddhas, and thus seek to bridge that gap.

The Daishonin, however, regards teachings that view the absolute or sacred as separate from human beings as incomplete. And he cites as an example the provisional, pre–Lotus Sutra Buddhist teachings, which do not set forth the principles or practice that enable ordinary people to attain Buddhahood in this lifetime. Rather, they espouse that one must first undergo countless kalpas of practice over many lifetimes before enlightenment can be achieved. In the provisional, pre–Lotus Sutra teachings, a virtually insurmountable gulf exists between Buddhas and ordinary people. As long as that divide exists between the world of Buddhahood and the nine worlds [the realm of ordinary beings], it naturally follows that there is no way for all people to attain enlightenment. In this worldview, ordinary people and the idealized Buddhas are poles apart, thus leaving ordinary people with

THE PRACTICE FOR TRANSFORMING OUR STATE OF LIFE

no option but to aspire for salvation through the assistance or intervention of such Buddhas.

This perceived separation between the nine worlds and the world of Buddhahood is demolished by the Lotus Sutra doctrine of three thousand realms in a single moment of life—in other words, the teaching that "the nine worlds have the potential for Buddhahood and that Buddhahood retains the nine worlds" (WND-1, 539). Here we can see the immense importance of the Lotus Sutra principle of the mutual possession of the Ten Worlds.

The Daishonin opened the way to actualizing this latter principle, which is the key to attaining Buddhahood in this lifetime, by establishing the practice of chanting Nam-myoho-renge-kyo. This constitutes in its fullest and most complete form the teaching of Buddhism that seeks enlightenment for all human beings.

The Mystic Law is the fundamental Law of the universe. Its universality transcends our individual selves. However, the Mystic Law also exists within our lives (see WND-1, 3). It both resides within us and transcends us. Put another way, the Mystic Law is inherent in our lives because it is the all-embracing Law that pervades everything in the universe.

Regarding the meaning of chanting Nam-myoho-renge-kyo, the Daishonin further states: "When we revere Myoho-renge-kyo inherent in our own life as the object of devotion, the Buddha nature within us is summoned forth and manifested by our chanting of Nam-myoho-renge-kyo. This is what is meant by 'Buddha'" (WND-1, 887). The expression "is summoned forth and manifested" points to the profound significance of the Mystic Law.

The Daishonin uses a wonderful metaphor to explain this principle of calling forth and revealing the inner Buddha nature: "When a caged bird sings, birds who are flying in the sky are thereby summoned and gather around, and when the birds flying in the sky gather around, the bird in the cage strives to get out" (WND-1, 887).

The singing of the caged bird refers to the chanting of Nam-myoho-renge-kyo by ordinary people who, shackled in the chains of fundamental ignorance and earthly desires, arouse faith in the Mystic Law. In other words, it is the chanting of Nam-myoho-renge-kyo with faith, determined to win over all obstacles and become happy without fail through the power of the Mystic Law.

The power of such strong, resolute chanting calls forth the Buddha nature in all living beings. Not only does the Buddha nature of [the protective gods] Brahma and Shakra and of the Buddhas and bodhisattvas throughout the universe manifest, but those chanting Nam-myoho-renge-kyo can also sever the chains of fundamental ignorance and illusion, and reveal their own Buddha nature. In other words, it is the power of our voices chanting Nam-myoho-renge-kyo that connects our lives with the Mystic Law pervading all phenomena in the universe.

The Daishonin's most important admonition in regard to attaining enlightenment through chanting Nam-myoho-renge-kyo is that we must not view the Law as something outside ourselves. If we think the Law exists externally, then we are reverting to the kind of divide between Buddhas and ordinary people found in the pre–Lotus Sutra teachings.

Throughout everything, Mr. Toda steadfastly continued to seek the Law that exists nowhere but within our own lives. And he stressed the importance of living true to oneself. His starting point was his profound realization in prison that the Buddha is life itself and his awakening to his identity as a Bodhisattva of the Earth.

He also often spoke of the spirit of faith we need in order to perceive the Mystic Law within us, saying: "You have to be resolved that Nam-myoho-renge-kyo is your own life!" and "Propagating the Mystic Law in the Latter Day of the Law simply means deciding 'My life is none other than Nam-myoho-renge-kyo!'" This is the spirit the Daishonin teaches in the passage "When you chant *myoho* and recite *renge*, you must summon up deep faith that Myoho-renge-kyo is your life itself" (WND-1, 3).

The Daishonin saw the power of the Mystic Law, which encompasses and sustains all things in the universe, as existing within human beings, and he established a means for actually manifesting that Law in their lives.

It is only by communing and fusing with the power ("other power") of the eternal, unchanging truth transcending our limited, finite selves that we can wholly activate our own power ("self-power"). At the same time, however, this eternal, all-encompassing "other power" actually exists inherently in our lives. The Daishonin writes: "People are certainly self-empowered, and yet they are not self-empowered. . . . People are certainly other-empowered, and yet they are not other-empowered" (WND-2, 62).[13] What this means, I believe, is that by relying neither exclusively on "other power" nor on "self-power," we can bring forth from within us the power that transcends us. Chanting Nam-myoho-renge-kyo enables us to do this.

In this way, Nichiren Buddhism opens up a broad new vision of a universal religion for the happiness of all humankind—one that transcends the approach of teachings that strictly divide the powers of self and other and that emphasize one over the other.

From Lecture on "On Attaining Buddhahood in This Lifetime,"
published in Japanese in January 2007.

3.9 A Practice Accessible to All

Chanting Nam-myoho-renge-kyo constitutes the entirety of the practice of Nichiren Buddhism; beyond that, ceremonies and formalities are of no importance.

Nichiren Daishonin sent many letters to his lay follower Toki Jonin. In one of them, titled "On the Four Stages of Faith and the Five Stages of Practice," he outlines the correct Buddhist practice for people in the Latter Day of the Law, clarifying that such practice lies in "making [the] single word 'faith' the foundation" (WND-1, 785).

The essence of Nichiren Buddhism is not ceremony or formality. It is the heart. It is our faith. The Daishonin further states that the practice of chanting Nam-myoho-renge-kyo with faith in the Gohonzon contains within it all other forms of practice. He explains with the following simple allegory: "The two characters that comprise the name Japan contain within them all the people and animals and wealth in the sixty-six provinces of the country, without a single omission" (WND-1, 788). Similarly, he says, the phrase "Nam-myoho-renge-kyo" contains within it the entirety of the Lotus Sutra. Therefore, the practice of chanting Nam-myoho-renge-kyo is itself the direct path to attaining Buddhahood. All other practices, especially those entrenched in formality, are secondary practices that, if given primary importance, can become an impediment to faith.

The Daishonin further teaches that even though we may not understand the profound meaning of Nam-myoho-renge-kyo, we can still gain the benefit of chanting daimoku. Here, employing another allegory, he states, "When a baby drinks milk, it has no understanding of its taste, and yet its body is naturally nourished" (WND-1, 788).

Though we may not understand Buddhist doctrine, if we simply chant free of doubt, then, just as a newborn baby gains nourishment from milk, we will naturally be able to imbue our lives with the great power of Nam-myoho-renge-kyo. Nichiren Buddhism is the Buddhism of the people; it exists for and is accessible to all.

In the same writing, Nichiren Daishonin states: "The five characters of Myoho-renge-kyo[14] do not represent the [Lotus Sutra] text, nor are they its meaning. They are nothing other than the intent of the entire sutra" (WND-1, 788). Nam-myoho-renge-kyo, which we chant, is the heart and essence of the Lotus Sutra. Fundamentally, it is the very spirit of Nichiren Daishonin. Accordingly, though we may not grasp its profound meaning entirely, when we chant with faith in the Gohonzon, we can come into contact with the Daishonin's spirit. We can bring forth within us the life state of the Daishonin that is one with Nam-myoho-renge-kyo. How truly fortunate we are!

From a speech at an SGI-Italy representatives conference, Milan, Italy, July 2, 1992.

3.10 Chanting Nam-myoho-renge-kyo Is the Key to Victory in Life

In this excerpt from The New Human Revolution, *the novel's protagonist Shin'ichi Yamamoto (whose character represents President Ikeda) is speaking in 1966 to members in Peru who have just started practicing Nichiren Buddhism.*

Those who challenge themselves earnestly, aligning their lives with the Mystic Law, kosen-rufu, and the SGI, lay the foundations for eternal happiness and realize ultimate victory in life.

I would like all of you to become such great victors. In that connection, allow me today to talk a little about the key requirements for victory.

The first is chanting Nam-myoho-renge-kyo.

Our health, courage, wisdom, joy, desire to improve, self-discipline, and so on, could all be said to depend on our life force. Chanting Nam-myoho-renge-kyo enables us to bring forth limitless life force. Those who base themselves on chanting Nam-myoho-renge-kyo are therefore never deadlocked.

The important thing is to continue chanting every day, no matter what happens. Nam-myoho-renge-kyo is the fundamental power of the universe. Please chant resounding daimoku morning and evening with the vibrant and energetic rhythm of majestic horses galloping through the heavens.

When we chant before the Gohonzon, we are facing the Buddha, so we should remember to have a respectful attitude. Other than that, though, we should feel free to express what's in our hearts honestly and directly to the Gohonzon.

The Gohonzon is the embodiment of the Buddha endowed with infinite compassion. We should therefore chant about our desires, our problems, and our aspirations, just as they are. When we're suffering, feeling sad, or experiencing hard times, we should take everything to the Gohonzon with an open heart, like a child who throws itself into its mother's arms and clings to her. The Gohonzon will "listen" to everything. Let's chant as if carrying on a conversation, confiding our innermost thoughts. In time, even hellish sufferings will vanish like the morning dew and seem but a dream.

If, for instance, we recognize that we have done something wrong, we should offer sincere prayers of apology and humbly reflect on our behavior. We can resolve never to repeat the same mistake again and set forth anew.

Also, when we encounter a crucial situation, we can firmly resolve to win and chant Nam-myoho-renge-kyo with the power of a lion's roar or the ferocity of an *asura* demon, as if to shake the entire universe.

Furthermore, in the evening, we can joyfully chant to the Gohonzon with profound appreciation for that day.

THE PRACTICE FOR TRANSFORMING OUR STATE OF LIFE

In *The Record of the Orally Transmitted Teachings*, Nichiren Daishonin cites the words "Morning after morning we rise up with the Buddha, evening after evening we lie down with the Buddha"[15] (OTT, 83). This means that those who continue to chant in earnest are always together with the Daishonin, the Buddha of the Latter Day of the Law. This holds true not only for this lifetime but even beyond death, with the Daishonin and all heavenly deities throughout the universe extending their protection to us. We can therefore feel a deep sense of security from the depths of our beings and be free of all fear. We can enjoy and live out our lives with complete confidence.

Chanting transforms suffering into joy and joy into greater joy. That's why it is important for us to single-mindedly chant Nam-myoho-renge-kyo, come what may, whether we are feeling happy or sad, in good times or in bad. This is the direct path to happiness.

From The New Human Revolution, *vol. 11,*
"Pioneering New Frontiers" chapter.

3.11 The Lotus Sutra Is a Scripture of Cosmic Humanism

Nichiren Buddhism is based on the Lotus Sutra, the scripture teaching the supreme enlightenment of Shakyamuni Buddha. The pinnacle of the Mahayana teachings, the Lotus Sutra was compiled in the first century CE. It sees the eternal life state of Buddhahood inherent within all people and teaches that anyone can reveal this lofty inner potential. And it calls on practitioners to carry on the struggle to lead people to enlightenment in the evil age after Shakyamuni's death. In this excerpt, President Ikeda discusses the profound meaning contained in the sutra.

"The scripture of the lotus flower of the Law"—the Lotus Sutra is the monarch of all scriptures. As a monarch, it does not reject any other teaching but acts to enable every other teaching to be fully effective.

Nichiren Daishonin writes:

> Ultimately, all phenomena are contained within one's life, down to the last particle of dust. The nine mountains and the eight seas are encompassed in one's body, and the sun, moon, and myriad stars are found in one's life. We, however, are like a blind person who is incapable of seeing the images reflected in a mirror, or like an infant who has no fear of water or fire. The teachings such as those of the non-Buddhist writings and those of the Hinayana and provisional Mahayana Buddhist scriptures all

> partially explain the phenomena inherent in one's life. They do not explain them as the Lotus Sutra does. (WND-1, 629)

Teachings apart from the Lotus Sutra offer only partial explanations of the Law of life. Though partially true, they do not have the capacity on their own to revitalize all aspects of life. They are more likely, in fact, to produce distortions. The Lotus Sutra, however, is the single essential Law that unifies all these partial teachings, places them in the proper perspective, and enables them to function effectively.

This is the wisdom of the Lotus Sutra. The "Life Span" chapter of the Lotus Sutra likens the wisdom of the Lotus Sutra to "a skilled physician who is wise and understanding" (LSOC, 268). Like a skilled physician, the wisdom of the Lotus Sutra has the power to cure those who are suffering.

The Lotus Sutra seeks to convey in an easily accessible way the truth that each of us has been a Buddha since the eternal past and will be so into the eternal future. And it was Nichiren Daishonin, the votary of the Lotus Sutra in the Latter Day of the Law, who made it possible for all people to actually experience this in their lives.

The Lotus Sutra teaches of a hidden treasure residing within us, as vast as the universe itself, that vanquishes all feelings of helplessness. It teaches us how to live vibrantly and vigorously, in rhythm with the infinite life of the universe. It teaches the true, great adventure of self-transformation.

The Lotus Sutra has a vastness that can enfold all people in a state of peace. It has cultural and artistic richness. It enables us to attain a boundless state forever imbued with the noble virtues of eternity, happiness, true self, and purity, and to live with the confidence, wherever we may be, that "this, my land, remains safe and tranquil" (LSOC, 272).

The Lotus Sutra has the drama of struggles of good over evil. It has a warmth that comforts the weary. It has a vibrant, pulsing courage that banishes all fear. It has joyous songs of living unbounded and at ease throughout past, present, and future. It has soaring freedom.

It has brilliant light, flowers, greenery, music, and scenes like epic works of art or cinema.

It offers brilliant psychology, life lessons, and guidelines for happiness and peace. It presents basic principles for healthy living.

It awakens us to the universal truth that changing our mindset changes everything. Avoiding both the desolation of individualism and the prison of totalitarianism, it possesses the power for creating a pure land of compassion in which people help and encourage one another.

Both communism and capitalism have reduced people to being a means to an end. But the Lotus Sutra, the monarch of all scriptures, embodies a fundamental humanism in which people are the end, not the means, where people are the protagonists, the monarchs. This message of the Lotus Sutra can be described as a "cosmic humanism"[16]—a magnificent theme to guide the twenty-first century.

From The Wisdom of the Lotus Sutra, vol. 1,
published in Japanese in March 1996.

3.12 Gongyo Encompasses the Heart of the Lotus Sutra

President Ikeda illuminates the significance of the "Expedient Means" and "Life Span" chapters of the Lotus Sutra, from which Soka Gakkai members recite passages during gongyo.

I once composed the following poem:

> Morning and evening,
> joyously attune your lives
> to the melody of the universe,
> as you recite the "Expedient Means"
> and "Life Span" chapters!

What wonderful efforts we are making toward the creation of peace and happiness when we recite these important chapters that comprise the heart of the Lotus Sutra, the highest of all the Buddhist sutras, and vibrantly chant Nam-myoho-renge-kyo, the supreme teaching of Buddhism and ultimate Law of the universe!

The Lotus Sutra was expounded to enable all living beings to attain enlightenment. When read in terms of its implicit meaning—namely, from the doctrinal standpoint of Nichiren Buddhism—the Lotus Sutra takes on profound significance as an "explanation" of the object of devotion (Gohonzon) of Nam-myoho-renge-kyo, the fundamental Law that opens the way for the enlightenment of all living beings throughout the entire world into the eternal future of the Latter Day of the Law.

The essence of this sutra is contained in the "Expedient Means" chapter, which expounds the "true aspect of all phenomena," and in the "Life Span" chapter, which reveals the Buddha's "attainment of Buddhahood in the remote past."

From the standpoint of Nichiren Buddhism, the "Expedient Means" chapter praises the wisdom of Nam-myoho-renge-kyo (the Mystic Law) as infinitely profound and immeasurable, and it elucidates the principle that all living beings are Buddhas. In particular, the section that clarifies the "true aspect of all phenomena" and the "ten factors of life" (the portion that we recite three times during gongyo) indicates that all the ever-changing forms and states of life (all phenomena) are without exception manifestations of Nam-myoho-renge-kyo (the true aspect). The Daishonin writes, "All beings and environments in the Ten Worlds . . . are without exception manifestations of Myoho-renge-kyo"

THE PRACTICE FOR TRANSFORMING OUR STATE OF LIFE

(WND-1, 383). All living beings are inherently entities of the Mystic Law. Therefore, all those who chant Nam-myoho-renge-kyo and work for kosen-rufu are assured of attaining the life state of Buddhahood just as they are.

We don't need to go to some faraway place to attain Buddhahood. We don't need to become someone special. We can commune dynamically with the universe as and where we are and fully reveal the brilliance of our own innate "true aspect"—that is, our true self as an entity of Nam-myoho-renge-kyo. That is the purpose of gongyo and the realm of faith. We can bring forth from within us the wisdom, courage, and compassion of the Mystic Law. We therefore have absolutely nothing to fear.

The term *life span* of "The Life Span of the Thus Come One" chapter contains the meaning of measuring the life span and benefits of the Buddha. Read from the perspective of the meaning implicit in its text, this chapter offers a detailed description of the eternal life span and the benefits of the "Thus Come One Nam-myoho-renge-kyo" (OTT, 123) extending from the infinite past. Here, the eternal nature of life is revealed, along with the fact that this constitutes the true nature of all living beings. Also revealed in this chapter is the mission of the Bodhisattvas of the Earth to spread this great Law and lead all living beings to enlightenment.

The verse section of the "Life Span" chapter, in particular, is a grand paean to the infinitely great, noble, and eternal life force we all possess.

The Daishonin notes that when we combine the Chinese character *ji* (self) of the opening line of the verse section—"*ji ga toku burrai*" (Since I attained Buddhahood) (LSOC, 270)—and the final Chinese character *shin* (body) of the closing line—"*soku joju busshin*" (quickly acquire the body of a Buddha) (LSOC, 273), this forms the word *jishin*, meaning "oneself" (see OTT, 140). From beginning to end, the verse section praises the "self" and the "life" of the Buddha, and, as such, it is also a paean to the state of eternal and absolute freedom inherent in our lives.

The verse section offers direct answers to the ultimate questions that form the basis of all thought, philosophy, and religion—in other words, the timeless questions of life, such as "What is the meaning of our existence?" "What is the true essence of our being?" "Where have we come from and where are we going?" and "What are life and death?" The verse section constitutes a teaching of hope and joy with the power to illuminate all humanity and all life for eternity.

In the verse section, we find the lines "*Ga shi do annon. Tennin jo juman.*" (This, my land, remains safe and tranquil, constantly filled with heavenly and human beings) [LSOC, 272].

There is still immense suffering in the world today—suffering as painful as being "consumed in a great fire" (LSOC, 272). Our noble movement for kosen-rufu, upholding the philosophy of the eternity of life, is firmly committed to creating a world where people live together in happiness and

THE PRACTICE FOR TRANSFORMING OUR STATE OF LIFE

peace—an ideal society that humanity has always longed for. This is the way to secure the right to lead a happy, fulfilled existence for all people in the twenty-first century, an aspiration shared by countless philosophers, religious leaders, and peace scholars.

From a speech at a world peace gongyo meeting,
Tokyo, Japan, September 8, 2002.

3.13 Gongyo—A Ceremony in Which Our Lives Commune With the Universe

President Ikeda explains the significance of gongyo and daimoku from the profound perspective of the universe and life.

Gongyo—reciting portions of the Lotus Sutra and chanting Nam-myoho-renge-kyo—is a ceremony in which our lives commune with the universe. It is an act through which, based on the Gohonzon, we can vibrantly draw forth the life force of the universe within the cosmos of our lives. We exist. We have life. The universe, too, is a giant living entity. Life is the universe and the universe is life. Each of us is a living entity, just like the universe. We are our own miniature universe.

One scholar, observing that the human body is made of the same elements produced by stars, has called human beings "children of the stars." Our bodies are a microcosm of the universe. Not only are they made of the same matter as the universe, but they also follow the same process of generation and disintegration, the same rhythm of life and death, that pervades the cosmos. All physical laws—such as gravity and the conservation of energy—also affect and operate in the microcosm of each living entity.

Earth takes 365 days, five hours, and forty-eight minutes to complete one revolution around the sun. It, too, operates according to a rigorous order. The human body, meanwhile, is said to have more than sixty trillion individual cells. When they function each day in a well-ordered fashion, correctly carrying out their respective jobs, we enjoy good health. The complexity and precision of the human body are truly wondrous. Likewise, if Earth were to veer even slightly from its present orbit around the sun, we would be in serious trouble. Everything hangs in a delicate balance, governed by the strict principle that life and the universe are one. The same is true of each individual life—of each microcosm.

Science has directed its attention to the investigation of real, yet invisible, natural laws. Such investigation has led to the invention of many machines and devices that apply those laws. An understanding of the principles of buoyancy, for instance, led to the development of seagoing vessels. Likewise, the discovery of the laws of aerodynamics led to

THE PRACTICE FOR TRANSFORMING OUR STATE OF LIFE

the invention of aircraft, and insight into the workings of electromagnetic waves paved the way for the development of radio and television. These natural laws, however, are only partial laws of the universe.

Buddhism, on the other hand, developed out of the search for and discovery of the ultimate Law of life that is the source and foundation of all other laws and principles. This ultimate Law of life is the Mystic Law.

The Mystic Law is also invisible, yet it, too, exists without a doubt. Nichiren Daishonin inscribed the Gohonzon so that we could bring forth the power of the Mystic Law from within our own lives. That is why Mr. Toda said, "I apologize for using such a simplistic analogy, but the Gohonzon can be likened to a happiness-producing device."

When we do gongyo—recite portions of the Lotus Sutra and chant Nam-myoho-renge-kyo before the Gohonzon—the microcosm of our individual lives harmonizes seamlessly with the macrocosm of the universe. It is a sublime ceremony, an action through which we fully open the storehouse of treasures within. We can thereby tap into the wellspring of life force in the depths of our own beings. We can access the source of inexhaustible wisdom, compassion, and courage.

The universe, in its essence, is Nam-myoho-renge-kyo; our life is an expression of Nam-myoho-renge-kyo; and the Gohonzon is an embodiment of Nam-myoho-renge-kyo. Since all three are Nam-myoho-renge-kyo, they are essentially one and indivisible. Therefore, when we chant

Nam-myoho-renge-kyo, our life and the universe are aligned around the Gohonzon—meshing together perfectly like cogs in a machine—and we begin to move in the direction of happiness and fulfillment.

We can be in rhythm with the universe 365 days a year—in spring, summer, autumn, and winter—and manifest the life force, wisdom, and good fortune that enables us to surmount any problem or suffering. When we rev up the powerful engine of life force that is Buddhahood, we can break through any impasse and keep moving forward, boldly steering ourselves in the direction of hope and justice.

From Discussions on Youth,
published in Japanese in March 1999.

3.14 Polishing Our Lives Through Chanting Nam-myoho-renge-kyo

President Ikeda discusses the benefits of our daily practice of chanting Nam-myoho-renge-kyo and reciting portions of the Lotus Sutra.

The Mystic Law is the key to polishing our lives. In "On Attaining Buddhahood in This Lifetime," Nichiren Daishonin writes:

> This is similar to a tarnished mirror that will shine like a jewel when polished. A mind now clouded by the illusions of the innate darkness of life is like a tarnished mirror, but when polished, it is sure to become like a clear mirror, reflecting the essential nature of phenomena [Dharma nature] and the true aspect of reality. Arouse deep faith, and diligently polish your mirror day and night. How should you polish it? Only by chanting Nam-myoho-renge-kyo. (WND-1, 4)

Our society today is rife with negative influences. People's lives are easily clouded and sullied. That is why we need this fundamental method for polishing and purifying our lives.

A life that has been thoroughly polished by chanting Nam-myoho-renge-kyo shines with wisdom, and this wisdom serves as a beacon guiding the way to victory in life. In "The Benefits of the Teacher of the Law" chapter of the Lotus Sutra, the wisdom of those who uphold the Mystic Law is likened to "a pure bright mirror in which forms and shapes are all reflected" (LSOC, 303). Just as a bright, clear mirror reflects every object as it is, a life that has been well polished can discern the true reality of all things in the world.

In *The Record of the Orally Transmitted Teachings*, Nichiren Daishonin comments on this passage as follows:

> The sutra passage is saying that persons whose six sense organs are pure will be like lapis lazuli or like bright mirrors in which one sees the major world system (or the thousand-millionfold world).
>
> Now when Nichiren and his followers chant Nam-myoho-renge-kyo, they see and understand the ten thousand phenomena [i.e., all phenomena], as though these were reflected in a bright mirror. (OTT, 149)

Lapis lazuli is one of the seven kinds of treasures. The purification of the six sense organs is one of the benefits achieved by practitioners of the Mystic Law that is outlined in the "Benefits of the Teacher of the Law" chapter. In other words, through Buddhist practice, we purify and enhance our mental and perceptual faculties as represented by our eyes, ears, nose, tongue, body, and mind—that is, our life in its entirety.

The "bright mirror" of a well-forged and polished life fully reflects the universe, society, and human life. The "bright mirror," fundamentally, is the Gohonzon—in other words, the life of Nichiren Daishonin. In a broader sense, it is the "bright mirror of the single mind [of faith]" (see OTT, 149) of all those who believe in the Gohonzon as disciples of the Daishonin.

This is the profound significance of faith in the Mystic Law. Through strong faith, we can elevate and transform our lives—spiritually and physically—to their purest and strongest possible state. The purification of our lives through faith is the driving force for our victory as human beings. That is why it is vital for us to persevere in faith until the very end of our lives.

From a speech at an arts division general meeting, Tokyo, Japan, May 10, 1987.

3.15 Change Starts From Prayer

Referring to the Daishonin's writings, President Ikeda discusses the profound significance of prayer in Nichiren Buddhism.

Nichiren Daishonin writes:

> The prayers offered by a practitioner of the Lotus Sutra will be answered just as an echo answers a sound, as a shadow follows a form, as the reflection of the moon appears in clear water, as a mirror collects dewdrops,[17] as a magnet attracts iron, as amber attracts particles of dust, or as a clear mirror reflects the color of an object. (WND-1, 340)

In this passage, the Daishonin states that the prayers of the votary of the Lotus Sutra are always answered. His use of natural principles and phenomena as analogies demonstrates his strong confidence in what he is saying.

Wherever practitioners of the Lotus Sutra chant Nam-myoho-renge-kyo, just as an echo answers a sound and a shadow follows a form, their prayers will unfailingly produce positive results there. The Daishonin teaches that our lives are transformed—both spiritually and physically—by prayer, which in turn exerts a positive influence on our environment.

Prayer is not something abstract. Many today may regard the intangible, unseen realm of life as nothing more than a product of the imagination. But if we were to view things only from a material perspective, then our relationships with people and things would largely appear to arise solely from the chaos of randomness. The penetrating insight of Buddhism, however, discerns the Law of life in the depths of chaos and apprehends it as the force that supports and activates all phenomena from within.

The Daishonin writes, "As life does not go beyond the moment, the Buddha expounded the blessings that come from a single moment of rejoicing [on hearing the Lotus Sutra]" (WND-1, 62). Because "life does not go beyond the moment," as he says, our focus should be on the power that emerges from within us at each moment to support us and give fundamental direction to our lives. Prayer—namely, chanting Nam-myoho-renge-kyo—is the only way for us to confront on this fundamental level the delusions inherent in life.

It thus follows that prayer is the driving force for maintaining a correct practice and tenacious action. Nothing is as insubstantial as action without prayer. For those who neglect prayer, things may appear to go quite smoothly for a while. They may even seem very upbeat. But once faced with adversity, they tend to fall into despair, their lives as fragile as a withered tree. Lacking self-mastery, they are tossed about like leaves on the turbulent waters of society.

The path up the hill of life doesn't follow a straight line. There are successes and mistakes. Sometimes we win and sometimes we lose. With each step on our way, with every curve and corner we navigate, we grow a little bit more. In this process, prayer functions as a powerful force preventing us from becoming arrogant in victory or devastated by defeat.

That's why none are stronger than those who base themselves on prayer. Our strong, focused prayer manifests as the power of faith and practice, which in turn activates the power of the Buddha and the Law. The main player in this drama is always the human being—it is we ourselves.

Prayer produces a change within our hearts, within the depths of our lives. This profound, intangible inner change does not end with us alone [but inspires a similar change in others]. Likewise, when one community changes, it will not be limited to that community alone. Just as a single wave gives rise to countless others, change in one community will create a ripple effect of change in other communities as well.

I wish to assert that the first step toward such social change is a change in the heart of a single individual.

This is also, I believe, where the deep significance of the Daishonin's statement that "Buddhism is reason" (WND-1, 839) lies.

To return to the passage from "On Prayer" that we are studying, "sound," "form," and "clear water" correspond to our attitude in prayer, while "echo," "shadow," and "reflection of the moon" correspond to the natural way in which prayers are answered. Just as these three analogies refer to phenomena that arise in accord with natural principles, the prayers of a practitioner of the Lotus Sutra will also be definitely answered in accord with the inexorable Law of life and in accord with reason.

Prayer in Nichiren Buddhism is free of all arrogance and conceit. The very act of sitting before the Gohonzon and chanting Nam-myoho-renge-kyo pulses with the humble spirit to transcend attachment to one's own shallow wisdom and limited experience to become one with the Law of life and the fundamental rhythm of nature and the universe, which were revealed through the Buddha's enlightened wisdom. Without being self-abasing, we concentrate all our actions into a single life moment—into our determined prayer—while recharging our lives to prepare for boundless, vibrant growth. That is the healthiest and most fulfilling state of life.

Let us chant to the Gohonzon about all of our problems in life and challenge them.

Prayer is essential. Let's never forget that everything starts from prayer. If we lose sight of prayer and fail to transform

THE PRACTICE FOR TRANSFORMING OUR STATE OF LIFE

our lives in actuality, then even the most eloquent speeches and high-minded arguments will all be just empty theory, pipe dreams, and illusions. Faith and the Soka Gakkai spirit, too, arise from praying strongly and deeply about our actual situations and realities.

In Nichiren Buddhism, prayer by itself isn't enough. Just as an arrow flying toward its target contains the full power and strength of the archer who shot it, our prayer contains all of our efforts and actions. Prayer without action is just wishful thinking, and action without prayer will be unproductive.

I therefore would like to point out that lofty prayer arises from a lofty sense of responsibility. Serious prayer will not arise from an irresponsible or careless attitude toward work, daily living, and life itself. Those who take responsibility for every part of their lives and give their all in every endeavor will make a habit of prayer.

From a lecture on Nichiren Daishonin's writing "On Prayer,"
published in the Seikyo Shimbun, *October 22, 1977.*

3.16 Chanting Nam-myoho-renge-kyo Freely

President Ikeda responds to a question from an Italian member about whether quantity or quality is more important in chanting Nam-myoho-renge-kyo.

A 100,000-lira note is worth more than a 10,000-lira note. It goes without saying that it is preferable to have the note with the greater value. In the case of daimoku, the important thing is to chant earnestly and with strong conviction. Of course, it would be even better to have lots of 100,000-lira notes! The bottom line is that both quality and quantity matter in chanting.

The principle of responsive communion is very important in Nichiren Buddhism. To use an analogy, when talking on the phone, if the connection is good, we'll be heard even if we speak softly, but if it's bad, then sometimes the other person won't be able to hear us even if we shout. In order for our prayers to be effective, we need to express them honestly and directly to the Gohonzon.

The Daishonin states, "What is called faith is nothing unusual" (WND-1, 1036). In other words, we can just be ourselves. He continues:

> Faith means putting one's trust in the Lotus Sutra, Shakyamuni, Many Treasures, the Buddhas and bodhisattvas of the ten directions, and the heavenly gods and benevolent deities, and chanting

Nam-myoho-renge-kyo as a woman cherishes her husband, as a man lays down his life for his wife, as parents refuse to abandon their children, or as a child refuses to leave its mother. (WND-1, 1036)

We should be honest and unpretentious when we chant to the Gohonzon. If we are suffering or feeling sad, then we should take that suffering to the Gohonzon without hiding it, expressing in our prayers what is in our hearts.

It is the Daishonin's wish that we all become happy. By coming in contact with and connecting with the life of the Daishonin [by chanting to the Gohonzon], therefore, we are certain to attain happiness. It is inconceivable that the Daishonin would fail to protect those who are striving as his emissaries to realize kosen-rufu.

Essentially, we practice Nichiren Buddhism for our own happiness and well-being. In chanting, too, the main thing is that we ourselves feel happy and satisfied. It's not a matter of formality; there are no rules specifying how long we have to chant and so on. While it is often helpful to set ourselves a target for the amount of daimoku we want to chant, when we're too tired or sleepy, or we find ourselves dozing off in front of the Gohonzon and just chanting out of force of habit, then it is far more valuable to get some rest and chant properly another time, when we're refreshed in body and mind.

The most important thing is that we are filled with a satisfying sense of revitalization after chanting. When we continue chanting in this way each day, we will naturally come to experience a life in which all our desires are fulfilled.

From a question-and-answer session during a North Italy representative leaders meeting, Milan, Italy, July 3, 1992.

3.17 Chanting With Unwavering Conviction

President Ikeda responds to the question of a member who asked: "When we were chanting daimoku together with you earlier, the desire and courage to realize my dreams came welling forth from my life. How can I chant with this kind of feeling and live with courage all the time?"

Even one daimoku can pervade the entire universe. Truly heartfelt and determined daimoku, therefore, has the power to move everything.

To illustrate, the words "I love you" can have a completely different impact depending on whether they are said from the heart or merely as an empty gesture.

Daimoku chanted with the deep conviction that one's life is the entity of the Mystic Law, or with the resolve to dedicate one's life to spreading the Mystic Law as an emissary of the Buddha, cannot fail to resonate with the Gohonzon or reach the universe. A person who chants in this way will definitely attain a state of complete freedom.

Of course, no one becomes an expert in anything right away. It is by overcoming obstacles again and again and continuing to press forward that we gain a degree of expertise or mastery in a given field.

The same holds true for faith. There may be times when we give in to self-defeat and our determination wanes, or when things don't go as we'd hoped and we begin to feel anxious or fearful. But the important thing is to continue chanting daimoku, no matter what. Whether our prayers are answered right away or not, we must keep chanting Nam-myoho-renge-kyo, without harboring any doubts. Those who maintain such faith will eventually attain the supreme path and highest pinnacle of value and savor the conviction that everything unfolded in the very best and most meaningful way. They will build immensely fulfilling lives and come to regard everything as a source of joy and a part of their mission. Such are the workings of the Mystic Law and the power of faith.

Why is the Gohonzon important? Because, through having faith in it, we can bring forth the Gohonzon, or the state of Buddhahood, that is inherent in our own lives. The Daishonin states that the Gohonzon is found only in the faith of each one of us (see WND-1, 832).

We ourselves and all human beings are worthy of respect because every single individual is an entity of the Mystic Law.

The Gohonzon is important above all because it enables us to manifest the Mystic Law that exists within us.

From a question-and-answer session during a North Italy representative leaders meeting, Milan, Italy, July 3, 1992.

3.18 Developing a Strong Inner Core

President Ikeda responds to the concern of a future division member who was failing to make any headway in solving a difficult problem even after having decided to challenge it by earnestly doing gongyo every day.

In Nichiren Buddhism, it is said that no prayer goes unanswered. But this is very different from having every wish instantly gratified as if by magic. If you chant to win the lottery tomorrow, or score 100 percent on a test tomorrow without having studied, the odds are small that it will happen. Nonetheless, viewed from a deeper, longer-term perspective, all your prayers serve to propel you in the direction of happiness.

Sometimes our immediate prayers are realized, and sometimes they aren't. When we look back later, however, we can say with absolute conviction that everything turned out for the best.

Buddhism accords with reason. Our faith is manifested in our daily lives, in our actual circumstances. Our prayers cannot be answered if we fail to make efforts to realize them.

Furthermore, it takes a great deal of time and effort to overcome sufferings of a karmic nature, whose roots lie deep in causes we made in the past. There is a big difference, for example, in the time it takes for a scratch to heal and that required to recover from a serious internal disease. Some illnesses can be treated with medication, while others require surgery. The same applies to changing our karma through faith and practice.

In addition, each person's level of faith and individual karma differ. By chanting Nam-myoho-renge-kyo, however, we can bring forth a powerful sense of hope and move our lives in a positive, beneficial direction without fail.

It's unrealistic to think we can achieve anything of substance overnight. If we were to have every prayer answered instantly, it would lead to our ruin. We'd grow lazy and complacent.

You may have a passing interest in painting, for example. But if you think you can simply dash off some paintings, suddenly hold an exhibition, and have your work snapped up by art collectors, you are hardly being realistic.

Suppose you spend all your money playing rather than working and are now destitute. Do you think someone giving you a large sum of money would contribute to your happiness in the long term?

It would be like making superficial repairs to a crumbling building without addressing the root problem. To create something fine and solid, it would be better to build anew from the foundation up. The purpose of our Buddhist practice is to transform our lives on a fundamental level, not superficially. It enables us to develop a strong inner core and solidly accumulate indestructible good fortune.

There are two kinds of benefit that derive from faith in the Gohonzon: conspicuous and inconspicuous. Conspicuous benefit is the obvious, visible benefit of being protected or being quickly able to surmount a problem when it arises—be it an illness or a conflict in personal relationships.

Inconspicuous benefit, on the other hand, is less tangible. It is good fortune accumulated slowly but steadily, like the growth of a tree or the rising of the tide, which results in the forging of a rich and expansive state of life. We might not discern any change from day to day, but as the years pass, it will be clear that we've become happy, that we've grown as individuals. This is inconspicuous benefit.

When you chant Nam-myoho-renge-kyo, you will definitely gain the best result, regardless of whether that benefit is conspicuous or inconspicuous.

No matter what happens, the important thing is to continue chanting. If you do so, you'll become happy without fail. Even if things don't work out the way you hoped or imagined, when you look back later, you'll understand on a much more profound level that it was the best possible result. This is tremendous inconspicuous benefit.

Conspicuous benefit, for instance, might allow you to eat your fill today but leave you worrying about your next meal. As an example of inconspicuous benefit, on the other hand, you may have only a meager meal today, but you are moving steadily toward a life in which you will never have to worry about having enough to eat. The latter is a far more attractive prospect, I think, and is the essence of practicing Nichiren Buddhism.

From Discussions on Youth,
published in Japanese in March 1999.

3.19 Faith Is a Lifelong Pursuit

President Ikeda responds to the concern of a future division member who said she feels guilty when she misses gongyo.

As long as we have faith in the Gohonzon, we are not going to suffer punishment or negative consequences from missing gongyo, so please put your mind at ease. Nichiren Daishonin says that chanting Nam-myoho-renge-kyo even once is a source of limitless benefit. So imagine the immense benefit you will accumulate when you continue earnestly to do gongyo and chant Nam-myoho-renge-kyo morning and evening. It is something we do for our own sake; it is a right, not an obligation.

The Gohonzon will never demand that you chant to it. Having appreciation for being able to chant to the Gohonzon is the heart of faith. The more you exert yourselves in faith—in doing gongyo and chanting daimoku—the more you stand to gain.

Also, Nichiren Daishonin writes nothing about the specific amount of daimoku we should chant. It is entirely up to each individual's awareness. Faith is a lifelong pursuit, so there's no need to be unnecessarily nervous or anxious about how much you chant.

You don't have to put unnecessary pressure on yourselves. Buddhism exists to free people, not to restrain them. Chanting every day, even a little bit, is important. For instance, the food you eat each day turns into energy that fuels your bodies. Your studies, too, become a valuable asset when you make steady efforts on a daily basis.

Our lives are created from what we do and how we live every day. For that reason, we should strive to live each day so as to continually improve ourselves. The driving force for this is our morning and evening gongyo.

Exerting ourselves in the practice of gongyo each day amounts to what we might call a "spiritual workout." It purifies our lives, gets our "motors" running, and sets us on the right track. It gets our bodies and our minds moving and sets a good rhythm for the day.

THE PRACTICE FOR TRANSFORMING OUR STATE OF LIFE

It is important to have the spirit to sit down in front of the Gohonzon. The spirit to keep challenging yourself to pray before the Gohonzon every day, to chant daimoku, even if only little, is truly admirable.

From Discussions on Youth,
published in Japanese in March 1999.

3.20 The Universal Language of Buddhas and Bodhisattvas

President Ikeda responds to the question of the effectiveness of reciting passages from the Lotus Sutra and chanting daimoku in a language one doesn't understand.

I would like to address the question of whether there is any value in reciting sutra passages and chanting daimoku without understanding their meaning.

Of course, it is better if you understand their meaning. That will strengthen your faith in the Mystic Law. But if you understand and yet fail to practice, it won't get you anywhere. Moreover, you cannot understand all of the profound significance of the Law through reason alone.

Birds and dogs, for example, have their own language,

their own speech. People do not understand it, but other birds and dogs do. There are many comparable examples among humans as well—codes, abbreviations, or foreign languages that are comprehended by experts or native speakers but unintelligible to others. Married couples also sometimes have their own language that only they understand!

In the same way, the language of gongyo and daimoku reaches the Gohonzon and the realms of the Buddhas and bodhisattvas of the ten directions and three existences. We might call it the language of the Buddhas and bodhisattvas. That is why our voices reciting the sutra and chanting daimoku before the Gohonzon reach all Buddhas, bodhisattvas, and heavenly deities, whether we understand what we are saying or not. They hear it and say in response, "Excellent, excellent!" rejoicing and praising us. The entire universe envelops us in the light of happiness.

Nichiren Daishonin teaches that through reciting the sutra and chanting daimoku, we can reach an elevated state of life in which, while engaged in our daily activities, we freely traverse the cosmos. In "Reply to Sairen-bo," the Daishonin writes: "Those who are our disciples and lay supporters can view Eagle Peak in India and day and night will go to and from the Land of Eternally Tranquil Light that has existed for all time. What a truly inexpressible joy it is!" (WND-1, 313).

When we chant before the Gohonzon, the door to our inner microcosm instantly opens to the macrocosm of the entire universe, and we savor a serene and boundless

THE PRACTICE FOR TRANSFORMING OUR STATE OF LIFE

happiness, as if gazing out over the entire cosmos. We feel a deep fulfillment and joy along with a feeling of supreme confidence and self-mastery, as if we hold everything in the palm of our hands. The microcosm enfolded by the macrocosm reaches out to enfold the macrocosm in its own embrace.

The Daishonin writes in "Letter to Niike," "When nurtured by the chanting of Nam-myoho-renge-kyo, . . . [we] are free to soar into the sky of the true aspect of all phenomena" (WND-1, 1030).

In "On Offerings for Deceased Ancestors," he also says: "Though he himself is like the wisteria vine, because he clings to the pine that is the Lotus Sutra, he is able to ascend the mountain of perfect enlightenment. Because he has the wings of the single vehicle [Mystic Law] to rely upon, he can soar into the sky of Tranquil Light [Buddhahood]" (WND-1, 821).

Just as we might climb the highest mountain peak to gaze down on the bright, clear scene of the world below, we can climb the mountain of perfect enlightenment, or supreme wisdom, the Daishonin says. We can attain a state of eternal bliss, experiencing moment after moment the infinite expanse and depth of life, as if soaring through the universe and savoring the sight of myriad beautiful stars, blazing comets, and glittering galaxies.

From a speech at an SGI-USA youth training session,
Malibu, California, February 20, 1990.

"IT IS THE HEART THAT IS IMPORTANT"

4.1 Living With an Awareness of the Importance of the Heart

Our inner transformation through revealing our inherent Buddhahood will transform not only our own lives but also our environment and the entire world. President Ikeda has always stressed this philosophy for achieving unshakable happiness, and this chapter introduces many important teachings on that subject.

I was talking with someone yesterday, and our conversation turned to the question of what is the ultimate message of Nichiren Daishonin's writings. We concluded that the first essential message is to base ourselves on the Gohonzon. It is to make the foundation of our faith "only Nam-myoho-renge-kyo" (WND-1, 903)—that is, to sincerely chant and practice the Mystic Law alone. The second essential message is that "it is the heart that is important" (WND-1, 1000). These two points, we agreed, are the crucial cornerstones of the Daishonin's writings.

The reason why the second is important is that faith is not just a matter of embracing the Gohonzon and chanting Nam-myoho-renge-kyo but also a matter of our hearts, or the attitude with which we practice. Are our hearts directed toward kosen-rufu? The innermost heart, the attitude in the depths of our beings, determines everything.

Whether we become happy, attain enlightenment, move in the direction of Buddhahood, or wind up in a state of suffering—everything is the exact result of the wondrous workings of our hearts or minds. This point cannot be overemphasized.

Just like us, the universe, too, has a nonmaterial aspect. Our heart of faith is communicated to the universe. The workings of our hearts or minds are truly amazing.

Selfishness, complaint, doubt, deviousness, conceit, arrogance, and so forth are all causes of unhappiness for both ourselves and others. When we allow ourselves to be ruled by such negative attitudes, we are like a plane that has lost its direction in a heavy fog. We can see nothing clearly. The distinction between good and bad, right and wrong, becomes blurred. We plunge not only ourselves but our passengers—our friends and others around us—into misery.

When afflicted by arrogance, our minds run amok, like a crazed horse galloping wildly in circles, unable to stop, until we lose all self-awareness and do harm to those around us.

This is not a normal human state. And though we may think ourselves better than others, the exact opposite is true. In fact, in Buddhism, the conceited and arrogant are the most dangerous people.

In contrast, a sincere concern for others, a dedicated commitment to our beliefs, a sense of responsibility toward fulfilling our mission for kosen-rufu, a wish to wholeheartedly encourage and support our fellow members, a feeling of appreciation, gratitude, and joy—these attitudes are causes that will produce boundless good fortune, not only for ourselves but also for our family and loved ones as well as our descendants. They give rise to strong protection by the heavenly deities—the positive forces of the universe—and enable us to advance directly along the path to attaining Buddhahood.

Let us therefore live with the Daishonin's words "It is the heart that is important" engraved deeply and indelibly in our lives.

From a speech at a divisional representatives conference, Tokyo, Japan, February 25, 1988.

4.2 Appreciation and Joy Multiply Our Good Fortune

Rejecting negativity and practicing faith based on appreciation and joy is the way to elevate our life state.

"It is the heart that is important" (WND-1, 1000), writes the Daishonin.

When we do something, do we approach it with a negative attitude—grumbling, "Oh, not again! I hate this!"—or a positive attitude—telling ourselves brightly, "All right, here's a fresh opportunity to gain good fortune!"?

This seemingly small, subtle difference in attitude can make a huge difference in our lives. It can change things 180 degrees. This is what the Lotus Sutra and the doctrine of three thousand realms in a single moment of life teach us.

The heart is invisible, and Buddhism provides a comprehensive understanding of the principles governing that invisible heart. It represents the highest form of psychology, neuroscience, and psychotherapy.

Appreciation and joy multiply our good fortune. Complaint and negativity erase it.

In the endeavor to spread Nichiren Buddhism, actions arising from our sincere wish to help others and teach them the greatness of the Mystic Law bring immense benefit and good fortune to fill our lives.

"It is the heart that is important"—there are no truer words than these.

"IT IS THE HEART THAT IS IMPORTANT"

Human beings are weak and easily susceptible to complaint, resentment, envy, and discouragement.

But this is where those who practice Nichiren Buddhism differ. They stop complaining, they stop being dissatisfied and negative. They attain an inner strength that makes them confident and positive. And their hearts overflow with appreciation and gratitude.

We often find that those who live in the city yearn for country life, while those who live in the country long for city life, or that those who are single dream of being married, while those who are married wish they were single again. That is a common tendency of the human heart.

But happiness doesn't lie somewhere far away. It is something we must achieve for ourselves through our present struggles in the here and now.

When we have a positive and appreciative attitude toward our communities, it will give greater confidence and impetus to our activities. The joy of kosen-rufu will spread.

From a speech at a Kyushu and Okinawa joint conference, Okinawa, Japan, March 3, 1998.

4.3 Those Who Smile Are Strong

President Ikeda urges us to regard difficulties as opportunities for attaining happiness and for leading positive, upbeat lives, creating hope where there is none.

Practicing Nichiren Buddhism doesn't mean that we are immune to life's problems. The storms of karma appear in many unexpected ways—as problems at home, at work, with our children, and so on.

But with each challenge we overcome, we carry out our human revolution and transform the destiny of our families and loved ones. In fact, trying times are opportunities to make a leap forward to greater happiness.

Life is long. Sometimes we will succeed, and sometimes we won't. There is no need to be embarrassed by a temporary setback. The important thing is to triumph in the end, to never lose our fighting spirit, no matter how difficult the situation.

Those who remain positive and cheerful in adversity are truly strong.

When I visited the Gandhi Smriti and Darshan Samiti [in 1992]—the national memorial to Mahatma Gandhi in New Delhi—there was a large portrait of Gandhi on the wall. His wide, toothless grin conveyed an unaffected sense of humor and enjoyment.

One museum official told me that while many of the photographs of Gandhi shown abroad usually depict him

"IT IS THE HEART THAT IS IMPORTANT"

with a serious, even stern expression, actually he was a person who laughed and smiled a lot. The official commented that Gandhi always said he would never have been able to survive his long and bitter struggle if he didn't have a good sense of humor.

Gandhi endured immeasurable persecution and suffering in his struggle for India's independence, but he was always smiling.

Those who can smile are strong. Those who lead good, positive lives are always bright and upbeat.

If you always seem stressed and gloomy, you'll bring down everyone else around you. You can't inspire or invigorate others that way. Precisely when things are tough, that's the time to encourage those around you with a bright smile.

If the situation seems hopeless, create hope. Don't depend on others. Ignite the flame of hope within your own heart.

From Nijuisseiki e no haha to ko o kataru *(Dialogue on mothers and children in the twenty-first century), vol. 3, published in Japanese in June 2000.*

4.4 Polishing Our Hearts to Shine Like Diamonds

Our hearts will not shine unless we polish them. When we exert ourselves in faith and polish our hearts like diamonds, we attain a state of genuine happiness.

What is the purpose of our Buddhist practice? It is for all of us, without exception, to become happy. That is also the purpose of our organization for kosen-rufu. Those who steadfastly uphold the Mystic Law will never be unhappy. It is important to have absolute confidence in this. That confidence, that conviction, will generate immense good fortune.

Buddhism teaches the four sufferings of birth, aging, sickness, and death. Our bright, hope-filled members in the future division and young men's and young women's divisions will also eventually grow old. The sufferings of sickness and death, too, are inescapable parts of life. Will you lead a life shining with solid happiness, accumulating ever more benefit and good fortune as you grow older? Or will you lead a life characterized by frustration and disappointment, growing sadder and lonelier with the passing years?

The Mystic Law embodies the principle that the sufferings of birth and death are nirvana. It enables us to be eternally youthful and vibrant, always bringing forth hope and actualizing our dreams.

The Mystic Law embodies the principle that earthly desires are enlightenment. The more numerous our problems, the more we can expand our life state based on faith and make

"IT IS THE HEART THAT IS IMPORTANT"

those problems the fuel for our happiness. We can positively transform everything, changing poison into medicine.

The time of youth, in particular, is fraught with problems and worries. But that's how it should be. You can't become great leaders without experiencing problems or making effort. Through effort and hard work, you strengthen yourself and grow.

Nichiren Daishonin writes, "It is the heart that is important" (WND-1, 1000).

Those who have diamond-like hearts of faith are radiant champions who enjoy an indestructible, diamond-like state of happiness. They are eternal victors. Wherever they go, wherever they dwell, is a royal palace. They enjoy a vast and lofty state of life, as if gazing serenely over the entire universe.

By contrast, there are those who, though giving the appearance of being fine and upstanding, are actually morally corrupt and dishonest.

We need to polish the diamond of our faith. A raw gemstone sparkles only when it is polished. The diamond of our faith is polished by chanting Nam-myoho-renge-kyo and working for kosen-rufu. A life dedicated to the mission of advancing kosen-rufu will unfailingly enter a path of enduring happiness—a wonderful state of constant joy.

Our Buddhist practice enables us to attain a vast and expansive state of life in which we can accept whatever happens with courage and joy, and keep moving positively forward.

From a speech at a Thai commemorative representatives conference, Bangkok, Thailand, February 2, 1992.

4.5 Mastering Our Minds

To effect a major transformation of our life state, we must free ourselves from the domination of our vacillating, weak minds; we must become the master of our minds and live accordingly.

"It is the heart that is important" (WND-1, 1000). The heart, the mind, is truly wondrous and unfathomable. The inner realm of life is boundless. We can also deepen it infinitely.

The mind can give rise to a life state of great joy, as if soaring freely and effortlessly through the vast blue sky. It can radiate compassion like the clear, bright, all-illuminating sunshine and warmly embrace those who are suffering. It can tremble with righteous anger and vanquish evil and injustice with the courage and ferocity of a lion. The mind is constantly changing, like an ever-unfolding drama or shifting panorama.

And the most wondrous thing about the mind is that it can manifest the world of Buddhahood. Even those beset by the deepest delusion and suffering can bring forth in the depths of their lives the state of Buddhahood that is one with the universe. This momentous drama of transformation is indeed the greatest of all wonders.

Buddhism recognizes the supreme nobility and potential

for phenomenal transformation inherent within the lives of all people. Based on that, Nichiren Daishonin taught that by thoroughly polishing their lives through chanting Nam-myoho-renge-kyo, anyone—no matter how steeped in ignorance and delusion—can reveal their Buddhahood and transform even the most evil and defiled land into a pure land.

Myoho-renge-kyo is the "mystic truth that is originally inherent in all living beings" (WND-1, 3).

And that is why, through our practice of chanting Nam-myoho-renge-kyo, we can polish the tarnished mirror of "a mind now clouded by the illusions of the innate darkness of life" into "a clear mirror, reflecting the essential nature of phenomena and the true aspect of reality" (WND-1, 4) and thus reveal our inner Buddhahood. In other words, we can manifest the "originally inherent mystic truth" (see WND-1, 3) and open the infinite potential that resides within us.

Myoho-renge-kyo is the Law inherent in our own lives. The moment-to-moment inner transformation we achieve through chanting Nam-myoho-renge-kyo leads not only to a fundamental change in our mindset but to a change in the entire way we live our lives, putting us on track to attain Buddhahood in this lifetime. And it further creates a groundswell for the great transformation of all humankind that is kosen-rufu. Myoho-renge-kyo is the dynamic pulse of change in all spheres.

The fact that Myoho-renge-kyo is the Law inherent within our lives raises another issue we must consider: that is, the relationship between the mind of delusion—a mind clouded by innate darkness—and the mind of enlightenment, or "*myo*"—a mind illuminated by the essential nature of phenomena and the true aspect of reality.

If we simply follow our easily swayed, unenlightened minds, our potential will quickly wither away. Or, even worse, we may give in to negative and destructive impulses. Such is the subtle nature of the workings of the mind. Because our minds are the key to attaining Buddhahood in this lifetime, we must overcome our own inner weaknesses. This is what our Buddhist practice is all about.

The deluded minds of ordinary people are always vacillating. We must not make this constantly changing, shifting mind our basis or guide. This is the meaning of the well-known sutra passage "Become the master of your mind rather than let your mind master you"[1] (WND-1, 502).

The Daishonin cites this passage about becoming the master of one's mind in many places in his writings, offering it as an important guideline for his followers. Becoming the master of one's mind means having a sound compass in life and the bright beacon of faith.

We must not let ourselves be mastered by our unenlightened minds that change and shift according to the circumstances. We need a teacher, or mentor, to help guide our minds in the right direction. In that sense, the true masters of the mind are the Buddhist Law and the teachings of the Buddha. Shakyamuni vowed to make the Law to which he had become enlightened the master or guide of his mind, and he took pride in living true to that vow. This is to live one's life "relying on the Law," which Shakyamuni emphasized in his final injunction to his disciples before he died.

To allow ourselves to be mastered by our minds is to make ourselves, our selfish impulses, our foundation. Ultimately, we will be pulled this way and that by our ever-moving minds, succumb to egoism, and sink into the depths of darkness or ignorance.

Conversely, to master our minds means to make the Law our foundation.

A teacher or mentor in Buddhism is one who leads and connects people to the Law, teaching them that the Law on which they should depend exists within their own lives. The disciples in turn seek the mentor, who embodies and is one with the Law. Looking to the mentor as a model, they exert themselves in their Buddhist practice. In this way, they lead a life that allows them to master their minds.

In other words, the existence of a mentor—one who embodies and lives in accord with the Law and teaches people about their vast inner potential—is indispensable for attaining Buddhahood in this lifetime.

I am who I am today because of my mentor, second Soka Gakkai president Josei Toda, who practiced in accord with the Buddha's teachings and dedicated his life to widely propagating Nichiren Buddhism in the modern age. Mr. Toda is always with me as my spiritual mentor. I still carry on a dialogue with my mentor in my heart, every moment, every day. This is the spirit of the oneness of mentor and disciple.

Those who always hold fast to their spiritual mentor as their model and compass and exert themselves as that mentor teaches are people who live based on the Law. Nichiren Buddhism is a teaching grounded in the oneness of mentor and disciple.

> *From* Lectures on "On Attaining Buddhahood in This Lifetime,"
> *published in Japanese in January 2007.*

4.6 Remaining True to One's Commitment in Faith

President Ikeda stresses the importance of maintaining a sincere spirit in faith, citing the example of the priest Sammi-bo, who though well versed in Buddhist doctrine succumbed to arrogance and abandoned Nichiren Daishonin's teachings.

Among the Daishonin's disciples was a priest named Sammi-bo, who abandoned his faith during the Daishonin's lifetime.

With his mentor's warm support and understanding, Sammi-bo went to study at Mount Hiei. During his time there, Sammi-bo wrote to the Daishonin, boastfully reporting that he had been asked to deliver a lecture for court nobles at a private Buddha hall in the imperial capital, Kyoto, and that he had "conducted himself fittingly"[2] (see WND-2, 342). The Daishonin responded with a stern rebuke:

> The ruler of Japan is simply the chief of this island country. To speak as you do of being "summoned" by persons who serve that ruler, of appearing before those "in high position," and of conducting yourself "fittingly" is, however I consider it, in the end an insult to me, Nichiren! (WND-2, 342–43)

The account that Sammi-bo relayed to his mentor evinced no pride in being his disciple or practicing the supreme teaching of Buddhism. While making a superficial gesture of respecting the Daishonin, in his heart Sammi-bo fawned on the powerful and, filled with self-importance, looked down on his mentor. He was arrogant, and the Daishonin keenly discerned this.

This is how Sammi-bo acted toward his mentor, who had done so much for him and taught him about the true essence of Buddhism. Sammi-bo was guided by self-interest, not by the teachings of his mentor. He was self-centered.

Arrogance is a form of ingratitude, and ingratitude is an ignorance of life's basic principles. Without such basic understanding, one cannot understand Buddhism. Arrogance, cowardice, and dishonesty—these were Sammi-bo's essential qualities.

The Daishonin added even more sternly:

> It would seem that Nichiren's disciples, after journeying to the capital [Kyoto], at first were careful not to forget their purpose, but later, led astray by the heavenly devil, they lost their senses completely....
>
> So you [Sammi-bo] have gone to the capital, and before much time has passed you are changing your name [to sound more aristocratic], a piece of utter nonsense. (WND-2, 343)

The Daishonin laments over the vanity and foolishness of his disciple in moving in court circles, forgetting his original aspiration to seek the Buddha way, adopting a pretentious new name, and even changing his accent:

> No doubt you have also changed your way of speaking and acquired the accent of the capital. Like a mouse that has changed into a bat but in fact is neither bird nor mouse, you are now neither a country priest nor a priest of the capital. You are behaving just like Sho-bo.
>
> You should just go on speaking like a country person—otherwise you will only sound ridiculous. (WND-2, 343)

With this one phrase about acquiring "the accent of the capital," the Daishonin exposed Sammi-bo's inner condition: enthralled by the glamour of the capital, he had been defeated by devilish functions.

Eventually, Sammi-bo renounced faith in the Daishonin's teachings, stopped practicing, and came to a sad end.

The Daishonin's great compassion led him to reflect later: "If I had scolded [Sammi-bo] more strictly, he might have been saved" (WND-1, 998). As this shows, sternly reprimanding those who succumb to arrogance is the proper approach, which requires firm compassion and accords precisely with the Daishonin's spirit.

The Daishonin boldly declared of himself, "I am merely the son of a commoner from a remote province" (WND-1, 1006). He affirmed that he was not of privileged birth or lineage but of common birth. He was not ashamed of this, but proud.

Because he was born among the common people, he understood their hearts. If he had been born to privilege or high rank, he would have been shielded by the authorities and never experienced the harsh persecutions that marked his life. As a child of the common people, the Daishonin lived his life among them. He understood their sufferings as if they were his own and propagated his great teaching of Nam-myoho-renge-kyo to relieve those sufferings. Through his own life, he taught and exemplified the true way to realize kosen-rufu for future generations.

Mr. Toda declared that academic background has nothing to do with faith. Of course, he valued learning, but he warned that if individuals who think their education makes them better than others were to become Soka Gakkai leaders, people wouldn't follow them. With such leaders, members would only suffer.

The Daishonin's teachings are just and impartial. He cites the words "Since the Law is wonderful, the person is worthy of respect"[3] (WND-1, 1097). And he writes, "If the Law that one embraces is supreme, then the person who embraces it must accordingly be foremost among all others" (WND-1, 61).

Important are individuals who work for kosen-rufu. Those who persevere wholeheartedly to spread the Mystic Law in even the most trying times are truly admirable. Graduating from a famous university or having high social status has absolutely nothing to do with faith.

Academic credentials do not define greatness or intelligence. The eyes of Buddhism focus on the people themselves.

From a speech at a Tokyo metropolitan area representatives conference, Tokyo, Japan, May 19, 2007.

4.7 When Our Life State Changes, the World Around Us Changes

The Buddhist principle of inner transformation means that when we achieve the great life state of Buddhahood, we cause ourselves, those around us, and the place we are to shine.

Nichiren Daishonin writes:

> Hungry spirits perceive the Ganges River as fire, human beings perceive it as water, and heavenly beings perceive it as amrita. Though the water is the same, it appears differently according to one's karmic reward from the past. (WND-1, 486)

How we perceive things differs according to our state of life. When our state of life changes, the realm in which we reside also changes. This is the essence of the doctrine of the "actual three thousand realms in a single moment of life" found in the Lotus Sutra.

Referring to the unending persecution he experienced throughout his life, the Daishonin says:

> Day after day, month after month, year after year I have been subjected to repeated persecutions. Minor persecutions and annoyances are too numerous even to be counted, but the major persecutions number four.[4] (WND-1, 240)

Yet even while exiled to Sado Island, the harshest of his persecutions, he still serenely declares, "I feel immeasurable delight even though I am now an exile" (WND-1, 386). The Daishonin calmly gazes down on his situation from the lofty heights of a life condition as vast and boundless as the universe.

Soka Gakkai founding president Tsunesaburo Makiguchi endured his wartime imprisonment for his beliefs with a similar state of mind, writing in letters from prison: "What I am going through is nothing compared to the sufferings of the Daishonin on Sado"[5] and "Depending on one's state of mind, even hell can be enjoyable."[6] This last sentence was censored and blacked out by the prosecutor.

Establishing such a towering state of life is the highest aim of humanity.

A single flower can completely transform a bleak atmosphere. The important thing, therefore, is to have the spirit, the determination, to improve your environment, to change it for the better, if even just a little. Especially as practitioners of Nichiren Buddhism striving earnestly in faith, we cannot fail to vibrantly transform our lives. We will definitely enjoy happiness and prosperity. This is an unchanging principle of Buddhism.

Our attitude changes everything. This is one of the great wonders of life, and at the same time, an undeniable reality.

A proverb says, "Do not complain that the rosebush has thorns but rejoice that the thornbush has roses." Our perception changes depending on our outlook, becoming bright, beautiful, and expansive.

Nichiren Daishonin speaks of the "wonderful workings of one mind" (OTT, 30). The focused mind of faith in the Gohonzon has power and functions that are truly immense and wondrous. When the fundamental engine of our "one mind"—our inner attitude, or resolve—starts running, the gears of all phenomena of the three thousand realms are set in motion. Everything starts to change. We move everything in a bright and positive direction.

When embraced by the great life state of Buddhahood, we ourselves, those around us, and the land in which we live will all shine with the light of happiness and hope. This is the power of Nam-myoho-renge-kyo of the actual three thousand realms in a single moment of life. At work here is the Buddhist principle of dynamic transformation.

From Lectures on the "Expedient Means" and "Life Span" Chapters of the Lotus Sutra, *vol. 3,* *published in Japanese in June 1996.*

4.8 Devoting Ourselves to Our Mission

Devoting ourselves to our mission in our daily lives is the way to embody the principle that "it is the heart that is important."

In life, not everything goes the way we hope from the very beginning. There are often cases in which, for various reasons, we have to spend long periods of our lives in places we would rather not be. How do we deal with this? How do we lead a life of satisfaction and victory in a way that is true to ourselves in such situations? That is the challenge.

All too many respond to those kinds of circumstances by bewailing their misfortune, resenting their environment and the people in it to the end of their days. There are countless people like this in the world. There are also people who are driven to seek worldly success and honor and the praise and admiration of others. As long as such things remain their sole goals in life, they are bound to suffer endless dissatisfaction and anxiety.

Desire has no limits, and as long as selfishness prevails, it is impossible to satisfy everyone. Not everyone in a company can be president.

Of course, it's natural to make efforts to change and improve our environment and circumstances. But it's even more essential that we resolutely protect where we are now, our own "fortress," or home ground, so to speak. We need to dedicate ourselves to our mission and, in that capacity, create a solid record of achievement in our own unique way.

"IT IS THE HEART THAT IS IMPORTANT"

Some people are never in the limelight, never in a position to receive praise and recognition from others. But "it is the heart that is important" (WND-1, 1000). A person's greatness is not determined by social status. Our happiness isn't determined by our environment. A vast universe exists in our hearts, in our lives. We practice Nichiren Buddhism to open up that boundless inner realm.

When we open that magnificent realm of the spirit, we will be champions wherever we might be. We will savor without end the wondrous delights of a truly profound existence.

Many people seek success and importance in the eyes of the world, but few aspire to become truly great human beings. Many wish to be showered with praise and attention, but few strive to build an inner happiness that will remain undiminished until the moment of their death and extend throughout the three existences of past, present, and future.

Death is the great final accounting of a person's life. Fame, wealth, social position, learning—these in themselves are of no avail in the face of death. Death is a struggle faced with nothing but one's life itself, stripped of all worldly trappings. It is a solemn moment, at which victory or defeat is impartially determined. Those who win in this struggle are true victors.

Our greatness and happiness as human beings are determined by the strength of our life force and our Buddhist faith and practice dedicated to kosen-rufu.

We are striving day after day for kosen-rufu, an unprecedented ideal in the history of humankind. It requires incredible perseverance and effort. Yet because of that, we are absolutely certain to build lives of true fulfillment.

How others view us is not important. Temporary successes or failures also do not matter. What counts is whether our faces shine with happy smiles at the very end of our lives. If we can look back and say: "My life was victorious. It was enjoyable. I have no regrets," then we are victors.

You, my friends in the youth division in particular, may now find yourselves in extremely trying and challenging situations. It may seem that impressive honors are beyond your reach. But that's fine. Just keep striving your hardest to realize your ideals, in the place of your personal mission. That's the way to build an eternally indestructible "fortress" of victory within your heart.

From a speech at a leaders meeting, Tokyo, Japan, November 12, 1989.

4.9 Nothing Is Ever Wasted in Buddhism

When we dedicate ourselves to working for kosen-rufu, illness and every other form of adversity act as tailwinds helping us to establish a state of eternal happiness.

In *The Record of the Orally Transmitted Teachings,* Nichiren Daishonin describes the workings of life as being "strict [or without a single exception]," adding that the three thousand realms, every single one of them, exist in our lives (OTT, 22).

None of us can escape the strict law of cause and effect operating in our lives. That is a fact. The cumulative tally of our deeds, words, and thoughts in this lifetime—the three categories of action—determines the course or trajectory of our lives throughout the three existences of past, present, and future.

That is why Nichiren Daishonin teaches that all of our efforts for kosen-rufu—chanting daimoku, talking to others about Buddhism, and taking action for others' happiness—create good causes and benefit in our lives (see WND-1, 4).[7] Consequently, there is no need to worry about how things may appear in the short term.

If you are ill, think of yourself as engaged in training for climbing the lofty peak of Buddhahood. Think of yourself as surmounting one slope after another, so that eventually you can stand on the summit and endlessly enjoy the wonderful view. Or think of yourself as swimming through rough seas toward a distant, shimmering island of hope and eternal happiness.

Live out your life with the spirit that everything you do is creating a record of brilliant achievement for your own wonderful eternal victory.

When you practice Nichiren Buddhism, nothing in your life is ever wasted. Please live without hesitation, fear, or regret. Never forget that everything is a tailwind propelling you forward to eternal happiness.

All rice shoots ripen within the year they are planted, though some ripen earlier and some later. In the same way, the Daishonin assures us, all people, as long as they persevere seriously in their Buddhist faith and practice, will attain the noble state of Buddhahood within this lifetime (see WND-2, 88).[8]

From a message to an Iwate Prefecture general meeting, Japan, September 16, 1996.

4.10 Cultivating a Lofty Life State Imbued With the Four Virtues

Those who dedicate their lives to the Mystic Law can attain a completely unshakable life state of eternity, happiness, true self, and purity. To do so, it is crucial to develop a deep faith that cannot be defeated by karma or adversity.

In *The Record of the Orally Transmitted Teachings,* Nichiren Daishonin states, "When, while in these four states of birth, aging, sickness, and death, we chant Nam-myoho-renge-kyo, we cause them to waft forth the fragrance of the four virtues" (OTT, 90).

The four virtues, or four noble qualities of the Buddha's life—eternity, happiness, true self, and purity—refer to the supreme state we can attain as human beings, a state of absolute freedom and happiness.

"True self" refers to a state of freedom as vast as the universe, in which we can enjoy our true, or greater, self.

"Eternity" refers to the dynamism of life that is ceaselessly renewing itself, the creative evolution of life that breaks through all stagnation.

"Purity" refers to the activity of purifying the narrow egoism of our lesser self through the powerful life force of our greater self.

And "happiness" refers to the joy of life as it pulses dynamically from moment to moment; it also corresponds to having a fully rounded character that imparts joy to all around us.

In this way, a person's character, when illuminated by the Mystic Law, will be firmly grounded in the "greater self," a state of boundless freedom that pervades the entire universe, qualitatively transforming even the energy of earthly desires focused on the egotistic "lesser self." In other words, the energy of earthly desires can be elevated and transformed into shining wisdom and compassion; it can be powerfully redirected to a higher level that transcends the individual and benefits others, the community, and society in general.

This is the Buddhist principle that earthly desires are enlightenment. It opens wide a brilliant path by which we can strive for our own perfection along with that of others, while actively working to build an ideal society.

What are the ingredients for happiness? This is one of life's fundamental questions.

The most crucial determinant for happiness is our own inner state of life.

Those with an expansive inner state of being are happy. They live out their days with an open and confident spirit.

People with a strong state of life are happy. They are not defeated by suffering and can calmly enjoy life as it unfolds.

Those with a profound state of life are happy. Savoring the deep significance of life, they are able to create a record of meaningful and enduring value.

People with a pure state of life are happy. They are always spreading refreshing joy to those around them.

There are countless individuals who are blessed with

"IT IS THE HEART THAT IS IMPORTANT"

wealth, social status, and other material advantages but are unhappy. And such external circumstances are changeable and impermanent; no one knows how long they will last.

But when you have established an unshakable inner state of happiness, no one can destroy it. Nothing can violate it. Creating this great life state is the aim of your Buddhist practice. The important thing is to never stray from the Gohonzon, to never stop advancing in faith.

In the course of life, you are bound to face all kinds of difficulties. At times, you may become stuck. That is when you need to strengthen your faith and chant daimoku in earnest. Difficult as it might be, once you surmount the steep mountain of your karma, a new horizon will open wide before you. Buddhist practice is the repetition of this process. Eventually, you will reach a state of absolute happiness that will never be destroyed.

Develop deep, strongly rooted faith. As long as a sapling has strong roots, and receives enough sunshine and water, it will grow into a tall, sturdy tree, even if it is buffeted by the elements. The same is true of our Buddhist practice and our lives. I hope that all of you will be courageous individuals who cheerfully spread the great light of happiness throughout this troubled world, your lives serving as personal proof of the true greatness of Nichiren Buddhism.

From a speech at an SGI-Europe general meeting,
Maidenhead, England, May 28, 1989.

TRANSFORMING SUFFERING INTO JOY

5.1 We Are the Protagonists of Our Own Lives

Faith in the Mystic Law ensures that by overcoming great pain and suffering we can build a life state of happiness and vibrant joy. President Ikeda has consistently stressed this life of unfettered, limitless hope. In this chapter, we will explore the key to overcoming all life's difficulties and to leading lives of victory.

We are each the scriptwriter of our own triumphant drama. We are also its protagonist. Shakespeare wrote: "All the world's a stage, / And all the men and women merely players."[1]

Buddhism teaches us that we each write and perform the script of our own lives. No one else writes that script for us. We write it, and we are the star who performs it. This extremely active life philosophy is inherent in the teaching of three thousand realms in a single moment of life.

We are each the author and the main character of our own stories. In order for it to be a wonderful production, it's essential that we become so familiar with the scenario that we can picture it vividly. We may need to rehearse it mentally. Sometimes it helps to write down our goals (for example, to pass an examination or to improve at work) and read them over and over again until they are deeply impressed in our minds.

There once was a young boy who had an accident that left one of his legs shorter than the other. His parents, however, never told him that anything was too hard or impossible for him to do. They treated him like any other child and encouraged him to play sports. They taught him that he could do whatever he believed he could and that if he was unable to do something, it was because he had decided he couldn't before even trying. Their conviction wasn't based on mere idealism or optimism. It was a belief in the latent potential of the human being.

The boy later became a star football player at school, and after graduation he succeeded in society as well. His life perfectly illustrates the following assertion, made by the Russian writer Maksim Gorky in one of his novels: "Talent is nothing but faith in yourself, in your own powers."[2]

Sir Walter Scott, the great Scottish author, wrote, "To the timid and hesitating everything is impossible, because it seems so."[3]

Thinking "It's impossible" or "It can't be done" has the effect of actually making anything and everything impossible. Similarly, if parents constantly tell their children they are hopeless or inept, the children will come to believe it and may wind up fulfilling that expectation.

Nichiren Daishonin cites a passage from the Flower Garland Sutra:

> The mind is like a skilled painter, who creates various forms made up of the five components. Thus of all the phenomena throughout the entire world, there is not a single one that is not created by the mind. . . . Outside of this mind there is no other phenomenon that exists. (WND-2, 844)

When we read the Daishonin's letters, we find that he constantly cites sutras and Buddhist scriptures to offer examples and documentary proof relevant to the situations or questions of the recipients, seeking to change their hearts, strengthen their determination, and give them conviction and self-confidence. His words always radiate hope and encouragement, like the sun. This is because he fully understood that when a person's heart changes, everything changes.

Many people ascribe others' success to favorable circumstances. They are likely to think, "If only I had such good luck" or "If only I didn't have this problem to deal with." But that ultimately is just complaining. There is no one who doesn't have problems.

A businessman once said to a friend: "You're always complaining about having so many problems. I know a place where there are at least ten thousand people, and not one of them has even a single problem or worry. Would you like me to take you there?"

His friend said, "Yes, please do!"

And guess where the businessman took him? To a cemetery. He was teaching his friend that as long as we are alive, we will have to deal with problems and sufferings. Challenging ourselves to find ways to overcome these problems gives richness and meaning to our lives.

Buddhism teaches that earthly desires lead to enlightenment. This means the greater our worries and sufferings, the greater the happiness we can transform them into through the power of chanting Nam-myoho-renge-kyo.

In Shakyamuni's day, there was a woman who had lost her beloved child to illness. Half insane with grief, she wandered the town clutching her dead child to her bosom and begged all those she encountered: "Please give me medicine for my child."

Feeling pity for her, someone took her to see Shakyamuni. When he heard her story, he said: "Do not fret. I will give you good medicine. Go into the town and bring me back some mustard seeds. However, they must be mustard seeds from a family where no one has lost a loved one."

In her quest, the woman walked all over the town, going from door to door. But there was not one family that had not lost a loved one. Finally, it dawned on her: all human beings die. She was not alone in her suffering. To gain insight into the eternity of life, she became a follower of Shakyamuni, and she later came to be respected as a sage.[4]

By employing the expedient means of sending her out in search of mustard seeds, Shakyamuni freed and restored peace to the heart of this woman who had been wrapped up in her own grief. He helped her awaken to a deeper wisdom based on the eternity of life.

The most important thing is to expand our state of life. When we think only of ourselves, we become increasingly caught up in our small egos, or lesser selves. In contrast, when we work toward a great and all-encompassing objective—for the sake of the Law, the happiness of others, and the welfare of society—we can develop big hearts and bring forth our greater selves through the "wonderful workings of one mind" (OTT, 30). With big hearts, we can savor truly immense happiness. Sufferings that may have once been a heavy burden in a lesser state of life will appear minor, and we are able to calmly rise above them. I hope all of you will lead lives in which you can demonstrate such brilliant, positive proof of the "wonderful workings of one mind."

From a speech at an SGI-USA representatives conference, Miami, Florida, March 9, 1993.

5.2 "Earthly Desires Lead to Enlightenment"

As the principle earthly desires lead to enlightenment from The Record of the Orally Transmitted Teachings *indicates, Buddhism enables us to transform all our problems and difficulties into the energy to advance.*

Buddhism teaches the principle that earthly desires lead to enlightenment. To explain this very simply, "earthly desires" refers to suffering and the desires and cravings that cause suffering, while "enlightenment" refers to happiness and an enlightened state of life.

Normally, one would assume that earthly desires and enlightenment are separate and independent conditions—especially since suffering would seem to be the exact opposite of happiness. But this is not the case in Nichiren Buddhism, which teaches that only by burning the "firewood" of problems and suffering can we obtain the "flames" of happiness. In other words, by using suffering as fuel, we gain the "light" and "energy" for happiness. And it is by chanting Nam-myoho-renge-kyo that we "burn the firewood of earthly desires."

When we chant Nam-myoho-renge-kyo, our problems and sufferings all turn into energy for our happiness, into fuel that enables us to keep moving forward in our lives.

The wonderful thing about faith in Nichiren Buddhism is that it enables those who suffer the most to attain the greatest happiness and those who experience the most daunting problems to lead the most wonderful, meaningful lives.

Problems come in all shapes and sizes. You may be dealing with some personal problem, you may be wondering how to help your parents live long and fulfilling lives, or you may be worried about friends who are sick or depressed and wish for their recovery. On a different level, you may be deeply concerned about the issue of world peace or the direction of the world in the twenty-first century. These are very noble concerns.

Through chanting Nam-myoho-renge-kyo, you can turn all these worries and concerns into fuel to propel yourselves forward—you can transform them into life force, into greater depth of character, and into good fortune. I therefore hope you will challenge all kinds of problems, chant abundantly about them, and develop yourselves along the way.

Faith means setting goals and striving to achieve each one. If we view each goal or challenge as a mountain, faith is a process whereby we grow with every mountain climbed.

From Discussions on Youth,
published in Japanese in March 1999.

5.3 "Changing Poison Into Medicine"

According to the Buddhist principle changing poison into medicine, with strong faith, we can transform the poison of problems and difficulties into the medicine of happiness and victory.

Life inevitably involves victory and defeat. There may be times of sorrow and suffering. But Buddhism teaches that earthly desires lead to enlightenment and the sufferings of life and death lead to nirvana. The greater our problems and suffering, the greater the joy and happiness we can transform them into through our Buddhist practice.

We practice this Buddhism for our own sake. The purpose of our faith and practice is to live true to ourselves. It is to increase our good fortune and open the way to happiness. Since this is the case, if we are easily swayed by trifling matters, upbeat one minute and down the next, we cannot say that we are truly practicing Nichiren Buddhism.

In the realm of the Mystic Law, no matter what happens, we can, in time, positively transform all poison into medicine.

In fact, there is really no clear-cut dividing line between poison and medicine. The same substance can act as either a poison or a medicine, depending on the dosage and the life force of the individual who takes it. Some have even described medicine as "poison that saves lives."

Similarly, there is no clear difference between what will function as poison or medicine when it comes to victory and defeat in life. For instance, if we triumph in the end, everything we experienced can be seen as medicine. On the other hand, if our lives end in defeat, then everything—even that which seemed to function as medicine along the way—becomes poison.

What do we mean by triumphing in the end? It means being victorious in faith. For this is our true victory as a human being—one that leads to our victory throughout the three existences of past, present, and future.

From a speech at a chapter leaders meeting, Tokyo, Japan, July 27, 1989.

5.4 Creating the Future With the Buddhism of True Cause

Buddhism teaches the principle of cause and effect in our lives—that our present situation is the effect caused by our past actions. Nichiren Buddhism, however, teaches the "true cause"—that we are not bound by our past but are always embarking from the present moment into the future.

It often seems that people begin to seriously consider the nature of cause and effect or what it means to lead a happy life only when they experience acute suffering themselves. When all is going smoothly, they tend not to give much thought to the truly important things in life. In that sense, difficulties play a crucial role in helping us lead deeper and more meaningful lives. In fact, that's how we should look at them.

No life is utterly without problems or difficulties. All too often, seemingly happy life circumstances can become causes of suffering and unhappiness. This is something we come to recognize more and more as we mature in years and experience.

A married couple's happiness, for instance, may be shattered when their child is born with a serious illness. All sorts of unanticipated events can assail us—a sudden economic downturn, a fire or accident, family discord, divorce, difficult personal relationships. They can even sometimes lead to lifelong suffering. It is truly the case that we never know what tomorrow brings. None can declare with certainty that they will never encounter misfortune.

Even those who enjoy security and tranquillity can come to feel that their lives have no meaning as they age. There are still others who always seem to be busily engaged in purposeful endeavors but are in reality simply trying to escape loneliness and emptiness by doing so, unwilling to reflect on themselves or their lives.

Behind a smile might lie sadness. After pleasure might come emptiness. Problems and suffering are inescapable realities of life. And yet, we must go on living. How, then, should we live? How can we change suffering into true joy? The Buddhism of Nichiren Daishonin has the answer to these important and fundamental questions.

Nichiren Buddhism is the Buddhism of true cause. It is a great, revolutionary teaching. It reveals that Nam-myoho-renge-kyo is the fundamental cause for attaining enlightenment and that, by simply embracing the Gohonzon, we can acquire in this lifetime all the practices and virtues of the Buddha.[5]

Nichiren Buddhism focuses on the present and the future. Its essence is for us to always keep advancing while looking toward and brightly illuminating the future.

Practicing this Buddhism doesn't mean that problems and suffering disappear. The reality of life is that within any of the Ten Worlds the other nine are always present—hence, the nine worlds characterized by delusion and suffering also exist within the world of Buddhahood. Likewise, the world of Buddhahood can express itself only within the reality of the other nine worlds.

The important thing is to remain undaunted when difficulties arise, to firmly believe that they are expressions of the Buddha's compassion and forge ahead with even stronger faith.

Some may weakly succumb to doubt and question why they still have problems even though they are practicing Nichiren Buddhism. But such a weak way of thinking will—in accord with the principle of three thousand realms in a single moment of life—come to permeate every aspect

The WISDOM *for* CREATING HAPPINESS *and* PEACE, Part 1

of their lives and create a state of even greater suffering. This is the opposite of having strong faith.

As ordinary people, we may not be able to fathom why a particular event happens at a particular time, but over the long term we will come to understand its meaning. We will also be able to positively transform the situation, changing poison into medicine. I can say this with complete confidence based on my personal experience of more than four decades of Buddhist practice. We may not understand the significance of a certain event until five or ten years later, or it may even take a lifetime. However, from the perspective of the eternity of life spanning the three existences, everything has meaning as an expression of the Buddha wisdom.

From a speech at a nationwide youth division leaders meeting, Tokyo, Japan, April 29, 1988.

5.5 Living With Joy Throughout All

In this selection, President Ikeda emphasizes that living with joy is the hallmark of a genuine practitioner.

Leo Tolstoy exclaimed: "Rejoice! Rejoice! The business of life, its purpose, is joy. Rejoice at the sky, the sun, the stars, the grass, the trees, animals, people."[6]

"Rejoice!"—that was one of the ultimate conclusions the great Russian writer and thinker reached in life.

Living with joy throughout all is the hallmark of a lofty state of being, of strength and happiness. In contrast, a life that greets everything with criticism and complaint is miserable, no matter how fine it might look from the outside.

In 1901, Tolstoy was excommunicated by the Russian Orthodox Church. He was seventy-two at the time, already advanced in years. The Church thought that taking this punitive measure would humiliate Tolstoy, who was widely admired around the world. But he was unruffled by the tactics of the Church authorities. He observed their actions with serene dignity.

"Rejoice, rejoice!" His conviction remained unshaken. In fact, he burned with a passionate fighting spirit.

Tolstoy's life was not untroubled. He struggled with his writing, with unhappiness in his family life, and with illness. But his spirit always and everywhere sought out and created joy.

This is also the Buddhist way of life. I hope you will all lead lives of pursuing and creating joy.

Nichiren Daishonin declared, "Nam-myoho-renge-kyo is the greatest of all joys" (OTT, 212). A life dedicated to kosen-rufu is a life of supreme joy. He also wrote:

> I feel immeasurable delight even though I am now an exile. (WND-1, 386)

✳

> The more the government authorities rage against me, the greater is my joy. (WND-1, 243)

✳

> The greater the hardships befalling [the votary of the Lotus Sutra], the greater the delight he feels, because of his strong faith. (WND-1, 33)

And at the time of the Tatsunokuchi Persecution, the Daishonin said to his loyal disciple Shijo Kingo, who accompanied him, "What greater joy could there be?" (WND-1, 767). "You should smile!" he was telling him.

When hardships occur, the Daishonin taught, "The wise will rejoice while the foolish will retreat" (WND-1, 637).

The more challenges we face, the more joyfully we should move forward and the more determinedly we should tackle them—this is the essence of Nichiren Buddhism and the most valuable way to lead our lives.

A joyless life is miserable. Those who are put off by everything, who are always negative, wear pained expressions, and do nothing but criticize and complain are not living as the Daishonin teaches in his writings.

Those who can find joy in everything, who can transform everything into joy, are genuine experts in the art of living.

In "Letter from Sado" the Daishonin writes, "Worthies and sages are tested by abuse" (WND-1, 303). Truly great individuals are distinguished by their ability to endure criticism and abuse and calmly lead joyful lives.

Finding joy in everything—when you brim with joy, you will lift the spirits of those around you, bring smiles to people's faces, and create value.

It is vital above all that leaders constantly think about how they can enable everyone to advance with joy.

From a speech at a divisional representatives meeting, Tokyo, Japan, June 28, 1993.

5.6 Both Suffering and Joy Are Parts of Life

As Nichiren Daishonin explains in a letter to his disciple Shijo Kingo, who was facing many difficulties, we should strive calmly to overcome every obstacle, unswayed by immediate events, and develop a state of supreme happiness.

I would like to share a passage from the Daishonin's writings that I'm sure all of you are very familiar with. It is from a letter of encouragement the Daishonin sent to Shijo Kingo, who found himself in difficult circumstances. Kingo had incurred his lord's disfavor by trying to convert him to the Daishonin's teaching, an act that also invited hostility from his fellow samurai retainers. The Daishonin writes to him:

> Suffer what there is to suffer, enjoy what there is to enjoy. Regard both suffering and joy as facts of life, and continue chanting Nam-myoho-renge-kyo, no matter what happens. How could this be anything other than [experiencing] the boundless joy of the Law? Strengthen your power of faith more than ever. (WND-1, 681)

Right now, your life may be filled with suffering. But just as pleasure never lasts forever, neither does suffering. In life, there is both suffering and joy. Sometimes we win, and other times we lose. Both suffering and joy are a part of life; this is life's reality. That is why, whether experiencing suffering or joy, we should keep chanting Nam-myoho-renge-kyo, just as we are, says the Daishonin. If we do that, we will attain a state of supreme happiness through the wisdom and power of the Mystic Law. We can lead a life in which nothing will defeat us.

The Daishonin uses the phrase "experiencing the boundless joy of the Law." "Experiencing" here means that we obtain and savor this joy ourselves. It comes down to us, not others. This joy is not bestowed on us by someone else or something outside us. Creating our own happiness and experiencing that happiness for ourselves; developing the inner strength and capacity to serenely enjoy life, regardless of its ups and downs—this is the meaning of "experiencing the boundless joy of the Law." The power of Nam-myoho-renge-kyo enables us to do this.

For that reason, we don't need to compare ourselves with others. We should simply live in a way that is true to ourselves, based on faith in the Gohonzon.

Please advance in good health and with clear goals, while cultivating positive, harmonious relations with those around you. By conducting yourself in this way, you will naturally become the kind of person others admire, are drawn to, and want to get to know. The Mystic Law enables you to utilize your potential to the fullest. When that happens, you can go anywhere and face anything with a sense of confidence and ease. You'll be able to do what you need to do, unswayed by immediate events and circumstances, and lead a life of deep satisfaction, without regrets. That is the mark of a true victor in life.

From a speech at a headquarters leaders meeting, Tokyo, Japan, April 21, 2005.

5.7 Difficulties Are a Driving Force for Growth

The great life state attained by Nichiren Daishonin, who surmounted a succession of hardships and persecutions, teaches us the importance of turning adversity into the energy to advance.

Nichiren Daishonin's life was a series of hardships and persecutions, including being exiled twice. Some of his disciples questioned where any peace and comfort was to be found in all this. But the Daishonin insisted that difficulties are in fact peace and comfort (see OTT, 115) and in his writings repeatedly made such statements as "What fortune is mine!" (WND-1, 402); "How delighted I am!" (WND-1, 402); "In future lives I will enjoy immense happiness, a thought that gives me great joy" (WND-1, 287); and "How can such joy possibly be described!" (WND-1, 396). He savored a state of life that he could only describe as "How fortunate, how joyful!" (WND-1, 642).

In the light of the Buddhist scriptures, difficulties are inevitable. The important thing is how we transform them, changing poison into medicine, and use them as the driving force for fresh growth and progress.

There is no point in feeling anxious or lamenting each time the harsh winds of adversity blow. If we have a powerful determination to change everything that happens into a strong "tailwind," we can surely open the way forward.

We of the Soka Gakkai have been able to create a history of tremendous development based on faith that is focused on the present and the future—namely, always looking from the present moment onward and moving forward, ever forward.

Without hardships, there is no true Buddhist practice. Without struggle, there is no genuine happiness. And that would not be real life. There would be no attainment of Buddhahood either. When we practice Nichiren Buddhism with this understanding, we will never reach an impasse.

The power of one's state of life is indeed wondrous. The power of one's inner determination is limitless. In identical situations or circumstances, people can achieve completely different results and lead completely different lives depending upon their life state and their determination.

Those who have a strong resolve to promote our movement for kosen-rufu will see clear blue skies of good fortune appearing rapidly in their lives, stretching ever further and further, as if the wind were sweeping away every dark cloud.

From a speech at a Nagano Prefecture general meeting, Nagano, Japan, August 4, 1991.

5.8 Polishing Ourselves Through Adversity

President Ikeda explains the significance of hardships we encounter in spite of practicing Buddhism to attain happiness.

Why do we have to endure hardships? The purpose of our Buddhist practice is to attain Buddhahood. Buddhahood is the state of absolute happiness. Though we are practicing Nichiren Buddhism to become happy, why then do we have to overcome obstacles? The reason is that we need to undergo the trials of difficulty to forge and strengthen within us the diamond-like and indestructible "self" of Buddhahood.

The diamond is regarded as the king of gemstones. It is the hardest of all minerals, possessing unmatched brilliance. A symbol of purity, its name derives from the Greek word *adamas* meaning "unconquerable" or "invincible."

How are diamonds formed? I'm not a scientist, but it is widely known that diamonds, like graphite, are made of carbon. Deep in the earth, this material is subjected to intense heat and pressure until it is transformed into the crystalline structure of a diamond.

This is similar to how we develop ourselves. Only when subjected to the concentrated pressure of hardships and the fierce heat of great adversity will the core of our lives, our deepest self, be transformed into the diamond-like and indestructible life state of Buddhahood. In other words, it is through experiencing hardships that we acquire the "diamond-like body," or the Buddha body—a brightly shining state of absolute happiness as indestructible as a diamond that cannot be crushed by any amount of suffering or delusion.

A smooth and uneventful kind of Buddhist practice without any difficulties cannot truly help us polish and forge our lives. It is only when we withstand the intense heat and pressure of great hardships that we can shine as "champions of life," sparkling like the most perfect of diamonds.

Such a diamond-like state of life shines with a pure, beautiful, and imperishable light. It is solid and indestructible when buffeted by the turbulent tides of society and the obstacles of corrupt and ill-intentioned forces. We can achieve this state of life through earnestly chanting Nam-myoho-renge-kyo and dedicating ourselves to kosen-rufu. Then our lives will forever be one with the Mystic Law, and we can strive for kosen-rufu with complete freedom throughout eternity. By correctly embracing and upholding the Gohonzon, we can become our greatest possible selves, continuing in this supreme state of Buddhahood in lifetime after lifetime.

Please lead brilliant lives that are diamond-like and indestructible. Indeed, may you all become diamonds of happiness that sparkle with the radiance of your beautiful hearts. To do so, please never fear hardships. Don't allow yourselves to be defeated by unfounded criticism. Rather, be grateful for all obstacles, because they help you polish and develop yourselves.

Those who show even stronger conviction in faith and engage even more joyfully in Buddhist practice the greater the hardships they encounter will truly live as diamond-like champions.

Please magnificently adorn this precious life with beautiful faith and beautiful friendship. Live out your days spreading the sublime diamond-like light of life far and wide and demonstrating the truth of the teachings and principles of Nichiren Buddhism.

From a speech at a Funabashi leaders meeting,
Chiba, Japan, July 13, 1987.

5.9 Winter Always Turns to Spring

President Ikeda encourages us to look to the future with confidence and determination.

Nichiren Daishonin writes, "Winter always turns to spring" (WND-1, 536). Those who believe in the Lotus Sutra may seem to be in winter, he says, but winter will definitely give way to spring.

These words of the Daishonin have enabled countless individuals to find their way forward to a springtime of rebirth, a springtime in life. It is one of our eternal guidelines, and its message, without a doubt, will continue to impart boundless hope to billions of people around the world who are searching for true happiness. Let us then consider the infinite compassion of the Daishonin that is embodied in these words.

He wrote them to encourage the lay nun Myoichi. Her husband had been a person of strong faith. After the Tatsunokuchi Persecution, he was stripped of his estate because of his faith in the Daishonin's teachings. Those who are in the right are often persecuted—that is the unfortunate way of our corrupt world, a constant we can observe in every country and every age. While the Daishonin was in exile on Sado, Myoichi's husband died, remaining steadfast in faith to the end of his life. He left behind his wife who was elderly and frail, a son who was ill, and also a daughter.

The Daishonin was very aware of the lay nun's situation. In his letter, he imagined how grieved her husband must have been to leave her and their children behind, worried about what would become of them when he was no longer there, and how he would also have been anxious about the fate of the Daishonin (see WND-1, 535–36).

As I mentioned, Myoichi's husband died while the Daishonin was still in exile on Sado, an island of freezing winters from which few exiles returned alive. His heart must have been filled with sorrow and concern for the Daishonin.

Thinking of his courageous disciple who had passed away amid severe hardship, the Daishonin writes:

> Perhaps your husband felt that certainly something would happen and this priest [Nichiren] would become highly respected. When I was exiled [to Sado] contrary to his expectations, he must have wondered how the Lotus Sutra and the ten demon daughters could possibly have allowed it to happen. Were he still living, how delighted he would be to see Nichiren pardoned![7] (WND-1, 536)

As this passage and other letters indicate, many of the Daishonin's disciples had expected that he would achieve a position of acclaim and honor. In reality, however, his life was filled with endless persecution. He was defamed and ridiculed throughout the land and subjected to unrelenting harassment. Among his followers were some who had expected their own reputations to rise along with the Daishonin's, but when their hopes in this regard were dashed they abandoned their Buddhist practice or joined the ranks of the Daishonin's opponents. They conspired with the authorities and began to maneuver behind the scenes to harm their former teacher and fellow practitioners.

Yet even amid all this, Myoichi's husband remained true and steadfast in his convictions. He must have dreamed of the Daishonin's triumphant return and been angered and pained at the mean-spirited betrayal by some of his followers.

The Daishonin knew what was going on in his disciples' minds. He was fully aware of everything. He refused to compromise in the slightest degree with evil and injustice and confronted persecution head-on.

That is why the Daishonin writes that Myoichi's deceased husband would surely have been delighted and overjoyed at the Daishonin's safe return from Sado—an outcome that no one at the time had expected. This passage powerfully communicates his wish that his faithful follower, who had stood by him through great hardships, could witness his victory and rejoice along with him.

In the same letter, the Daishonin writes that Myoichi's late husband would also have been glad to see that the Daishonin's prediction of a Mongol invasion had come true, affirming the correctness of his assertions. Though foreign invasion, of course, was a tragic event for the country, such a reaction from a disciple was simply a matter of human nature, he points out, "the feelings of ordinary people" (WND-1, 536).

No doubt upon reading this, the lay nun Myoichi felt she could hear the Daishonin's voice saying, "We are united in our joys and sufferings."

The Daishonin's words "winter always turns to spring" are written with regard to the circumstances just described. He is telling her, in effect: "Your husband died in 'winter.' But 'spring' has now arrived. Winter always turns to spring. Live out your life to the fullest. Those who remain true to their convictions are sure to attain Buddhahood. You cannot fail to become happy. Your husband is most certainly watching over you and your family."

In addition, with deep care and compassion, the Daishonin assures Myoichi that he stands ready to look after her children if the time ever arises (see WND-1, 536). Such limitless kindness and warm humanity are the lifeblood of the compassionate Buddhism of Nichiren Daishonin. There is not the slightest trace of authoritarianism. How wonderful!

The words "winter always turns to spring" can also be read as an expression of the Daishonin's own conviction and actual proof, having experienced the spring of victory after weathering the bleakest circumstances during his exile on Sado.

The Daishonin faced persecution after persecution, trials that could not be surmounted without the power of Buddhahood. Ordinarily, someone subject to such ongoing persecution would most likely fall ill, have a nervous breakdown, commit suicide, or end up being killed. The Daishonin, however, triumphed over every adversity. He survived and lived on. For the sake of all humankind, he transmitted the Buddhism of the Three Great Secret Laws for the eternal future of the Latter Day of the Law. We must be deeply aware of his immense compassion in doing so.

The lay nun Myoichi was no doubt profoundly moved by the Daishonin's message calling on his followers to observe his victory of "winter turning into spring" and to adopt it as a model in their own lives.

We also need to attain our own "spring of happiness"—not only for ourselves but also for the sake of our fellow members who have striven alongside us for many long years. It is important for us to set an example so that those coming after us can look at us, rejoice, and say: "How wonderful! Those who continue practicing Nichiren Buddhism become outstanding people and attain happiness!"

Over the past decade, I have attained a "spring of victory" that no one could have imagined. It is all due to my single-minded commitment to do this for the sake of kosen-rufu and for my fellow members.

Seniors in faith have a responsibility to demonstrate victory, for the sake of their fellow members who have been striving valiantly for kosen-rufu. By victory, of course, I do not mean the external trappings of worldly success or superficial honors. True victory exists in realizing the great uncrowned state of having joyfully and confidently fulfilled one's mission in life, as a human being and as a practitioner of Nichiren Buddhism.

Spring is the time when flowers bloom. But in order to bloom, flowers need the cold of winter. What would happen if there was no winter?

In autumn, plants that bloom in spring prepare to enter a period of dormancy, or recharging. They start saving energy for the coming spring. If there is a sudden warm spell during their dormancy in winter and they are awakened, the buds waiting for spring's arrival start to open before they are ready, and when the winter cold returns, they wither and die. To prevent that from happening, plants will not bloom unless they have fully experienced the cold of winter. This is the "wisdom" of plants that enables them to bloom in spring.

Life and Buddhist practice also follow this principle. A winter of adversity is the time to recharge our batteries and temper ourselves for the arrival of a wonderful spring. In life's winters, the eternal and indestructible energy for attaining Buddhahood is stored up, and life force as vast as the universe is forged. This energy, in addition, grows in response to adversity and hardship. And all who practice the correct teaching of Buddhism will without fail experience the coming of spring.

But if, in the difficult times of life's winters, we try to avoid or doubt the realm in which we strengthen our faith, and as a result we fail to accumulate enough strength and good fortune, we will never get anywhere nor be able to lead a truly satisfying life. The crucial thing is how we challenge ourselves and how meaningfully we spend our time during life's winters. What matters is how deeply we live with the conviction that spring will definitely arrive. In the realm of nature, the flowering springtime always comes when the time is right. That is the rhythm of life and the universe. But far too many people in the world are still in the midst of winter when they reach the end of their lives. To avoid that fate, we need to align our lives with the rhythm of the universe that calls forth spring. And our Buddhist practice based on faith in the Mystic Law is what enables us to do that.

In that sense, faith in the Mystic Law functions as our wings to eternal happiness. Every time we overcome difficulties, we accumulate good fortune and elevate our state of life. By attaining Buddhahood in this lifetime, we are able to soar serenely through the vast skies of life in a state of supreme happiness and fulfillment throughout eternity. This is the teaching of Buddhism and the rhythm of life.

From a speech at a headquarters leaders meeting, Tokyo, Japan, April 29, 1990.

5.10 The Principle of Lessening Karmic Retribution

The principle of lessening karmic retribution represents a radical rethinking of the concept of karma, enabling us to engage positively with adversity through strong faith.

Nichiren Daishonin offered the following encouragement to the Ikegami brothers, Munenaka and Munenaga, who were in the midst of a struggle against serious obstacles: "The blessings gained by practicing the correct teaching [the Mystic Law], however, are so great that by meeting minor sufferings in this life we can change the karma that destines us to suffer terribly in the future" (WND-1, 497).

Through "the blessings gained by practicing the correct teaching"—that is, "the blessings obtained by protecting the Law"[8]—the grave negative effects of karma that we would otherwise have experienced in the future are transformed and received as minor effects in the present. We need to be deeply convinced of this principle, called lessening karmic retribution. And, to a degree that accords with the depth of our faith, we can experience its reality in our own lives.

For instance, suppose you meet with an accident, but it is very minor and not a disaster that involves many people. This could be an instance of receiving the effects of negative karma in a lessened form. You can probably think of many similar examples.

In this way, we can clearly see the significance of hardships from the perspective of the eternity of life across the three existences of past, present, and future. In other words, by undergoing hardships, we can transform in this lifetime the cycle of negative causes and effects in our lives and magnificently reveal within us the brilliant, vibrant state of Buddhahood.

The Daishonin discussed these principles of lessening karmic retribution and the blessings obtained by protecting the Law in terms of his own life in works such as "The Opening of the Eyes" and "Letter from Sado," which he composed while in exile on Sado Island. Though the Buddha of the Latter Day of the Law, the Daishonin strove as an ordinary person to demonstrate, for the sake of his followers into the eternal future of the Latter Day, the reason why we encounter difficulties. He also taught us the essence of "faith for overcoming hardships." This is a crucial guideline both for our personal lives and for the realm of kosen-rufu.

Three years ago [in October 1985], I was hospitalized for the first time in my life, for ten days. Objectively speaking, I could have collapsed at any moment. After all, I had been working relentlessly for forty years since joining the Soka Gakkai, and for nearly thirty years since I had inherited the mantle of our organization's leadership from Mr. Toda. I had been pushing myself to the limit, even though when I was younger the doctors had said I probably wouldn't live to see the age of thirty. I was constantly on the go. I was always fighting against adversity.

The media made a big fuss about my hospitalization. There were also many unfounded speculations, and some people moved to act against me motivated by self-interest and calculation. But I understood exactly what was going on. Personally, I felt that my illness was a gift arising from the Buddha's great compassion. I was convinced it was teaching me that the time had come to stand up again on my own and start in earnest on completing my work for kosen-rufu.

Now, I thought, is the time to speak the full truth. Now is the time to offer, from every angle, thoroughgoing guidance for the sake of future generations. I resolved that I must convey the Soka Gakkai's true greatness and its profound significance and spirit.

Until then, I thought I had done my utmost to build a solid organization and teach all that had been necessary. But now, with my illness, I pledged to teach ten or twenty times more and to work ten or twenty times harder. And I began, and continue, to do so.

What I am saying is that you are bound to encounter obstacles and difficulties in life of one degree or another. But please know that they all derive from the Buddha's compassion aimed at helping you become strong, like tall, sturdy trees.

With that conviction, please forge ahead as champions of faith, overcoming all challenges and opening the way forward in your lives and for kosen-rufu with ever greater strength, resilience, and joy with each obstacle you face.

From a speech at a nationwide youth division leaders meeting, Tokyo, Japan, April 29, 1988.

THE PRINCIPLE OF CHERRY, PLUM, PEACH, AND DAMSON

6.1 "Still I Will Bloom"

Buddhism teaches the principle of cherry, plum, peach, and damson—that every being is beautiful and valuable as it is, without trying to be something else. Everyone possesses the seed of a precious mission. The purpose of our lives is to make that seed sprout, flourish, and blossom. On a visit to Yamagata Prefecture, President Ikeda explains this principle and urges us to dedicate our lives to our mission.

This is my first visit to Yamagata in nine years. Wishing to see you all as soon as possible, I took the train here from Niigata. From the train window, I could see blue streams and green forests amid the lingering mountain snow. Golden forsythia, bridal veil, daffodils, and cherry blossoms were in beautiful bloom.

The WISDOM for CREATING HAPPINESS and PEACE, Part 1

Observing the scenery, I was reminded of how, in *The Record of the Orally Transmitted Teachings*, Nichiren Daishonin states that the cherry, plum, peach, and damson each embody the ultimate truth just as they are, without undergoing any change (see OTT, 200).[1] This teaching provides us with a basic model for the way we should live our lives.

The cherry tree blossoms as a cherry tree, living to fulfill its own unique role. The same is true of the plum, peach, and damson trees. Each of us should do likewise. We each have a unique personality. We have a distinct nature and character, and our lives are each noble and worthy of respect. That's why we should always live with a solid self-identity, in a way that is true to ourselves.

Each of us has a mission and a way of life that is ours alone. We don't need to try to be like anyone else. The cherry tree has its own life and inherent causes for being a cherry. The plum, peach, and damson also each have their own inherent causes. And in the same way, from the viewpoint of Buddhism, we each have a mission we were born to carry out in this world, and each one of us has our own inherent causes to be who we are. Practicing the Mystic Law enables us to experience the joy of discovering this.

The most fundamental happiness in life is to bring forth our inner Buddhahood through the power of faith in the Mystic Law.

Some of you may envy those who live in bustling cities such as Tokyo. Others might wish to have a glamorous job or live in a big luxurious house. But in Tokyo, you can't

THE PRINCIPLE OF CHERRY, PLUM, PEACH, AND DAMSON

enjoy this natural environment [of Yamagata] with its pure, clean air, the bright moonlight or twinkling stars at night, or beautiful mountains draped softly in their white mantles, like Mount Zao standing out against the morning sky. At the same time, our happiness in life does not depend on the land or environment in which we live, our workplace, or the size of our homes.

The grass always seems greener on the other side. To those living in Yamagata, life in the big city might seem appealing, but city dwellers long for the beautiful natural environment of Yamagata. The key is to give full play to our capabilities and carry out our mission in our own communities, wherever we are, without being swayed by immediate circumstances or events.

A writer once remarked, "Whether seen by others or not, still I will bloom."[2] The Gohonzon is aware of all our actions. It is important to live in our own unique way, always embraced by the Mystic Law, whether or not anyone is watching. This is what the principle of cherry, plum, peach, and damson teaches.

From a speech at a Yamagata Prefecture general meeting, Yamagata, Japan, April 18, 1983.

6.2 Bringing Out Our Positive Qualities

In this excerpt from The New Human Revolution, *the novel's protagonist Shin'ichi Yamamoto (whose character represents President Ikeda), after attending a student division meeting, encourages a young person who is worried about being timid by nature.*

Shin'ichi said: "Gentleness and timidity can be seen as two different expressions of the same underlying nature. When that underlying nature takes the form of gentleness, it's a strength; when it takes the form of timidity, it can be a weakness. When that underlying nature consistently acts as a weakness, it can become the cause of unhappiness.

"For example, people with a fiery temper by nature may often end up arguing with coworkers. This could alienate those around them, making for strained relations. In some cases, their hotheadedness could even lead to them being fired or quitting. And since that is their underlying nature, the same problem is sure to crop up wherever they go.

"Our basic underlying natures don't change, but through our Buddhist practice, we can redirect our natures in a positive manner. Nichiren Daishonin says, 'When one comes to realize and see that each thing—the cherry, the plum, the peach, the damson—in its own entity, without undergoing any change, possesses the eternally endowed three bodies [of the Buddha]' (OTT, 200).

"Buddhism teaches the way for each of us, just as we are, to attain happiness while bringing out the best of our innate disposition and potential—in the same way that the cherry, plum, peach, and damson each manifest their own unique nature.

"People with fiery tempers are often also passionate, with a strong sense of right and wrong. By exerting themselves in Buddhist practice, they will no longer lose their tempers about unimportant things but become people strongly committed to opposing evil and injustice.

"Likewise, people who tend to be too agreeable or easily manipulated by others are often very kindhearted and able to get along well with others. Through practicing Buddhism, they can bring out this latter strong side of their natures. Positively transforming ourselves in this way is what we call human revolution. The important thing is how to make that transformation happen.

"Basically, the key is to chant Nam-myoho-renge-kyo and continue developing your life. It's crucial to reflect on yourself and discover your problematic qualities and life tendencies.

"We all have faults. Perhaps we tend to blame others when something bad happens to us, or we lack perseverance, or are unwilling to listen to the opinions of others. These faults can become negative tendencies obstructing our personal growth and happiness.

"But unless someone points these negative tendencies out to us, we may not be aware of them. That's where our seniors in faith and fellow members come in. They can draw our attention to them and support us in the effort to overcome them. We also need to chant earnestly to challenge and transform our negative tendencies.

"In addition, we can also forge and develop ourselves through Soka Gakkai activities. As Nichiren Daishonin writes, 'The flaws in iron come to the surface when it is forged' (WND-1, 497).

"Refusing to allow our weaknesses to defeat us and triumphing in one activity after another is the way we train and strengthen ourselves; it is the path of human revolution for each of us to win over our negative tendencies. Soka Gakkai activities are the 'place of practice' or 'training ground' where we develop and strengthen our lives. By dedicating ourselves to the mission of kosen-rufu and continuing to strengthen and improve ourselves, we can also transform our karma."

From The New Human Revolution, *vol. 16,*
"Heart and Soul" chapter.

6.3 Live True to Yourself

In a speech at a gathering commemorating the anniversary of second Soka Gakkai president Josei Toda's death, President Ikeda introduces President Toda's guidance and stresses the importance of living true to oneself.

To know oneself, to know the nature of human beings, to know the preciousness of life—herein lies the important significance of religion.

President Toda remarked:

> Whether one is suffering because of poverty, a business failure, a bitter quarrel with one's spouse, an injury caused by tripping over a hibachi [a charcoal brazier]—ultimately, all these things are a reflection of one's life. That is, they are outward expressions of one's inner state of being. When viewed in this way, everything in our lives occurs as a result of the changes unfolding within us. That's why it is important for us to strive to change for the better and ceaselessly create our own happiness.
>
> You therefore have to be true to yourself and take responsibility for your own life. Indeed, it's vital to recognize that you have no choice but to do so. It's a mistake to blame others or things outside you for your circumstances, to constantly think: "If only he or she would do this or that" or "I'd be

happy if only the situation in society were such and such."

However, human beings are weak. They are easily controlled by others or their external circumstances, no matter how they may resolve to be true to themselves, to follow their own convictions. . . .

This is why I believe the only way to make one's life shine with supreme strength, brilliance, and happiness is to base one's life on Buddhism, which teaches the principles of three thousand realms in a single moment of life and the mutual possession of the Ten Worlds.[3]

People who have vibrant life force are happy. People with strong conviction are happy. They can lead positive, successful lives. Those who are weak, in contrast, are miserable. They create misery and unhappiness for themselves. Practicing Nichiren Buddhism enables us to become as strong as we possibly can. To live in such a way that we can perceive everything in terms of faith and are always determined to overcome everything through faith means to walk the path to eternal happiness.

You yourself are precious beyond measure—every one of you. The Daishonin taught this to his disciples while he himself was facing major persecution. And the Soka Gakkai's first and second presidents, Tsunesaburo Makiguchi and Josei Toda, faithfully embraced the heart of Nichiren Buddhism and taught it to people from all walks of life.

THE PRINCIPLE OF CHERRY, PLUM, PEACH, AND DAMSON

With great conviction, let us continue to forge ahead powerfully along this path, which is directly connected to Nichiren Daishonin.

President Toda once gave the following guidance to members of the youth division:

> To believe in your own mind is especially important when you are young. Yet it is difficult to trust one's mind. This is particularly true during one's youth, a time of emotional turmoil and confusion. . . .
>
> I've seen the American cartoon *Popeye*. The main character, Popeye, is so weak that he is constantly being beaten up by others. But when he eats spinach, he instantly acquires strength and easily triumphs over his adversaries. This is because he believes in the power of spinach. . . .
>
> We all need to have something we believe in. "I have the Gohonzon. Therefore, I will be able to overcome any problem. Everything will be fine."—if you have such firm conviction, you can do anything. . . .
>
> If you feel that this is the path in life for you, that it's the right way to go, then believe in the Gohonzon and make it the core of your convictions. You will definitely be able to overcome any obstacle, including illness and poverty. But it requires the essential ingredient of faith. . . .
>
> For youth, the stronger your faith, the more invincible you will be in any situation. Young people

need to have something to believe in. You must trust your own hearts.

Yet because the human heart can be such an unreliable thing, it is important that you make the Gohonzon the foundation of your faith. If you do so, I am sure you will be able to lead your lives with confidence and ease. Please lead your lives that way and help others do the same.[4]

Mr. Toda dearly loved young people and held the highest hopes for them. Nothing gave him greater pleasure than seeing the energetic endeavors of the youth division members who brimmed with powerful conviction in faith.

From a speech at a representatives gathering commemorating April 2, the anniversary of second Soka Gakkai president Josei Toda's death, Tokyo, Japan, April 3, 1993.

6.4 Appreciating Your Uniqueness

President Ikeda encourages an SGI-USA member who asked how to deal with his lack of self-confidence.

No one has absolute confidence in themselves. In fact, it is quite normal not to have much confidence. In many

THE PRINCIPLE OF CHERRY, PLUM, PEACH, AND DAMSON

cases, people who go around bragging about their confidence are merely arrogant, always clashing with and greatly disliked by those around them. A person can be miserable with either too much or too little self-confidence.

The important thing is that all of you shine in your own way, win in your own daily endeavors, and develop your lives in the way most suitable and natural for you. All you need to do is just keep on improving yourself as you steadily advance toward your goal.

After all, you are you, not someone else. There is no need for you to compare yourself with others; it's *your* life. The important question is, What do you really feel and think in the depths of your being? Buddhism expounds the principle of cherry, plum, peach, and damson, each having their own unique characteristics, and the related principle of illuminating and manifesting one's true nature (see WND-1, 746).

Cherry blossoms are cherry blossoms, and peach blossoms are peach blossoms. A cherry blossom can never become a peach blossom. Nor is there any need for it to try to do so. It would be perfectly miserable if it did. Similarly, you are none other than yourself. You can never be someone else, however much you might wish it. What matters is that you become the kind of person who can cherish, praise, and feel content with your own precious, irreplaceable life.

Chanting Nam-myoho-renge-kyo is fundamental to this, enabling you to reveal your innate Buddhahood just as you are. Not only will chanting give you a wonderful, fundamental self-confidence, it will also adorn and dignify your life with the brilliance of your true and highest potential.

Please have absolute confidence in yourself, because you are living the noblest possible life, with a beautiful heart.

From a question-and-answer session with
SGI-USA Culture Department representatives,
Nagano, Japan, August 7, 1992.

6.5 Developing Your Own Individuality

In Dialogue of Hope, *addressed to junior high school students, President Ikeda talks about individuality and being oneself.*

Seeking to show their individuality or stand out from the crowd, some young people rush to adopt the latest fashions. But often, all they end up doing is looking just like everyone else. What sense is there in that?

Quite frankly, it almost seems as if there is some kind of set image of what individualism is, with everyone trying to conform to that image. But that image, in most cases, is just something created by the mass media and people trying to turn a profit, a fashion or trend that has been deliberately manufactured.

THE PRINCIPLE OF CHERRY, PLUM, PEACH, AND DAMSON

That's why being truly individualistic is actually quite difficult. First, you need to have a solid sense of who you are. You have to open your own eyes and look at the world, open your ears and listen to what others are saying, use your brain and think for yourself, and have the courage to follow through with your convictions.

It's much easier to just conform and be like everyone else. Even when people try to free themselves from the constraints that are holding them back, they often find themselves adopting someone else's standards. Japanese people have a strong tendency for this kind of mass conformity.

Genuine individuality isn't just a matter of style or outward appearance; it emanates from the inside out.

Someone has said that your individuality is a singular treasure that only you possess. It may be difficult for you to know exactly what that treasure is right now, but you definitely possess such a treasure, which you share with no one else. Every one of you does, with absolutely no exception!

If there are those who claim they don't possess this treasure, then it is because they themselves have decided they are worthless. Such thinking causes one to destroy one's own precious treasure.

Of course, even when trying to "be themselves," there are many people who don't know what that means. That's quite natural. In fact, all too often what people think of as being true to themselves or exercising their individuality is something they have borrowed or copied from others. That's why, if you think who you are right now is all there is to you, you are very much mistaken. Human beings have the capacity to change. Who you are now is really no more than the starting point for an even more wonderful you in the future.

Telling yourself, for instance, "I'm a poor speaker, so I'll stay in the background," is not living true to yourself. Instead, suppose you earnestly challenge yourself with the spirit to become a person who, though maybe not naturally a good talker, can bravely speak out and stop someone from bullying another, or can speak up for what's right at a crucial moment. Then, by making that kind of effort, your own unique character will shine in a way that is different from those who are naturally good speakers. That will be your individuality.

Your individuality starts to shine only when you strive with all your might, challenging yourself with every last ounce of your energy. It won't if you don't develop yourself. Only through making efforts to improve and grow will your individuality shine—just as a sword is forged in the flames. Your individuality is your own unique weapon for making the most of your life. It is your jeweled sword.

People who have splendidly developed their individuality are beautiful. Everyone finds them attractive. Theirs is not a fleeting, temporary beauty, but an enduring, lifelong one. Such people's spirit is as bright and clear as the skies over the high plains in summer. They are never envious or jealous of others.

In Japan, there is a tendency to try to drag down people who have real individuality and character. There is a narrow-minded mentality that seeks conformism, as exemplified by the Japanese proverb "The nail that sticks out gets hammered down." This is inspired by the jealousy and resentment of people who have no solid sense of identity or self-confidence and are always concerned about what others are doing, thinking, or saying, allowing themselves to be swayed this way and that.

In contrast, people who have worked hard and long to develop their own identities take delight in seeing others develop theirs to the fullest too. They support and encourage them in their efforts. They take joy in others' successes. And they have the capacity to work for the happiness and welfare of others.

I hope all of you will become such bighearted, truly beautiful people. Become people whom others admire and respect.

From Dialogue of Hope,
published in Japanese in June 2003.

6.6 Be a Shining Presence Like the Sun

In Discussions on Youth, *President Ikeda talks with high school students and other young people about the keys to finding their unique mission and becoming a shining presence.*

When you live in a way that is true to yourself, your real value as a human being shines through. Buddhism teaches the concept of "illuminating and manifesting one's true nature" (see WND-1, 746). This means to reveal your genuine innate self, your true inherent potential, and bring it to shine, illuminating all around you. It refers to your most refined individuality and uniqueness.

The important thing is to be patient, to have the confidence and determination that you will achieve something meaningful in the future. Don't be impatient in your youth. Your true substance as human beings will be determined ten, twenty, or thirty years from now. What matters is the kind of people you become then and whether you are fulfilling your mission then. Each of you has a mission that only you can fulfill. If you did not have such a mission, you would not have been born.

There are many kinds of mountains in this world. Some are high and some are low. And there are a great many different kinds of rivers. Some long, some short. Despite their differences, however, all mountains are mountains and all rivers are rivers.

There are serene mountains like the ones in the ancient

Japanese capital of Nara, and there are rugged mountains like Kyushu's Mount Aso [Japan's largest active volcano]. Then there are the grand snowcapped peaks of the Himalayas. All of these mountains are beautiful and impressive in their own way.

The same is so with rivers. There is Hokkaido's Ishikari River, home to magnificent salmon, as well as Nagano's Chikuma River, which has inspired countless poets. There is the Yellow River in China, and the Amazon in South America, rivers so wide that in some places the opposite shore cannot be seen. Each of these rivers has its own special beauty.

The same is true of people. Each of you has a unique mission in life. Moreover, you have encountered the Mystic Law while still young. You have a mission that is yours and yours alone. That is an indisputable fact, one in which I would like you to have conviction and pride.

You won't find your mission by standing still. Please challenge yourselves in something; it doesn't matter what. Then, by your making consistent efforts, the direction you should take will open up before you quite naturally. It's important, therefore, to have the courage to ask yourselves what you should be doing now, at this very moment.

The key, in other words, is to climb the mountain before you. As you ascend its slopes, you will develop your "muscles," increasing your strength and endurance. Such training will enable you to challenge still higher mountains. It is vital that you continue making such efforts. Chanting

The WISDOM for CREATING HAPPINESS and PEACE, Part 1

Nam-myoho-renge-kyo will enable you to bring forth the life force necessary to succeed.

Chant Nam-myoho-renge-kyo and climb the mountain in front of you. When you reach the summit, wide new horizons will stretch out before you. Little by little, you will understand your own mission.

Those who never forget that they have a unique mission are strong. Whatever problems they have, they will not be defeated. They will transform all their problems into fuel for growth toward a hope-filled future.

The important thing, therefore, is to resolve to be a shining presence like the sun. If you do so, all darkness will be dispelled. Live confidently, determined to be the sun in your environment, no matter what happens.

Of course, in life, there are both sunny days and cloudy ones. But even on cloudy days, the sun still shines. The same is true for people. Even when we are struggling, we mustn't let the light go out in our hearts.

All people have a unique mission that only they can fulfill. But that doesn't mean you should simply wait for someone to tell you what yours is. It is important that you discover your mission on your own.

Precious gems start out buried underground. If no one mines them, they'll stay buried. And if they aren't polished once they've been dug out, they will remain rough and dull.

THE PRINCIPLE OF CHERRY, PLUM, PEACH, AND DAMSON

All of you, my young friends, possess a jewel. You are each like a mountain with a hidden treasure. What a shame it would be to spend your entire life without uncovering it!

It is often said that everyone is a genius at something. Being talented doesn't just mean being a good musician, writer, or athlete—there are many kinds of talent. For instance, you may be a great conversationalist or make friends easily or put others at ease. Or you may have a gift for nursing, a knack for telling jokes, selling things, or economizing. You may be someone who is always punctual, patient, steady, kind, or optimistic. Or you may love new challenges, be strongly committed to peace, or bring joy to others.

Each of you is as unique as a cherry, plum, peach, or damson blossom (see OTT, 200), as Nichiren Daishonin explains. Please bloom in the way that only you can.

Without a doubt, you each possess within you a jewel, your own innate talent. How can you discover that talent? The only way is to challenge yourself to the limit. Your true potential will emerge when you give everything you've got to your studies, sports, or whatever you take on.

The most important thing is getting into the habit of challenging yourself to the limit in this way. In a sense, the results you get don't matter all that much. The actual grades you receive in high school, for instance, won't decide the rest of your life. But the habit of challenging yourself to the limit will in time bear fruit. It will distinguish you from others without fail and bring your unique talents to shine.

It has been said that we can only become as big as our

dreams. That is why you should have big dreams. But it's important to remember that dreams are dreams and reality is reality. If you want to realize your dreams, you have to take a hard look at reality and then make all-out efforts toward your goals.

Mr. Toda once said, "Young people must have the determination to excel at something." Determination, tenacity of purpose, is crucial. Halfhearted effort will not make the precious jewel of your unique talents shine.

From Discussions on Youth,
published in Japanese in March 1999.

6.7 Advancing Freely and Steadily

President Ikeda prefaced a question-and-answer session with Bharat [India] Soka Gakkai members by stating that "open discussion in which participants can speak freely and ask anything on their minds is a Buddhist tradition dating back to the times of Shakyamuni." In this excerpt, he offers encouragement to a men's division member who said he found it difficult to master the qualities of eloquence, wisdom, and compassion that the guidance of the Soka Gakkai suggests we aspire to.

Just be yourself. All you have to do is keep chanting Nam-myoho-renge-kyo and advance freely in a manner that is true to yourself. That is what the Buddhist principle of "illuminating and manifesting one's true nature" (see WND-1, 746) is all about. By practicing Nichiren Buddhism, we can bring our true self to shine. If this were not the case, we'd be frauds. Naturally, we should exert ourselves in our human revolution, but there is absolutely no need to resort to false or contrived eloquence, compassion, or wisdom.

What's important is to continue making effort daily, chanting and praying for the happiness of others, doing your best to be kind and considerate to those around you, and polishing your own character. But, as Mr. Toda often pointed out, if you can't treasure your spouse or those closest to you, you won't be able to treasure others. Compassion, he said, doesn't flow forth so easily.

Surely the correct path and most dignified way to live

is to advance just as we are, as ordinary people, striving to improve ourselves even just by small increments based on chanting Nam-myoho-renge-kyo. Nichiren Buddhism is a great teaching that is open to all people; it does not make irrational or unreasonable demands.

From a question-and-answer session on the occasion of a Bharat [India] Soka Gakkai meeting, New Delhi, India, February 16, 1992.

6.8 Everyone Has a Noble Mission

When we base our lives on the principles of Nichiren Buddhism, we can create a diverse and harmonious world where individuality is affirmed and differences respected.

Spring is near. The plum trees have bloomed, the peach trees have flowered, and soon it will be time for the cherry trees to blossom. The English Romantic poet Shelley wrote, "If Winter comes, can Spring be far behind?"[5] No matter how long and bitter the winter may be, spring always follows. This is the law of the universe, the law of life.

The same applies to us. If we seem to be weathering an endless winter in our lives, we must not abandon hope. As

THE PRINCIPLE OF CHERRY, PLUM, PEACH, AND DAMSON

long as we have hope, spring will come without fail. Spring is a time of blossoming.

Buddhism, as I have mentioned many times, teaches the principle of cherry, plum, peach, and damson (see OTT, 200). The cherry has its distinct beauty, the plum its delicate fragrance. The peach blossom has its lovely color, and the damson has its delightful charm. Every person has a singular mission, unique individuality, and way of living. It's important to recognize that truth and respect it. That is the natural order of things. That is how it works in the world of flowers. There, myriad flowers bloom harmoniously in beautiful profusion.

Unfortunately, in our human world, things do not always work this way. Some find it impossible to respect those who are different, so they discriminate against them or harass and torment them. They violate their rights as individuals. This is the source of much suffering and unhappiness in the world.

All people have a right to flower, to reveal their full potential as human beings, to fulfill their mission in this world. You have this right, and so does everyone else. That is the meaning of human rights. To scorn and violate people's human rights destroys the natural order of things. We must develop ourselves to become people who prize human rights and respect others.

From Discussions on Youth,
published in Japanese in March 1999.

6.9 Building a Harmonious World of Brilliant Diversity

In a lecture at the East-West Center in Hawaii, President Ikeda discusses the principle of cherry, plum, peach, and damson and Buddhism's respect for diversity and affirmation of the worth of all people.

In the teachings of Nichiren, we find the passage "The cherry, the plum, the peach, the damson . . . without undergoing any change . . ." (OTT, 200). These words confirm that there is no need for all to become "cherries" or "plums," but that each should manifest the unique brilliance of his or her own character.

This metaphor points to a fundamental principle of appreciation for diversity that applies equally to human beings and to social and natural environments. As the concept of "illuminating and manifesting one's true nature" (see WND-1, 746) indicates, the prime mission of Buddhism is to enable each and all to blossom to the fullest of their potential. The fulfillment of the individual, however, cannot be realized in conflict with, or at the expense of, others but only through active appreciation of uniqueness and difference, for these are the varied hues that together weave the flower gardens of life.

Nichiren's teachings also contain the following parable: When you face a mirror and bow respectfully, the image in the mirror likewise bows to you respectfully (see OTT, 165).

I think this beautifully expresses the all-encompassing causality that is the heart of Buddhism. The respect we demonstrate for the lives of others returns to us, with mirrorlike certainty, ennobling our lives.

The Buddhist principle of dependent origination reflects a cosmology in which all human and natural phenomena come into existence within a matrix of interrelatedness. Thus, we are urged to respect the uniqueness of each existence, which supports and nourishes all within the larger, living whole.

From a lecture at the East-West Center, "Peace and Human Security: A Buddhist Perspective for the Twenty-First Century," Honolulu, Hawaii, January 26, 1995.

6.10 The Wisdom for Fostering the Positive Potential in All People

In a peace proposal commemorating the twenty-third SGI Day in 1998, President Ikeda discusses the Buddhist principle of cherry, plum, peach, and damson as a source for creating new value, transcending all differences to build a world of harmony and peaceful coexistence.

Education does not mean coercing people to fit one rigid and unvaried mold; this is mere ideological indoctrination. Rather, it represents the most effective means of fostering the positive potential inherent in all people—self-restraint, empathy for others, and the unique personality and character of each person. To do this, education must be a personal, even spiritual encounter and interaction between human beings, between teacher and learner.

The teachings of Buddhism employ the analogy of flowering fruit trees—cherry, plum, peach, and damson—each blossoming and bearing fruit in its own unique way, to express the value of diversity. Each living thing, in other words, has a distinct character, individuality, and purpose in this world. Accordingly, people should develop their own unique capabilities as they work to build a world of cooperation where all people acknowledge both their differences and their fundamental equality, a world where a rich diversity of peoples and cultures is nourished, each enjoying respect and harmony....

THE PRINCIPLE OF CHERRY, PLUM, PEACH, AND DAMSON

The late Dr. David L. Norton, the respected American philosopher who was well versed in the educational philosophy of Tsunesaburo Makiguchi, shared his view of the Buddhist model of diversity in a 1991 address:

> For the reorganized world that must come, our responsibility as educators is to cultivate in our students a sensibility of respect and appreciation of cultures, beliefs, and practices that differ from their own. This can only be done on the basis of the recognition that other cultures, beliefs, and practices embody aspects of truth and goodness, as the blossoms of the cherry tree, the sour plum, the sweet plum, and the pear tree each embody beauty in a distinctive aspect. To achieve this means that our students must abandon the supposition that the beliefs and practices with which they are most familiar have a monopoly on truth and goodness. This supposition is called parochialism, or narrow-mindedness when it is the innocent result of ignorance, but it breeds the aggressive absolutism of the "closed society" mentality.[6]

Soon after World War II, as the East-West ideological confrontation escalated, second Soka Gakkai president Josei Toda spoke of the underlying unity of the human race, calling for the realization of a "global family." His appeal grew from the same roots as what today is called "world citizenship" and sought to transcend the constraints of self-centered and bigoted nationalism. There are, of course, those who believe a clash of civilizations to be unavoidable. My view is that such a clash would not occur between civilizations but between the savage elements that lurk within each civilization. If people from different cultural traditions are willing to work over time to build tolerant and enduring links, rather than indulging in the temptation to dominate and forcibly influence others, the very nature of culture is such that humanity will be enriched by their interaction, and their differences will give birth to new values.

The role of religion must be to provide the wisdom which can propel the effort toward mutual development and improvement. In this connection, Buddhism teaches that one meaning of *myo* (mystic) is "to open" (see WND-1, 145). The constant seeking after improvement and growth, the desire to open up latent potentialities, is a special characteristic of human life. What is urgently sought today is religion that responds to this desire for growth and fulfillment.

The sad historical reality, however, is one of endless strife, bloodshed, and tragedy originating from religion and religious differences. As Nichiren wrote, "The true path [of life] lies in the affairs of this world" (WND-1, 1126). I interpret this as meaning that if we are to avoid repeating the errors of the past, religions must give first priority to serving the needs of real people in their daily lives and finding solutions to the problems facing human society. In this way, they must provide the spiritual basis for peaceful competition.

A hopeful future can be opened up by overcoming what Toda criticized as narrow self-centeredness and by promoting the humanitarian competition that Makiguchi advocated, the shared work of value-creation among people committed to living together as global neighbors. Indeed, this is the core objective of the SGI's movement of what we call "human revolution."

*From a peace proposal commemorating
the twenty-third SGI Day,
January 26, 1998.*

HAPPINESS FOR BOTH OURSELVES AND OTHERS

7.1 "'Joy' Means That Oneself and Others Together Experience Joy"

Buddhism teaches that we should strive for the mutual happiness of ourselves and others, without sacrificing the interests of either. President Ikeda has consistently affirmed that happiness must be mutual and that we must not seek our happiness at the expense of others. In this selection, referring to the writings of Nichiren Daishonin, President Ikeda explains how we should aim to live as Buddhists pursuing happiness for both ourselves and others based on compassion and wisdom.

Nichiren Daishonin declares: "'Joy' means that oneself and others together experience joy. . . . Both oneself and others together will take joy in their possession of wisdom and compassion" (OTT, 146).

Both ourselves and others matter. Caring only about one's own happiness is selfish. Claiming to care only about the happiness of others is hypocritical. Real "joy" lies in both ourselves and others becoming happy together.

Second Soka Gakkai president Josei Toda said: "Becoming happy yourself is no great challenge; it's quite simple. But the essence of Nichiren Buddhism lies in helping others become happy too."[1]

The passage I just quoted from the Daishonin plainly states that true happiness means possessing both wisdom and compassion—in other words, the life state of Buddhahood. If one has wisdom but lacks compassion, one's life will be closed and constricted. Such wisdom, then, is not genuine. To have compassion but lack wisdom or behave in a foolish manner is to be of no help to anyone, including oneself. And compassion that is incapable of helping anyone cannot be said to be genuine.

Only faith in the Mystic Law encompasses both wisdom and compassion. The Daishonin clearly states: "Now, when Nichiren and his followers chant Nam-myoho-renge-kyo, they are expressing joy in the fact that they will inevitably become Buddhas eternally endowed with the three bodies" (OTT, 146). This in itself is "the greatest of all joys" (OTT, 212).

Mr. Toda maintained that "individual happiness and social prosperity must go hand in hand." The individual happiness referred to here is not self-centered; rather, it means cultivating true humanity—developing into a person who possesses wisdom and compassion and helping others do the same.

The Lotus Sutra (Nam-myoho-renge-kyo) has the power to actualize both individual happiness and social prosperity.

From The Wisdom of the Lotus Sutra, vol. 5,
published in Japanese in September 1999.

7.2 The Bodhisattva Way Enables Us to Benefit Both Ourselves and Others

The bodhisattva way teaches that our happiness is inextricably linked with serving others.

There are countless people in the world whose hearts have been wounded in some way. We need to extend a healing hand to such individuals. Through such efforts, we in fact heal ourselves.

When beset by some misfortune, people tend to think that no one could possibly be as unhappy or unlucky as they are. They feel sorry for themselves and become blind to everything but their own situation. They wallow in their suffering, feeling dissatisfied and hopeless, which only saps their life force further.

At such times, what gives someone the strength to go on living? It seems to me that it is human bonds—the desire to live for the sake of others. As long as we are wrapped up in ourselves, there is no happiness. When we courageously take action for others, the wellspring of our own life is replenished.

When we look after and care for others—that is, help others draw forth their life force—our own life force increases. When we help people expand their state of life, our state of life also expands. That is the wonderful thing about the bodhisattva way. The practice for benefiting others is one and the same with the practice for benefiting ourselves.

To speak only of benefiting others leads to arrogance. It conveys a sense of self-righteousness, as if we are somehow doing others a favor by "saving" them. Only when we recognize that our efforts on others' behalf are also for our own sake will we be filled with humble appreciation for being able to develop our lives.

Our lives and the lives of others are ultimately inseparable. It is vital, therefore, that we follow the bodhisattva way.

From The Wisdom of the Lotus Sutra, *vol. 4,*
published in Japanese in December 1998.

7.3 The Path of Mutual Respect and Growth

The aim of Buddhism is the pursuit of happiness, a life of mutual elevation in which we seek happiness together with others, respecting and supporting one another as fellow seekers.

Buddhism is the pursuit of happiness. The purpose of faith is to become happy; we carry out Buddhist practice for the sake of our own happiness.

Aniruddha, one of Shakyamuni's ten major disciples, known as the foremost in divine insight, once dozed off while Shakyamuni was preaching. Deeply reflecting on his behavior, he vowed never to sleep again. As a result of his unremitting practice, he eventually went blind. Later, though, he is said to have opened his mind's eye and thereby gained extraordinary powers of discernment.

One day, Aniruddha attempted to mend a tear in his robe. However, because he could not see, he was unable to thread the sewing needle. In his frustration, he muttered, "Is there no one who will thread this needle for me and so gain good fortune [from helping a practitioner of Buddhism]?"

Someone approached him and said, "Allow me to accumulate good fortune."

Aniruddha was stunned. For it was unmistakably the voice of Shakyamuni.

"I couldn't possibly trouble you," he protested, adding: "Surely one such as yourself, World-Honored One, does not need to gain any benefit."

"On the contrary, Aniruddha," Shakyamuni responded, "there is no greater seeker of happiness in the world than myself."[2]

Shakyamuni went on to teach Aniruddha, who was still not convinced by his words, that there are things that one must continue to pursue eternally. For instance, in seeking truth, there is never an end, a point at which we can say, "This will do." Similarly, in our efforts to lead others to enlightenment, there is no limit at which we can say, "I have done enough." The same goes for our practice to develop and perfect ourselves.

The pursuit of happiness also has no bounds. Shakyamuni told Aniruddha: "Of all the powers in the world, and in the realms of heaven or human beings, the power of good fortune is foremost. The Buddha way, too, is attained through the power of good fortune."[3]

Shakyamuni's words "There is no greater seeker of happiness in the world than myself" have important meaning.

Buddhism is not about turning one's back on life or escaping reality, or acting as if one has already attained enlightenment and risen above considerations of happiness and unhappiness. In particular, thinking oneself alone to be special has nothing to do with Buddhism.

Rather, genuine practitioners of Buddhism are those who, as humble seekers of happiness, earnestly pursue their Buddhist practice together with and in the same way as everyone else. They take action with courage and joy, more determined than anyone to never pass up an opportunity to accumulate good fortune. Such people never arrogantly think, "This is good enough," but continue to exert themselves out of a desire to gain still more fortune and benefit and to develop a state of eternal happiness. The spirit of Buddhism pulses in this resolve to keep improving and challenging oneself without end.

Shakyamuni's simple offer to thread Aniruddha's needle conveys his infinitely profound spirit and attitude toward life. His conduct is a natural expression of his egalitarian philosophy to regard his fellow practitioners as equals.

In *The Record of the Orally Transmitted Teachings*, the Daishonin states, "It is like the situation when one faces a mirror and makes a bow of obeisance: the image in the mirror likewise makes a bow of obeisance to oneself" (OTT, 165).

Believing in others' Buddha nature, we respect and treasure them from the bottom of our hearts. When we treat others in this manner, the Buddha nature within them responds, on a fundamental level, with respect toward us in return.

Broadly speaking, when we interact with others with true sincerity, more often than not they will come to respect and value us as well. And this is all the more so when our actions are based on prayer—chanting Nam-myoho-renge-kyo.

Conversely, denigrating others only leads to being denigrated oneself. And those whose lives are tainted by feelings of hate toward others will come to be reviled by others in turn.

The WISDOM *for* CREATING HAPPINESS *and* PEACE, Part 1

Let us open the path to mutual respect and harmonious coexistence so as to bring an end to this vicious circle that has long been part of human destiny.

From a speech at a European representatives conference, Frankfurt am Main, Germany, June 11, 1992.

7.4 Treasuring the People Right in Front of Us

President Ikeda introduces a story by the great Russian writer Leo Tolstoy to address three crucial approaches to living wisely.

Tolstoy wrote many very accessible stories and folk tales. He composed them for ordinary people who lived off the land, and for the young boys and girls who would inherit the future.

Today, I would like to share with you one of those stories, titled "Three Questions."

The story concerns an emperor who, in directing the affairs of state, finds himself wondering about three questions.

The first question is, When is the best time to start a task, to know the right time for every action, so that I have no regrets?

The second question is, What kind of person do I need most and to whom I should pay attention to?

The third question is, What affairs or tasks are the most important?

The emperor very much wants to know the answers to these questions, because he is sure that if he has the answers, he will be able to succeed in everything he does. He makes it known throughout the land that he will richly reward anyone who can tell him the right answers to these questions. Many learned people come to see him, and they offer many answers. But the emperor is not convinced by any of them.

The learned are not necessarily wise.

I will leave out the details of the story, but in the end the emperor gains the true answers to his questions from a sage who lives among the people.

This wise man replies that the most important time is now, this very moment; the most important person is the one in front of you right now; and the most important task is doing good to others, caring about others' happiness.

This moment, this instant is important, not some unknown time in the future. Today, this very day, is what matters. We must put our entire beings into the present—for future victory is contained in this moment.

Likewise, we do not need to look for special people in some far-off place. People are not made important simply by virtue of their power, learning, fame, or riches. The most important people are those in our immediate environment right now. They are the people we must value. Wise individuals consider the unique characteristics of those around them and make it possible for them to bring out their full potential. This is also the way to win the trust and respect of everyone.

Whenever I travel abroad, I always endeavor to sincerely greet and connect with the very first people I meet after getting off the plane—and then do the same with all those I meet thereafter. This is how my efforts to foster friendship start.

It is not important whether you are unknown or unremarkable in the world's eyes. What matters is that you know you have done your best, in a way that is true to yourself, for the sake of others, for your friends, and for people in society at large. Those who can declare that with confidence are champions of the human spirit, champions of life.

From a speech at an Asian commemorative general meeting,
Hong Kong, May 16, 1993.

7.5 We Are Enriched by Helping Others

Buddhism is the way to happiness for both self and others, and to victory for all. Serving others as we pursue that aim enriches us as human beings and becomes a precious personal treasure.

While sowing the seeds of happiness in the life of one person after another may seem like a long, roundabout process, it is actually the most fundamental groundwork for changing our planet as a whole.

Although it takes a long time for a tree to grow from a tiny seed, when it does grow big and tall, it will bear abundant flowers and fruit, and people will find rest in its cool shade. Each of us must strive to become such a tall tree.

Nichiren Buddhism is the path for attaining happiness for ourselves and others. It advocates neither sacrificing others nor sacrificing ourselves. It may be noble to sacrifice oneself for others, but it is not something we can expect of everyone. If we did, it would lead to a very unnatural situation.

Our real aim is the happiness of both ourselves and others. We need a path that empowers everyone to be a victor in life. That means, while we strive for others' happiness, we do so with a deep sense of appreciation for them—"All of my struggles to help him have made me into a much better person. How wonderful!" "The efforts I made to support her have made me so much stronger. How grateful I am!" The fact is, the harder we strive for kosen-rufu, the greater the good fortune and wisdom we will acquire. Soka Gakkai activities benefit others and ourselves at the same time.

For example, you meet and talk with someone, you chant for someone's happiness, or you write a postcard or letter to someone. Perhaps someone you arranged to meet didn't show up, but you continue to stay in touch and meet with them again and again. These may seem like small things, and you may sometimes feel you're not getting anywhere. But when you look back later, you'll see that none of your efforts were wasted. You'll see that going to meet others and encouraging them has made you a stronger, bigger person. You'll discover that chanting for a friend's happiness has enriched your own life enormously. The more time passes—ten years, twenty years on—the more you'll see that your every action has become a precious treasure for you.

And the day will come when those you have reached out to will show their appreciation. Someday they will happily tell others that you helped them stand up in faith or become the people they are today.

Your aim is to play that role in the lives of as many people as you can. There is no greater treasure in life than this.

From Discussions on Youth II,
published in Japanese in September 2000.

7.6 The Bodhisattva Practice of Respecting All People

In his dialogue with Brazilian Academy of Letters president and renowned journalist Austregésilo de Athayde, President Ikeda discusses the actions of the bodhisattva as taught in the Lotus Sutra and the significance of the bodhisattva way in Buddhism.

Our happiness does not exist apart from the happiness of others. The Buddhist's foundation for action is the spirit of compassion. Compassion has two aspects—relieving suffering and providing ease. It seeks to eliminate people's anxieties and fears and impart joy, reassurance, and hope.

As a Buddhist—and, indeed, as a human being—taking action for people's happiness is only natural. But sometimes the simplest things can be the most difficult. The essence of the teachings of Buddhism is simple: treasure each person. A Buddha is one who strives and works tirelessly for the happiness of every individual.

In Buddhism, those whose actions are based on the spirit of benefiting others, or altruism, are called bodhisattvas. Numerous bodhisattvas appear in the Buddhist scriptures—for instance, Manjushri, Universal Worthy, Maitreya, Perceiver of the World's Sounds, and Medicine King, to name but a few. These bodhisattvas use their unique qualities to serve living beings, working to protect and save them from various forms of suffering and misfortune. For example, Manjushri does so with wisdom, Universal Worthy with learning, and Maitreya with compassion. Perceiver of the World's Sounds relieves the sufferings of living beings through his power to perceive what is taking place in the world. Medicine King, as his name indicates, cures illnesses with beneficial medicines.

Of all the many bodhisattvas, Nichiren Daishonin focuses on Bodhisattva Never Disparaging in the Lotus Sutra as a model for practice. As the bodhisattva's name indicates, he never disparages anyone, showing the highest respect for all.

In the Lotus Sutra, Bodhisattva Never Disparaging greets people respectfully, saying: "I have profound reverence for you, I would never dare treat you with disparagement or arrogance. Why? Because you will all practice the bodhisattva way and will then be able to attain Buddhahood" (LSOC, 308). This is a distillation of the Lotus Sutra's spirit of respect for the dignity of all human beings. As described in the sutra, Bodhisattva Never Disparaging presses his hands together in reverence and bows to all whom he meets.

Nichiren Daishonin identifies the actions of Bodhisattva Never Disparaging as the essence of the practice of Buddhism, writing, "The heart of the Buddha's lifetime of teachings is the Lotus Sutra, and the heart of the practice of the Lotus Sutra is found in the '[Bodhisattva] Never Disparaging' chapter" (WND-1, 851–52).

The behavior of Bodhisattva Never Disparaging is based on his conviction that all living beings are noble because they possess the Buddha nature. By revealing their Buddha nature—the universal nobility or dignity inherent within them—any and every individual can open the way to an unparalleled life. Advancing on this path together with others is the practice of the bodhisattva way.

> *From* A Dialogue on Human Rights in the Twenty-First Century, *published in Japanese in February 1995.*

7.7 Accumulating Treasures of the Heart

The bodhisattva way constitutes what is most important in life and the supreme memory that we engrave in our lives.

By helping others become happy, we, too, become happy. This is also a tenet of psychology. How can those who have lost the will to live under the weight of inconsolable suffering or deep emotional wounds get back on their feet? All too often, the more they dwell on their problem, the more depressed and discouraged they become. But by going to support and help someone else who is also suffering, they can regain the will to live. Taking action out of concern for others enables them to heal themselves.

There are many people in the world who feel that working for others' welfare is not worth the effort. Some even view the merest mention of charity and compassion with derision. Such arrogant disregard for others causes untold suffering in society.

An American missionary supposedly once asked Mahatma Gandhi: "What religion do you practice and what form do you think religion will take in India in the future?" Two sick people happened to be resting in the room. Pointing in their direction, Gandhi replied simply: "My religion is serving and working for the people. I am not preoccupied with the future."[4] For Gandhi, politics and government were also a matter of service and, as Rabindranath Tagore said, of helping "the most destitute."[5]

It's all about action. In essence, altruistic bodhisattva practice is the very heart of religion, of Buddhism, and also of humane government and education.

We have a tremendous mission. The Daishonin writes, "More valuable than treasures in a storehouse are the treasures of the body, and the treasures of the heart are the most valuable of all" (WND-1, 851). To focus only on the "treasures of the storehouse"—finances or the economy—will not improve the economic situation. Things may improve for a while, but this will ultimately not contribute to the welfare of society. It is people, it is the heart, that matters most. The heart determines everything. When we possess the "treasures of the heart," when our lives overflow with good fortune and wisdom, we will naturally be endowed with abundant "treasures of the body" and "treasures of the storehouse."

HAPPINESS FOR BOTH OURSELVES AND OTHERS

What is left at the end of our lives? It is our memories, the memories that we have engraved in our hearts and minds.

I met the Russian novelist Mikhail Sholokhov when I visited Moscow in 1974. He told me: "When one lives to an old age, the most painful experiences in life become difficult to recall. The older one grows, the colors of the events in one's life fade and everything from the happiest times to the saddest starts to pass away." After pausing for a moment, he continued with a smile, "When you turn seventy, Mr. Ikeda, you will know that what I am saying is the truth." His words are profound, indeed.

Everything passes. Both the soaring joys and crushing sorrows fade away and seem but like a dream. However, the memory of having lived one's life to the fullest never disappears. The memories of having worked wholeheartedly for kosen-rufu, in particular, are eternal.

Surely all that remains and adorns our lives in the end is what we have done or contributed to the world in our lifetime in terms of how many people we have helped become happy, how many people appreciate us for having helped them change their lives for the better.

The Daishonin writes, "Single-mindedly chant Nam-myoho-renge-kyo and urge others to do the same; that will remain as the only memory of your present life in this human world" (WND-1, 64).

From The Wisdom of the Lotus Sutra, *vol. 5,*
published in Japanese in September 1999.

7.8 The Supreme Path of Benefiting Others

In this selection, President Ikeda emphasizes that the supreme way to work for the happiness of others is to share with them the Mystic Law.

The reality of life is that people usually cannot even help themselves, much less make their own families happy. Many political leaders and celebrities pretend to be caring and altruistic, but how many are actually dedicating their lives to the welfare of others?

Our members in the early days of our movement were virtually all poor. Most had no particular social status or higher education. But they possessed a lofty spirit. They were determined to help everyone they encountered become happy. They burned with a sense of great mission as trailblazers for humanity.

There is no nobler way of life than to be committed to helping others, to empowering them to become happy.

I will never forget the words of one of the members who pioneered the movement for kosen-rufu in Peru: "Other than my blood and my bones, what sustained me in this life was just my wish for the happiness of the people of Peru." Those were his last words.

HAPPINESS FOR BOTH OURSELVES AND OTHERS

Mr. Toda said:

> You can give food to the hungry and money to those in need, but you cannot distribute those things equally to all who are wanting. There is a limit to material aid. And the recipients may be glad, but they may also become dependent upon you and think they can continue to receive this support without any effort on their part. The greatest offering one can make is the offering of Buddhism. This allows people to gain fresh life force, enabling them to do their work and to become healthy again. This inner strength, like water welling up from the earth, is limitless.

This is, indeed, the supreme path of benefiting others.

From Discussions on Youth II,
published in Japanese in September 2000.

FACING ILLNESS

8.1 Struggling With Illness Can Forge Invincible Spiritual Strength

Birth, aging, sickness, and death are challenges everyone must face. We are all likely to confront the challenge of illness at some time in our lives. Buddhism regards illness not as something to be feared but as an opportunity for the human revolution that leads to attaining the life state of Buddhahood. Through Buddhism, we are able to transform illness into a force for victory in life. In this chapter, we explore President Ikeda's guidance on the subject of birth, aging, sickness, and death based on Buddhism.

Buddhism recognizes illness as one of the fundamental sufferings that human beings experience—one of the four sufferings of birth, aging, sickness, and death. In seeking a solution to illness, both Buddhism and medical science share a common goal. Both ask what is necessary for people to enjoy vibrant mental and physical well-being and to lead fulfilling lives.

Health is not simply the absence of illness. A truly healthy life is creative—one in which we keep challenging something, creating something, and moving forward to expand our horizons as long as we live.

My mentor, second Soka Gakkai president Josei Toda, said that people today make two basic mistakes: they confuse knowledge with wisdom and wrongly associate sickness with death.

Knowledge and wisdom are not the same. The relationship between the two can be discussed from many perspectives.

Speaking very generally, we can say that medical science combats illness through knowledge. Buddhism, on the other hand, develops human wisdom so that we may balance our lives and strengthen our life force. By doing so, we can use medical knowledge as an aid in the process of healing ourselves.

It is therefore foolish to ignore or reject medical science. To do so on religious grounds would amount to fanaticism. We need to make intelligent use of medical knowledge to conquer illness, and Buddhism can help us bring forth the wisdom to do that effectively.

Wisdom is essential for both health and long life. It is also a vital ingredient for happiness. If we wish to create an age in which people enjoy good health, we must first create an age that is founded on wisdom.

As for the relationship between sickness and death, illness does not necessarily lead to death. Nichiren Daishonin writes, "Illness gives rise to the resolve to attain the way" (WND-1, 937). Just as he says, illness can motivate us to take stock of ourselves, to reflect on the essence of life and our way of living. Through struggling with illness, we can gain a much fuller understanding of life and forge invincible spiritual strength.

I was a rather sickly child. Later, I also suffered from tuberculosis, and the doctor said I might not reach the age of thirty. But that experience allowed me to understand the feelings of those afflicted with poor health. It also made me treasure every single moment, never waste a minute, and live with all my might, doing everything I could while alive.

There are many people with healthy bodies whose lives are ailing. And there are also those who suffer from physical illness but whose lives are vibrant. As long as we are alive, we are bound to experience illness of some kind. That's why having the wisdom to know how to deal successfully with illness is so important.

From Kenko no chie *(The art of health),*
published in Japanese in February 1997.

8.2 Transforming the Sufferings of Birth, Aging, Sickness, and Death

President Ikeda encourages members to resolve never to be defeated by illness and to strive for a life of eternity, happiness, true self, and purity.

Illness is one of the four universal sufferings that no one can escape. In that sense, our entire lives are a battle against illness, so there's no need to fear it. By the same token, we shouldn't make light of illness. It's important to quickly take practical measures to get well.

Nichiren Daishonin writes: "Could not this illness . . . be the Buddha's design, because the Vimalakirti and Nirvana sutras both teach that sick people will surely attain Buddhahood? Illness gives rise to the resolve to attain the way" (WND-1, 937).

We can use the suffering of illness as fuel to strengthen our faith and also to develop a deeper and more expansive state of life. In the light of the Mystic Law and viewed from the perspective of eternity, the struggle against illness is a test to enable us to attain happiness and victory.

True health is found in a positive attitude toward life that refuses to be defeated by anything.

The sufferings of birth, aging, sickness, and death can be transformed into a winning life imbued with the four noble virtues of eternity, happiness, true self, and purity. This is the life of Soka, or value creation.

FACING ILLNESS

Falling ill is not a form of failure or defeat. It doesn't happen because our faith is weak. When the suffering of illness occurs amid our efforts for kosen-rufu, it is the working of devilish influences trying to obstruct our attainment of Buddhahood. As such, we mustn't let illness intimidate us. The Daishonin teaches us how to bring forth courage to face illness and attain Buddhahood in this lifetime.

When you experience illness, the important thing is to rouse even stronger faith. Keep chanting Nam-myoho-renge-kyo with the determination to make this illness an opportunity to demonstrate the tremendous power of faith and achieve truly amazing growth as a human being.

The Daishonin writes: "Nam-myoho-renge-kyo is like the roar of a lion. What sickness can therefore be an obstacle?" (WND-1, 412).

The Mystic Law is the ultimate source of power for overcoming the sufferings of illness. It is the best of all medicines for our life. Mr. Toda often used to say, "The human body is one big pharmaceutical factory."

If you are suffering from illness, it is important to keep chanting earnestly and persistently for the treatment you are now receiving to yield its greatest possible effectiveness and for the great life force of the Buddha to manifest itself in your body and vanquish the devil of illness. If you base your struggle with illness on faith in the Mystic Law, you can definitely transform all poison into medicine.

The Daishonin teaches, "*Myo* [of *myoho*, the Mystic Law] means to revive" (WND-1, 149).

In a letter to a follower with a sick family member, he says: "[This illness] cannot be the work of demons. Probably the ten demon daughters [protective deities in Buddhism] are testing the strength of your faith" (WND-1, 899). In other words, the benevolent forces of the universe cannot fail to protect the practitioners of the Mystic Law. He is telling the family, "You can overcome this!"

In another letter, the Daishonin writes: "The sun breaks through the pitch-black dark" and "The Lotus Sutra is compared to the sun" (WND-1, 315). As Soka Gakkai members who chant Nam-myoho-renge-kyo and base our lives on the Mystic Law, a bright sun of hope shines ever in our hearts. We can dispel all darkness and cast off even the heaviest chains of karma.

In struggling against illness for both ourselves and others, we can attain a state of shining health.

Chant daimoku, trusting in the power of the Gohonzon. Strive fearlessly and patiently. Refuse to accept defeat. Never retreat a single step. In the end, you are certain to triumph!

[Concerning emotional or psychological disorders, such as depression:]

Life is long, and there is no need to rush things. I think it's prudent in the case of psychological disorders to seek professional advice and take time to get proper care and treatment. Everyone's situation is different. There is no universal prescription or panacea. But there is one point I wish to emphasize: I can affirm that none of you who uphold the Mystic Law is destined to be unhappy.

We should warmly support and watch over those struggling with mental health issues, keeping their long-term welfare always in mind, and also sincerely encourage their family members. Those caring for others with emotional or psychological disorders face a great challenge, too, and they should try to find creative ways to take a break and refresh themselves.

Showing care and support for those suffering from emotional illnesses will lead to the cultivation of a truly deep spirit of compassion and also to the creation of a richly humanistic society.

Those who have experienced great suffering can develop into outstanding people. Those who have undergone painful trials can help many others. Such individuals have an important mission. This is the teaching of Nichiren Buddhism and the bodhisattva way of life.

Mr. Toda remarked: "Outwardly, we might look like a 'Bodhisattva Poverty' or 'Bodhisattva Sickness,' but that is merely a role we're playing in the drama of life. We are in fact bona fide Bodhisattvas of the Earth!" He also said, "People who have battled serious illness really understand the profundity of life."

Everything in life has a meaning.

Nichiren Daishonin writes, "Even the jewels and treasures that fill the major world system are no substitute for life" (WND-1, 1019). Though one may be ill, this has no bearing on the inherent nobility, dignity, and beauty of one's life. Everyone, without exception, is an infinitely precious and noble treasure.

> From "To My Young Friends—Leaders of a New Age,"
> published in Japanese, July 25–27, 2012.

8.3 Chanting Nam-myoho-renge-kyo Is the Wellspring of Life Force

Daimoku is the wellspring that enables us to face illness and transform it into an opportunity for human revolution.

My wife and I chant earnestly every day for all our members to lead lives of health and victory as they advance on the path of kosen-rufu.

Some of our members may be struggling with illness. But being ill doesn't mean one has to be unhappy or that one can't take action for kosen-rufu. Those who embrace the Mystic Law are guaranteed to become happy.

The Swiss philosopher and educator Carl Hilty said, "Sickness is . . . just a passageway to a higher step in life."[1]

Those who have experienced illness themselves are

FACING ILLNESS

more considerate of others. The experience of illness makes us more compassionate. Illness teaches us many things. It makes us look death in the face and think about the meaning of life. It makes us realize just how precious life is. It is all just a passageway leading us upward to a more elevated life. It is a learning experience. And for those who base themselves on the Mystic Law, everything becomes energy for creating happiness, fuel for self-improvement.

Mr. Toda said with great conviction: "[The benefit of the Gohonzon] is that it supercharges our life force. Such powerfully charged life force transforms a state of mind in which we grumble and complain about our problems, suffering, poverty, and other misfortunes into a state of mind filled with light and joy." He also said, "The power of daimoku is colossal. It can transform a life imbued with painful karma into one that is like strolling in a beautiful garden, or like a pleasant dream."

When you are suffering, chant daimoku. When you are stuck, chant daimoku. If you do, life force and courage will emerge, and you will be able to change your situation. Our Buddhist practice is the engine for victory in all things.

From a speech at a leaders training course, Nagano, Japan, August 15, 2005.

8.4 Turning Illness Into an Impetus for Growth

Referring to Nichiren Daishonin's writings, President Ikeda affirms that Buddhism enables us to make illness into a positive value as an opportunity to achieve absolute happiness.

It is said that those who overcome a major illness deeply savor the taste of life. In Nichiren Buddhism, illness is regarded as an impetus for achieving the supreme objective of Buddhahood. The misfortune of a severe illness can become the stepping-stone to a state of absolute happiness that endures for all eternity.

A famous passage from the Daishonin's writings states: "Could not this illness of your husband's be the Buddha's design, because the Vimalakirti and Nirvana sutras both teach that sick people will surely attain Buddhahood? Illness gives rise to the resolve to attain the way" (WND-1, 937). With these words, the Daishonin warmly encourages a female follower whose husband is suffering from illness. This guidance conveys his boundless and freely flowing wisdom and compassion.

It is certainly true that a painful illness can motivate us to begin chanting daimoku more earnestly and abundantly than usual. Such times of suffering are precisely when we need to make the flame of our faith burn higher than ever. What matters is whether we make our illness a starting point for embarking on a course to greater happiness or the beginning of a decline toward misery.

FACING ILLNESS

The power of chanting Nam-myoho-renge-kyo not only produces a strong life force to help us overcome illness but also transforms the karma in the depths of our being. It elevates our inner "self" to the world of Buddhahood and enables us to attain immeasurable good fortune that leads to an indestructible state of absolute happiness.

We can then brilliantly transform the negative condition of illness beyond the neutral condition of health into a more expansive, positive condition—moving our lives in the direction of happiness. What enables us to draw forth that power is indomitable faith—faith that can courageously turn even adversity into a springboard for tremendous growth.

Of course, faith cannot immediately cure every kind of illness. People have their own karma, and the strength of each person's faith also differs. In addition, a struggle with illness can have a variety of profound meanings that cannot be fathomed by ordinary wisdom.

As long as we have strong faith, however, there is not the slightest doubt that we can transform our condition in the direction of health, happiness, and Buddhahood. From the perspective of life existing throughout the three existences of past, present, and future, we can move our life in the best possible direction, in the direction of happiness.

It is important to continue chanting earnestly and to keep our passionate commitment to kosen-rufu burning brightly in our hearts as long as we live. Such strong, thoroughly forged determination in faith is the primary force for serenely overcoming the sufferings of birth and death.

From a speech at a Wakayama Prefecture
commemorative general meeting,
Wakayama, Japan, March 24, 1988.

8.5 Falling Ill Is Not a Sign of Defeat

Illness is not a sign of defeat or misfortune. For those dedicated to the Mystic Law, the drama of birth, aging, sickness, and death is also the joyous stage for a life of eternity, happiness, true self, and purity.

Mr. Toda said: "It is natural for us to fall ill. At the same time, we possess within us the power to cure our own illness." This was a message he often shared.

Nichiren Daishonin states that birth, aging, sickness, and death are "the aspect or characteristics of the three-fold world" (OTT, 127). Illness itself is just one aspect of human life. Falling ill is by no means a sign of defeat in life. Moreover, it would be utterly lacking in compassion to presume that someone's faith is weak simply because they have gotten sick. Offering heartfelt encouragement to those who are battling illness is an expression of genuine caring.

FACING ILLNESS

Whenever one of his followers fell ill, the Daishonin would encourage that person with all his heart and being.

The "lion's roar" of Nam-myoho-renge-kyo is the ultimate weapon for battling illness. We must absolutely never forget the Daishonin's words "Nam-myoho-renge-kyo is like the roar of a lion. What sickness can therefore be an obstacle?" (WND-1, 412).

To use the struggle against illness to develop an even greater sense of fulfillment and inner richness is to lead a life of value creation. That is why it is so important to have the "heart of a lion king" with which to fight through to the end against all obstacles. We must possess an indomitable and unyielding spirit. It is for this very reason that we need to exert ourselves in faith and practice every day, chanting Nam-myoho-renge-kyo for both ourselves and others, and forge a strong determination grounded in faith that will remain steadfast and unwavering in the face of any attack by the devil of illness.

When the lay nun Toki, the wife of Toki Jonin, became seriously ill, the Daishonin repeatedly sent her letters of encouragement, seeking to impart hope and strength.[2] "Do not burden your mind with grief" (WND-1, 656), he tells her. The important thing is to have a fighting spirit, to possess the spirit of a votary of the Lotus Sutra. He also says, "Take care of yourself" (WND-1, 656). It is vital that we take practical steps toward restoring our health when we are ill.

No one intends from the outset to be defeated by illness. But should a particular illness interfere with our daily activities or our work, or cause us to lose courage and self-confidence, we may gradually be overtaken by despair. In the case of the lay nun Toki, she may have begun to feel a sense of resignation because of her slow recovery. The Daishonin urges her to summon the resolve to live out her life to the fullest.

Of course, there are people who have strong faith but who die young. However, there is definitely some profound meaning behind this. The value of one's life is not determined by the number of years one has lived. The Daishonin asserts, "It is better to live a single day with honor than to live to 120 and die in disgrace" (WND-1, 851).

The Daishonin speaks of "the treasure of faith" (WND-1, 955), emphasizing to the lay nun Toki the importance of rousing the will to go on living, or, we might say, enthusiasm for life.[3]

For us, each day of life is a day that we can directly contribute to kosen-rufu; our efforts each day lead directly to the fulfillment of the great vow for kosen-rufu. Therefore, we absolutely must not be defeated by illness or any other obstacle.

The Daishonin says that illness is "the Buddha's design," because it can spur us to arouse the "resolve to attain the way" (WND-1, 937).[4]

The ultimate purpose for living long and healthy lives is so that we can take compassionate action to benefit others who are struggling amid the realities of society. It is only natural, of course, that we chant for good health and longevity for our own sakes as well. Needless to say, to ruin one's health on account of immoderate habits or plain neglect runs entirely counter to a way of life of value creation.

We have to exercise wisdom in our daily lives—for example, taking time to refresh ourselves and resting if we become fatigued. Good health is something we have to secure for ourselves by acting with prudence and good sense. Health is the badge of honor of the wise.

What is the purpose of striving for good health and longevity? It is so that we can use our lives to the fullest to work for the sake of the Law, for the happiness and welfare of our families, our fellow members, and our fellow human beings, and to accomplish our individual missions and realize the great vow for kosen-rufu.

It is vital therefore that we actively take on the challenges of the sufferings of birth, aging, sickness, and death amid our efforts for kosen-rufu. Doing so is actual proof that the four noble virtues of Buddhahood—eternity, happiness, true self, and purity—exist eternally within us.

The sufferings of birth, aging, sickness, and death are not causes for lamenting. Rather, they together form the brilliant stage of life upon which we enact a drama that resounds with the triumphant strains of eternity, happiness, true self, and purity. Through this drama of birth, aging, sickness, and death, we perform a joyous play of human victory.

From The World of Nichiren Daishonin's Writings, *vol. 3, published in Japanese in March 2005.*

8.6 The Buddhist View of Illness

In this excerpt from The New Human Revolution, *the novel's protagonist Shin'ichi Yamamoto (whose character represents President Ikeda), during a visit to Kansai, encourages men's division members suffering from poor health.*

Shin'ichi said: "The 'Life Span' (sixteenth) chapter of the Lotus Sutra teaches the principle of prolonging one's life through faith. In other words, through our Buddhist practice, we can extend how long we live. If we continue to strive with strong faith in the Mystic Law, there is no illness that we cannot surmount. Please chant abundantly and live a long, healthy life! . . .

"In discussing the origins of illness, the Daishonin cites a passage from T'ien-t'ai's *Great Concentration and Insight*, which states: 'There are six causes of illness: (1) disharmony of the four elements; (2) improper eating or drinking; (3) inappropriate practice of seated meditation; (4) attack by demons; (5) the work of devils; and (6) the effects of karma' (WND-1, 631)."

Let us look at these points in closer detail.

Listed as the first cause of illness is "disharmony of the four elements." The four elements are earth, water, fire, and wind. According to traditional Eastern thought, nature and all things in the universe, including the human body, are made up of these four elements. "Disharmony of the four elements" refers to unseasonable weather and other conditions of discord in the natural world, which have a powerful influence on the human body and can cause various illnesses.

The second and third causes of illness—"improper eating or drinking" and "inappropriate practice of seated meditation"[5]—refer to a lack of control in one's dietary habits and other aspects of day-to-day living. When our daily lives fall out of rhythm, our diet may suffer. Also, insufficient sleep and exercise may cause disorders in our internal organs, muscles, or nervous system.

The "demons" in number four—"attack by demons"—refer to external causes. These include microorganisms, such as bacteria and viruses, as well as the stress we experience in our daily lives.

Number five, "the work of devils," indicates the various inner impulses and desires that disrupt the healthy functioning of our minds and bodies. Afflictions that prevent us from practicing Buddhism also arise from the workings of such negative functions.

Number six, "the work of karma," refers to causes that derive from the inner depths of our lives. This indicates sickness that stems from distortions or deeply rooted tendencies in our lives. Buddhism views such distortions as karma.

The origins of illness are divided into these six different categories, but in actuality, many illnesses have overlapping causes. In the case of influenza, for example, the cause is a virus. This could be looked at as an "attack by demons." Infection can, however, be triggered by changeable weather—in other words, by "disharmony of the four elements." In addition, a poor physical condition brought about by an unhealthy lifestyle—"improper eating and drinking"—can be a contributing factor. Negative functions may also be at work in the depths of one's life to keep one from engaging in Buddhist practice, and there are also cases when karma may be an important consideration.

Shin'ichi went on to give a detailed explanation of the six causes of illness in light of the Daishonin's writings: "In short, one of the first steps in avoiding illness is taking care to dress appropriately for the weather and environment. Leading a well-balanced life, not overindulging in food or drink, and getting enough sleep and exercise are all vital too.

"In this way, we can avoid the first three causes of illness. Faith means employing the wisdom to do so. And with the help of medical science, we can also avoid the fourth cause of illness, which includes such things as germs and viruses. But no matter what the sickness, the speed with which we recover depends upon our life force. And faith is the wellspring of that life force.

"At the same time, if the root cause of an illness is the work of negative functions or the effect of karma, then even the best efforts of medical science alone cannot bring about a cure. It is only through strong faith in the Gohonzon that we can defeat such negative functions in our life and transform our karma."

FACING ILLNESS

[The following is in response to a diabetic man taking daily insulin injections. The man said that he had lost all hope in life because his doctor has told him he would never be cured.]

Shin'ichi said: "If you exert yourself wholeheartedly in faith, your life will be filled with hope, supreme happiness, and fulfillment, even if you have a chronic illness. The Daishonin writes: 'Nam-myoho-renge-kyo is like the roar of a lion. What sickness can therefore be an obstacle?' (WND-1, 412). Nam-myoho-renge-kyo is a lion's roar. A lion's roar will send even the fiercest animals running. In the same way, when faced with chanting Nam-myoho-renge-kyo, no ailment can be an obstacle to one's happiness or to kosen-rufu.

"People today have been described as being only 'half healthy,' meaning that we are all afflicted with some kind of illness and that our physical health will decline as we age. But is sickness necessarily the cause of unhappiness? Absolutely not. It is being defeated by illness and losing hope that makes us unhappy. We become unhappy when we forget our mission to strive for kosen-rufu.

"There are many people with perfectly healthy bodies who are unhappy because they are ailing spiritually. On the other hand, there are many Soka Gakkai members who, while struggling with illness or disability, are not only genuinely happy but also work for the happiness of others.

"At life's most fundamental level, health and sickness are one. There are times when we manifest a healthy condition and times when we manifest illness. The two conditions are interconnected. Thus, by making earnest efforts in faith and fighting against illness, we can establish a state of genuine health both mentally and physically.

"It may be hard to have to take insulin injections for the rest of your life. But if you think about it, eating and sleeping are also things we must do every day to live. Try to view your injections as just one more thing that's been added to your daily routine. It won't do any good to let it get you down.

"I hope you will live in such a way that others struggling with the same condition will marvel and say: 'Look how energetic he is, despite his diabetes!' 'Look at what a long life he is enjoying!' 'Look how happy he is!' If you are able to do that, you will be a brilliant example of the power of Buddhism. That is your mission in life. Don't allow yourself to be defeated. Keep going! Never give up!"

Shin'ichi then addressed all present, saying: "The Daishonin will not fail to protect those who dedicate their lives to kosen-rufu. When his disciple Nanjo Tokimitsu was ill, the Daishonin sent him a letter in which he wrote, 'You demons, by making this man suffer, are you trying to swallow a sword point first, or embrace a raging fire, or become the archenemy of the Buddhas of the ten directions in the three existences?' (WND-1, 1109). In sternly rebuking the devilish functions causing his disciple to suffer, the Daishonin protected him. We are all embraced by this great conviction and compassion of the Daishonin.

"I hope all of you will also be filled with certainty and indomitable resolve not to be defeated by those negative forces. Muster your courage. I also used to suffer from poor health, and a doctor said I probably wouldn't make it to age thirty. But I'm strong and healthy now and able to handle the most demanding of schedules. You can all become healthy too!"

From The New Human Revolution, *vol. 10,*
"Crowned Champions" chapter.

8.7 "Faith" Means to Continue to Believe Until the Very End

This story of a young child who overcame the suffering of illness and the fear of death to create an inspiring drama shows us that no matter how ill we may be, through strong faith we can triumph in life in the end.

The law of life and death is universal, permeating the entire universe. But it manifests itself in distinct, unique ways that are different from person to person. It is very complex, involving innumerable factors.

Buddhism teaches that our lives are governed to a large extent by our karma, which is formed by our actions in past lifetimes. We are subject to the effects of immutable karma (fixed karma), which determines how long we live and the basic course of our lives. We are also subject to the effects of mutable karma (unfixed karma), which we may or may not experience in this lifetime. If we compare these two types of karma to sickness, immutable karma is like a serious or even fatal disease, while mutable karma is like a relatively minor illness, such as a cold.

The word *karma* is Sanskrit for "action." Our every action—what we think, say, and do—is engraved in our lives. Good actions produce good, fortunate results, and bad actions produce bad, unfortunate results. They are bound to manifest themselves eventually.

The energy, both positive and negative, that is engraved in our lives through our actions does not disappear at death. It continues into our next existence, carried over in a way we might think of as resembling the law of the conservation of energy in physics.

But Nichiren Buddhism teaches that we can change all such karma. We can transform even fixed karma—or rather, we must do so. No matter what sufferings or hardships we may encounter, we must live out our lives fully, fighting our hardest until we triumph. Those who win in the end are true victors in life.

Victory is not decided halfway through. If we win in the end, we can look back on everything in our life up

FACING ILLNESS

to that moment and realize that it all had meaning. But if we are defeated in the end, everything will have been meaningless, no matter how smoothly things may have been going until then.

If members persevere with strong faith to the very end, they will be victorious, even if they should die from illness. There are many who, while suffering from illness, have chanted for kosen-rufu and the happiness of others and continued to reach out to encourage those around them right up to the very moment of death. Their lives and their bravery in the face of death have given courage and inspiration to countless others. Such people will quickly be reborn with healthy bodies.

I knew a young girl who was diagnosed with a brain tumor at age eleven and died at fourteen. But throughout her illness, she was always happy and bright. She even cheered up the adults in the hospital with her sunny, positive presence. No doubt her illness caused her terrible pain, but she continued to chant daimoku and to encourage others.

When she was near death, she said to one of her last visitors: "I don't care about my illness anymore. I've stopped chanting for myself. There are so many others worse off than me. I'm chanting with all my heart that they will take faith as soon as possible and find out for themselves just how wonderful the Gohonzon is."

To her parents, she said brightly: "What if this had happened to you, Dad? We'd be in terrible trouble! And it would be just as bad if it had happened to you, Mom. And if it had happened to my little brother, I'm sure he wouldn't have been able to handle it. I'm glad that it happened to me instead of any of you. . . . I'm sure this is the result of a promise I made before I was born. If my life can somehow touch and inspire those who know me, I will be happy."

Hearing of this girl's struggle with illness, I sent her a bouquet of roses. I also sent her a Japanese fan on which I had written the words "Light of Happiness" and a photograph I had taken of a field of irises in bloom. I heard that she was thrilled when she received them.

To those around her, she left the following words: "Faith means to continue to believe until the very end." And she demonstrated those words with her own life.

At her funeral, a long line of people came to pay their respects. In her brief fourteen years, she had told over a thousand people of the greatness of the Mystic Law.

She won. That's what I believe. Everything that happened to her had meaning. Or rather, through her struggle, she gave meaning to her suffering.

She said that her illness was the result of a promise she had made in her past lifetime. Buddhism teaches the concept of voluntarily assuming the appropriate karma. This is when practitioners of the Mystic Law voluntarily choose to be born into painful situations so they might demonstrate the power of Buddhism to others through their struggles and subsequent triumph. This is the bodhisattva way of life.

If those who embrace the Mystic Law were blessed with every form of happiness from the start, no one would ever come to know how powerful and effective Nichiren Buddhism is. That's why we voluntarily choose to be born with problems and suffering so that we can show others what human revolution looks like. It is as if we are performing a part in a play, a great drama.

From Discussions on Youth II,
published in Japanese in September 2000.

8.8 "Laugh Off the Devil of Illness"

The example of a women's division member who triumphed brilliantly over illness teaches the importance of never losing hope and employing strong faith to change winter into spring.

One day after a women's meeting, I learned that a woman I knew well was going to be hospitalized. I had known her from her student days, and I also knew her parents.

She had developed a lump under her chin and gone to see the doctor about it. He examined her and, though a precise diagnosis would have to wait until further tests, he thought it was serious. She had always been in the best of health and very energetic and active, so this news surprised me. I could imagine how unsettling it must have been for her.

I immediately composed a poem as a message of encouragement and had someone convey it to her verbally:

> Confidently live out your life
> and triumph over all,
> laughing off
> the devil of illness
> to become a queen of longevity.

The next day, I inscribed the poem on a decorative card and sent it to her.

I sent another message to her the day before she was hospitalized: "Don't worry. Be confident. My wife and I are chanting for you. Put your mind at ease, and whatever you find out, don't let yourself be intimidated by illness. You mustn't let yourself be defeated. Again, there's nothing to worry about. Take care."

I continued to send her messages the following day (the day she was hospitalized) and the day after that. She was undergoing several days of tests, so I wanted to give her as much encouragement as I could. I told her: "Stay cheerful. Remember, from the standpoint of the eternity of life, we are 'Buddhas in life' and 'Buddhas in death' (see WND-1, 456). It's a pity to make life a painful affair. Remain positive and upbeat, no matter what."

I had a women's division member go in my stead to visit her at the hospital. She was apparently in high spirits, happy to have received my messages, and chanting with a firm determination to beat the devil of illness.

Two weeks later, the day before she was to receive the results of her tests, I sent her another message, this time asking someone to convey it by phone: "How are you doing? I am chanting in earnest for you, so everything will be fine. You will get better. This encounter with illness will deepen your prayers and become a source of strength as a personal experience in faith."

The test results showed that she had cancer—a malignant lymphoma. She was also found to have a tumor about the size of a fist deep in her abdomen. Surgery was not possible, so she would have to undergo chemotherapy. This would involve one round of chemotherapy a month for ten months. For the first two or three months she would have to remain in the hospital, but after that, she could receive treatment as an outpatient.

She said that her doctors told her she would suffer severe side effects from the chemotherapy, including hair loss, lack of appetite, and nausea.

Because she hadn't yet experienced any symptoms of pain or discomfort, this discussion of her treatment drove home to her for the first time that she was dealing with something life threatening.

The news of her illness was a great shock for her elderly parents and the rest of her family. They must have been distressed and worried beyond imagination.

She sent me a letter expressing her determination in

which she wrote: "Because of your constant encouragement, I have been able to accept my diagnosis calmly. I will follow your advice to 'laugh off the devil of illness,' determined to fight on cheerfully and win."

A person of firm resolve is strong. Resolute prayer strengthens our life force.

Everyone in her hospital ward was suffering from similar illnesses. Some of them openly expressed their misery and said they would rather die than continue the harsh treatments. Observing their plight, she was well aware of the tough battle that lay ahead of her. It was only natural that one might feel anxious and afraid in such a situation. But she decided to face this challenge with unflinching courage.

Strangely, she experienced no pain or discomfort after her first chemotherapy treatment. I was very happy to hear her first joyous report.

Her hair soon began to fall out, but her second treatment also went well, and she was allowed to leave the hospital. Her appetite remained good, and she even gained weight. Not only that, the tumor in her stomach shrunk to one-third its original size.

I received that report while I was on a visit to Russia. I immediately sent her a message congratulating her and telling her not to overexert herself.

Praying for her to make a full recovery, my wife also wrote her a postcard saying: "You have achieved victory in the first stage. Please continue to be patient and take things slowly until you achieve complete victory. Remember, laugh off the devil of illness!"

After several more months of outpatient treatment, she completed her chemotherapy. The tumor in her stomach had almost completely disappeared.

She had to be careful over that nearly one-year period, because the chemotherapy had weakened her immune system. But aside from losing her hair, she experienced no painful side effects. She even returned to work. She was so cheerful throughout that no one would ever have imagined she was ill unless she told them. Her doctor, too, was genuinely surprised.

I received a letter from her that was filled with joy and appreciation. I had been kept well informed of her progress, and I was very happy to hear of the successful outcome of her battle with illness. She wrote that she had constantly reminded herself of my advice to "laugh off the devil of illness," which she had found a great source of encouragement and strength.

She is now even more active than she was before her illness, and a growing number of people come to her for advice about dealing with health problems because they know that she successfully overcame a serious illness.

She sincerely shares her experience with and encourages each of them wholeheartedly. Nothing provides greater reassurance and hope than words of encouragement brimming with conviction based on personal experience.

Overcoming illness is profoundly meaningful, not only

in terms of one's own well-being, but also because it enables one to inspire and help many others who are going through similar struggles.

All sorts of things happen in life. It is a continuous series of changes. What matters in the end is never to be defeated by anything—to keep fighting and not lose hope.

Life is a struggle against our inner tendencies to give up when things are tough, to compromise and accept less. Please win in the struggle with yourself, vowing not to give up, not to be defeated.

We mustn't avoid difficulties. We must win out over our problems and sufferings. It is up to us to create our own treasures through our own efforts. "I am happy. I have won!"—those who can create value in life so that they can say this with confidence are people who shine with true brilliance and character.

From Haha no uta *(Ode to mothers),*
published in Japanese in August 1997.

8.9 Four Mottoes for Good Health

President Ikeda proposes four guidelines for good health based on the perspective of Buddhism and faith.

FACING ILLNESS

I'd like to speak to you a little about health. Once, when I was talking with members of the Kansai doctors division and young women's division nurses group, I proposed four mottoes for leading a healthy life. They were just some simple personal thoughts I shared with the members, based on the perspective of Buddhism and faith. The doctors and nurses I was speaking with, however, agreed that my advice was also medically sound.

The four mottoes are:

1. Do an invigorating gongyo.
2. Lead a balanced and productive lifestyle.
3. Contribute to the welfare of others.
4. Eat wisely.

Medically speaking, such factors as diet, exercise, sleep, and stress relief are often mentioned as fundamental to good health, and all of those basic elements are included in the four mottoes I suggested.

(1) Do an invigorating gongyo.

When our gongyo and chanting become sluggish or half-hearted, we feel physically sluggish too. Many of you can probably relate to this.

The good fortune and benefit we derive through chanting vigorously are immeasurable. Our bodies, hearts, and minds begin to exhibit their limitless latent potential.

Additionally, sitting up straight and breathing deeply is also considered to be very beneficial for one's health from a medical viewpoint. Enhanced respiratory function improves our cardiovascular system.

A member of the doctors division also commented that using our voices is an important way of relieving stress. Once people stop using their voices, they tend to age more quickly.

Sitting properly with our palms pressed together as we do gongyo and chant Nam-myoho-renge-kyo is, in every sense, the most solemn and meaningful activity, in accord with the underlying principles governing the universe. Our individual bodies and minds, as the microcosm, are aligned and merged with the fundamental rhythm of the universe, the macrocosm. Day after day, our beings are rejuvenated. This is the first foundation for health and long life.

(2) Lead a balanced and productive lifestyle.

Sufficient sleep is another important foundation for good health. Not getting enough sleep is like leaving a car's engine constantly running. Eventually, it will malfunction or break down.

Mr. Toda used to say that the sleep we experience before midnight is twice as deep as the sleep after midnight, so we should go to bed as early as we can. This appears to be supported by medical science.

Manage your time wisely, and try to do your gongyo early and get to bed early. That will prepare you for a fresh start the next morning. Developing the wisdom and self-control to put this into practice will benefit your health.

Getting stuck in an unhealthy cycle of staying up late, either out of routine or force of habit, and then oversleeping and waking up without ever feeling refreshed is definitely not putting faith into correct practice in daily life.

Recently, there has been some focus on the benefits of "mini naps"—brief naps of five or ten minutes' duration—in promoting health and productivity. The key is to make good use of rest periods during the day so that you can take care of your health.

(3) Contribute to the welfare of others.

Physical activity is, of course, a crucial factor in improving health. And more particularly, activity in the form of our efforts to contribute to the promotion of Buddhism, the happiness of others, and the good of society are an incredible source of inner revitalization and energy for living vibrantly.

In contrast, if we stop taking action for others, regarding such efforts as a bother, and shut ourselves up in a shell of self-interest and uncaring individualism, then we will find our bodies and minds begin to stagnate and often grow more susceptible to illness as a result.

Movement is a defining characteristic of animals, including human beings. We need to move. If we aren't active, we are no different than objects of stone or wood. When living beings with the power of motion cease to be active, they begin to decline.

The same is true of water in a river. When the water stops flowing, it becomes cloudy and stagnant. In the realm of the Mystic Law, too, those who have stopped practicing because they found contributing to the welfare of others a chore are people who have allowed the clear water of their faith to become cloudy, causing them to spiritually stagnate.

You, on the other hand, are making noble efforts day and night to contribute to the welfare of others—spreading the teachings of Nichiren Buddhism, encouraging your fellow members, and striving for the development of your communities.

Sometimes you may think, "Wouldn't it be nice to just stay home tonight and relax and watch TV?" But in joyfully taking action for the happiness of others and your fellow members, you are leading lives infinitely more fulfilling and worthwhile.

We are said to live in a stressful society today. Our environment is filled with potential causes of stress.

In a certain respect, stress can be described as an attack on our spirits from outside. We need to fight back against it. If we remain still, we will be overwhelmed by its pressure, which will destroy us both physically and mentally.

One effective response to stress is to meet it by stepping forward and taking action. In that sense, our actions based on faith in the Gohonzon are actions for reviving and reinvigorating ourselves in perfect accord with the Law of life.

I have spoken many times of the importance of walking.

It is said that a good way to get regular exercise is to walk ten thousand steps a day.

Some say that aging starts when our legs begin to give out. Every step we take for our Soka Gakkai activities is hugely beneficial in terms of maintaining strength and promoting health.

Nichiren Daishonin writes, "If one lights a fire for others, one will brighten one's own way" (WND-2, 1060).

Contributing to the welfare of others, imparting the light of hope to those around us, also brightens our own life with fresh hope and makes it shine with good fortune and benefit.

(4) Eat wisely.

Overeating can lead to obesity. The Great Teacher T'ien-t'ai of China listed improper eating or drinking as a cause of illness (see WND-1, 631). How do we correct unbalanced eating habits? How do we effectively control the desire to eat more than we need to? This is where we need to apply wisdom and good sense.

The members of the doctors division and nurses group voiced specific concern about eating too much late at night, because some members tend to eat meals after attending nighttime Soka Gakkai activities.

Medically speaking, it is desirable to stop eating three hours before going to bed. But if you're really hungry and find that impossible, then it's best to eat vegetables or some other low-calorie food.

The WISDOM *for* CREATING HAPPINESS *and* PEACE, Part 1

You are all very important both for kosen-rufu and for your families. You mustn't put yourselves at risk by becoming too overweight, diabetic, or being afflicted by some other serious illness.

Eating wisely will help you lead pleasant, enjoyable lives. Take responsibility for looking after your own health.

I hope that you will enjoy excellent physical and mental health and lead wonderful lives, adorning this noble existence with victory and happiness as you strive with vibrant faith and in joyful camaraderie.

From a speech at a joint meeting for representatives of Kumamoto and Oita Prefectures, Kumamoto, Japan, September 28, 1990.

CREATING A BRILLIANT FINAL CHAPTER IN LIFE

9.1 Enjoying a Rewarding and Fulfilling "Third Stage of Life"

None of us can avoid physical aging with the passage of time, but the members of the Soka family, practicing the Mystic Law, becoming more youthful and vibrant and accumulating more good fortune with each passing year, encourage one another and adorn their lives together with victory in human revolution. Nichiren Daishonin encouraged a disciple with the words "You will grow younger, and your good fortune will accumulate" (WND-1, 464). Life is often divided into three periods— the first stage of study, the second stage of independence and work, and the third stage of the fulfillment and completion of our lives. Here President Ikeda offers guidance on enriching that third period of life.

Buddhism in general is focused on solving the sufferings of birth, aging, sickness, and death. However, the essence of Nichiren Buddhism lies not in simply overcoming these four sufferings. In *The Record of the Orally Transmitted Teachings*, the Daishonin states: "The words 'four sides' [of the treasure tower] stand for birth, aging, sickness, and death. We use the aspects of birth, aging, sickness, and death to adorn the towers that are our bodies" (OTT, 90). Nichiren Buddhism thus teaches a deeper understanding of those four sufferings, observing that they can be transformed into treasures that add dignity and splendor to "the towers that are our bodies," to the treasure tower of our lives themselves.

There is a saying: "The foolish regard old age as winter; the wise regard it as a golden time." Everything depends upon our attitude, how we approach life. Do we look at old age as a period of decline ending in death or as a period in which we have the opportunity to attain our goals and bring our life to a rewarding and satisfying completion? Is old age a descending path leading to oblivion or an ascending path taking us to new heights? The same period of old age, especially in terms of the richness and fulfillment one can experience during those years, will be dramatically different depending upon one's outlook.

Let's try to make the third stage of life a third stage of *youth*. Youth is not something that fades with age. Our attitude toward life is what makes us young. As long as we maintain a positive attitude and a spirit of challenge, we will continue to gain depth and richness, and our lives will shine with the brilliance of gold or burnished silver.

I think we can say that one of the most important challenges of the third stage of life is how to live in a way that is true to ourselves until the very last and show this to those around us.

People's memories and recollections about a person who has passed away, the example of that individual's life, can be a great source of encouragement and strength to them.

What can we contribute, what can we leave as a legacy for others in our third stage of life? After all is stripped away—wealth, renown, social status—the only thing that remains after one's death is the example of how one has lived one's life as a human being.

Nichiren Daishonin writes, "If one lights a fire [lantern] for others, one will brighten one's own way" (WND-2, 1060). In an aging society, this spirit of contributing to the welfare of others is very important. It ultimately means brightening our own way as well.

Nichiren Buddhism teaches that since we owe a debt of gratitude to all living beings, we should pray for all of them to attain Buddhahood (see WND-2, 637).

Valuing people, treasuring human relationships—these are vital requirements for creating a society in which people can truly enjoy long and fulfilling lives.

What matters is how much we can improve the quality of our lives during our time here on Earth—however long it may be. There is a difference between simply living a long life and living a rich and rewarding life. For example, a life can be fulfilled and productive even if it is short by time's measure.

What matters is that we live each day without regret, moving forward in our work for kosen-rufu, that we continue to cherish in our hearts a shining purpose and reason for living, whatever our age. Living this way each day is the key to a life of profound satisfaction and fulfillment.

The memory of striving arduously in our Buddhist practice for both the happiness of ourselves and others and earnestly chanting Nam-myoho-renge-kyo is eternal, enduring throughout the three existences of past, present, and future. It remains indelible in our lives, even if we should succumb to Alzheimer's disease. It is clearly recorded in the "diary of the heart."

Soka Gakkai activities are the greatest source of pride in life. When we chant and take action for the happiness of others, we, too, become happy. No way of life is more worthwhile.

Nichiren Daishonin writes, "Single-mindedly chant Nam-myoho-renge-kyo and urge others to do the same; that will remain as the only memory of your present life in this human world" (WND-1, 64).

We have nothing to worry about. The good fortune and

benefit we accumulate through our Buddhist practice will never age. Even should we suffer from Alzheimer's, they will remain latent in the depths of our beings.

Fundamentally, society must learn to value and respect the elderly, even those who suffer from Alzheimer's or other forms of cognitive decline, as venerable seniors, as predecessors who have made important contributions to society. With the rapid graying of society, all of us will be called upon to care for the elderly in one form or another.

A graying society will have to revise its values, placing cooperation above competition, quality over efficiency, and spiritual richness over material richness. It will be a time when we ask not what others can do for us but what we can do for others—a time for seeking ways to make a contribution, while striving to stay fit and healthy. That is the life of creating value.

The Greek philosopher Plato is said to have advised, "We should recall in the vigor of the young people around us our former youthful vigor and allow their energy to revive us."

At Soka Gakkai discussion meetings, which are attended by people of all ages, the elderly have a chance to absorb the energy of the young, while the young have the opportunity to learn from the experience and wisdom of the elderly.

Nothing is wasted in Buddhism. In that sense, it is a model for an aging society.

The key is to keep hope alive in our lives, to hold on to our ideals. It is to press ahead with our mission as long as we are alive.

The American poet Henry Wadsworth Longfellow wrote:

> For age is opportunity no less
> Than youth itself, though in another dress,
> And as the evening twilight fades away
> The sky is filled with stars, invisible by day.[1]

Let us join together in making the final years of our lives as brilliant as a night sky filled with sparkling stars.

A life lived to the fullest to the very end is beautiful. That's why it is crucial to maintain the spirit and lively activity of our youth throughout our lives. We mustn't use our age as an excuse to become inactive or withdraw from life.

Many of Shakyamuni's senior disciples grew self-satisfied and complacent as they aged. They felt they had attained a certain status and degree of enlightenment, and that this was enough. They had practiced a long time; Shakyamuni's enlightenment was marvelous, they thought, but they would never match it, so they contented themselves with the state they had attained.

Shakyamuni, however, said this was mistaken. When he

made his prophecy in the Lotus Sutra that Shariputra [who represents the persons of the two vehicles—voice-hearers and cause-awakened ones] would become a Buddha in future ages, he declared that his disciples must apply themselves vigorously to their Buddhist practice all their lives. He sternly urged them to keep striving, for this was the only way to attain Buddhahood. The senior disciples awakened to their own complacence, renewed their efforts, and were filled with joy. With this, persons of the two vehicles, who were said to be unable to attain Buddhahood, were able to become Buddhas as well (see LSOC, 86–89).

"Strengthen your faith day by day and month after month" (WND-1, 997)—these words of the Daishonin epitomize the spirit of the Lotus Sutra and the Soka Gakkai.

The American poet Samuel Ullman wrote in his well-known prose poem "Youth":

> Youth is not a time of life; it is a state of mind. . . .
>
> Youth means a temperamental predominance of courage over timidity of the appetite, for adventure over the love of ease. This often exists in a man of sixty more than a boy of twenty.[2]

Youth is not a matter of chronological age. As long as one has a burning passion for kosen-rufu, one can still be a youth at ninety.

Faced with the inescapable realities of aging and death, how can people make their final chapter in life and in society a brilliant and active one, lived true to themselves? This will be the most important question for our rapidly graying society in the twenty-first century.

Nichiren Buddhism and the Soka Gakkai alone offer a genuine solution to this challenge. With that conviction, let us continue the grand journey of hope that is kosen-rufu, creating a triumphant history of lives lived to the fullest.

From Daisan no jinsei o kataru *(A discussion on the third stage of life—Aging in contemporary society), published in Japanese in October 1998.*

9.2 Striving to the End With a Spirit of Ceaseless Challenge

Exploring the profound Buddhist teaching of perpetual youth and eternal life, President Ikeda speaks of the golden value of old age.

The struggle against aging is really a struggle against the fear of facing new challenges. The aging process occurs more rapidly in those who start thinking that they've done enough, who lose the spirit to foster younger people, and who remain attached to the past. Those who keep challenging themselves to the end are the most admirable and youthful of all. Such people are ever young and true victors of life. Come to think of it, the German writer Johann Wolfgang von Goethe was over eighty years old when he completed his masterpiece *Faust*.

The Soka Gakkai's founding president, Tsunesaburo Makiguchi, continued advancing and challenging himself until the final moments of his life. He was fifty-seven when he encountered Nichiren Buddhism and fifty-nine when he founded the Soka Kyoiku Gakkai (Value-Creating Education Society; forerunner of the Soka Gakkai). In his seventies, he was still energetically traveling by train all the way to Kyushu to offer personal guidance and share Buddhism with others. He was fond of using the expression "We youth."

About a month before Mr. Makiguchi passed away, he wrote a postcard from his prison cell saying, "I am avidly reading the philosophy of Kant." Such passionate seeking spirit and thirst for knowledge are no doubt the source of youthfulness.

The Buddhist teaching of perpetual youth and eternal life does not mean, of course, that we never age or die. It refers to our state of life, our life force. The Lotus Sutra states, "If a person who has an illness is able to hear this sutra, then his illness will be wiped out and he will know neither aging nor death" (LSOC, 330). And the Daishonin writes, "If we consider the power of the Lotus Sutra, we will find perpetual youth and eternal life before our eyes" (WND-1, 413).

In other words, we are promised that, if we believe in and uphold the Mystic Law, we will never be defeated by illness, we can forever advance through life with a youthful spirit regardless of our age, and we can establish an eternal and indestructible state of happiness. This is nothing extraordinary. The precious members of the Many Treasures Group, who are always vibrantly active, are perfect examples of this.

In a certain respect, it's only natural that we dislike growing old, for it makes us think of the inevitable reality of death. But each period of life has its own distinct and precious value.

What is the true significance of old age? It is not a time to look back with nostalgic longing on our youth. I believe it is the climax, the period of life that should be the most satisfying and fulfilling, the time when we shine with the brilliance and glory of a magnificent sunset. It's not a period of gloom and sadness. As the French writer Victor Hugo said, "There is an indefinable dawning in radiant old age."[3]

I feel that society today, unfortunately, has averted its gaze from the fundamental reality of death and, in the process, has lost sight of the golden value of old age.

The Daishonin encourages us to "first of all learn about death, and then about other things" (WND-2, 759). We must not avert our gaze from death but face it head-on and come to terms with it. If we can do that, we will come to appreciate old age in its own right and its true value will surely start to shine.

From the Buddhist perspective of the eternity of life, death is just a departure into the next phase of life.

The Daishonin describes the Mystic Law as "the great lantern that illuminates the long night of the sufferings of birth and death" (WND-1, 1038). Those who embrace the eternal Mystic Law are not afraid of death. They are not worried or troubled by it. They are able to freely savor the journey of life, experiencing a state of mind in which both life and death are a joy.

Nichiren Buddhism teaches the fundamental means for transforming a life bound by the four sufferings of birth, aging, sickness, and death into a joyous life characterized by the four virtues of eternity, happiness, true self, and purity.

From Sho-ro-byo-shi to jinsei o kataru
*(Discussions on life and death),
published in Japanese in November 2006.*

9.3 The Secret to a Vigorous Old Age

In this selection, President Ikeda discusses the best approach to enjoying a vigorous old age.

What is the secret to longevity? Of course, individual differences must be taken into account, and there are many diverse opinions on this subject. But we of the Soka Gakkai would naturally agree that an important key to long life is our practice of chanting Nam-myoho-renge-kyo.

Other than that, it is generally said that mental attitude has a vital influence on longevity. In that respect, I would like to share some attributes commonly listed as having a positive influence on longevity:

(1) Not worrying about things too much.

In a Buddhist scripture, Shakyamuni states:

> The past should not be followed after,
> the future not desired.
> What is past is got rid of and the future has not come.
> But whoever has vision now here, now there,
> of a present thing,
> Knowing that it is immovable, unshakable,
> let him cultivate it.
> Swelter at the task this very day.[4]

It is foolish to endlessly suffer and agonize over the past, or to needlessly fret and worry about the unknown future. Instead, we should concentrate on taking care of the things that we have to do today. What is important is that we live each day earnestly and conscientiously. This is the Buddha's message.

Those who live long lives are for the most part optimists. I hope that you will live each day joyfully and with genuine optimism.

(2) Having a goal or aim.

French President Charles de Gaulle once remarked that the end of hope is the beginning of death.[5]

Hope is life. To lose hope is to lose one's vital spirit.

To practice Nichiren Buddhism is to always live with hope. It means to take it upon oneself to create hope, actualize it, and continue to advance in ever higher spirits toward still greater hope. And faith is the driving force that enables us to do this.

(3) Having a sense of humor and the ability to laugh.

In Europe, there is an old saying: "A joyful heart is good medicine."

The German philosopher Immanuel Kant also noted that laughter has a positive effect on our health, functioning like a physician.[6]

True humor is not flippant; it is an expression of an open, relaxed, and generous heart.

Let us live with "a joyful heart." To do that, we must win in life each day, continuously pressing forward with powerful life force.

(4) Striving in some work or mission.

The Nobel Peace Prize laureate Albert Schweitzer is reported to have said: "I have no intention of dying so long as I can do things. And if I do things, there is no need to die. So, I will live a long, long time."[7] He in fact lived to the age of ninety.

We can presume that the source of vitality that allowed him to live so long was the conviction that he had a mission to fulfill, and that as long as he did, he could not and would not die.

In addition to the four points I have listed, there may be other factors contributing to longevity. However, these four points are all contained in the teachings of Nichiren Buddhism and can be cultivated through our Soka Gakkai activities.

The members of the Soka Gakkai are advancing with hope, joyful hearts, and a sense of mission toward the great objective of kosen-rufu. All of you who make your way together with the Soka Gakkai are naturally leading the most admirable and fulfilling of lives.

The Daishonin assures Nichigen-nyo, the wife of Shijo Kingo, "You will grow younger, and your good fortune will accumulate" (WND-1, 464).

I hope that you will all deeply experience the immense power of the Mystic Law.

> *From a speech at a Soka Gakkai headquarters leaders meeting, Tokyo, Japan, September 25, 1992.*

9.4 A Source of Hope and Inspiration for a Happy Aging Society

Soka Gakkai members are taking the lead in creating a happy aging society in which all can enjoy a wonderful old age.

Birth, aging, sickness, and death are fundamental issues of existence that no one can escape. As the population ages at an unprecedented rate in many countries, people are living longer than ever, and time spent in the so-called twilight years of life is increasing, posing numerous new challenges for individuals and society. We of the Soka family, especially our Many Treasures Group members, therefore, have an even greater mission to take up these issues and find new approaches and solutions.

No matter how much wealth or power one may possess, such things vanish like a fleeting dream in the face of the unrelenting reality of old age and death. What is crucial, then, is the philosophy one upholds and the life one has lived. In *The Record of the Orally Transmitted Teachings*, Nichiren Daishonin states, "Passing through the round of births and deaths, one makes one's way on the land of the Dharma nature, or enlightenment, that is inherent within oneself" (OTT, 52). The Mystic Law is the eternal and indestructible Law governing all things in the universe. As people who chant Nam-myoho-renge-kyo based on faith in the Mystic Law and are committed to realizing kosen-rufu, our lives, too, are eternal and indestructible, diamond-like and imperishable. I firmly believe that, as entities of Nam-myoho-renge-kyo, our lives will continue advancing steadfastly and calmly "on the land of the Dharma nature, or enlightenment"—imbued with the four noble virtues of eternity, happiness, true self, and purity—throughout the cycle of birth and death. As such, we have nothing to fear.

In one of his letters, Nichiren Daishonin warmly encourages and praises the lay nun Toki (the wife of Toki Jonin), who devotedly nursed her over-ninety-year-old mother-in-law until the latter passed away peacefully. This sincere disciple also faced her own health problems, which had perhaps been caused in part by exhaustion from caring for her mother-in-law. Nevertheless, she refused to be defeated by illness. Encouraging her, the Daishonin writes, "There is nothing to lament when we consider that we will surely become Buddhas" (WND-1, 657).

There is no reason to lament and ask yourself why, after so many years of sincere and diligent practice of Nichiren

Buddhism, you should have to fall ill, or a family member should require nursing care, or some other such situation. Your practice has enabled you to lessen your karmic retribution and makes it possible for you to change poison into medicine. When families practicing Nichiren Buddhism pull together to overcome such obstacles based on faith, they will be able to open the way to attaining Buddhahood in a profound and substantial manner.

Brimming with powerful conviction in faith and shining brightly as treasure towers, our Many Treasures Group members are making the final chapters of their lives truly joyful. Their examples are an unsurpassed source of hope and inspiration for the realization of a happy aging society where long life is genuinely celebrated.

My mentor, Josei Toda, declared, "Smile amid the raging winds and fight on until your final day!"

My wise friends of the Many Treasures Group, together let us always brim with hope and forge ever onward!

From an editorial titled "Wise Members of the Many Treasures Group, Forge Ever Onward!" published in Japanese in the Daibyakurenge, *April 2014.*

The WISDOM *for* CREATING HAPPINESS *and* PEACE, Part 1

9.5 Building an "Eternal Palace" in Our Lives

President Ikeda teaches the importance of our final years as an opportunity to employ all our accumulated experience to promote the happiness of others as well as continue to advance our own efforts to attain true mastery of life.

While residing at Mount Minobu, Nichiren Daishonin sent letters of encouragement to the elderly lay priest of Ko and his wife, the lay nun of Ko—disciples who lived on faraway Sado Island.

The Daishonin concluded one of his letters to the couple, writing: "No place is secure. Be convinced that Buddhahood is the final abode" (WND-1, 491). Where is our final abode, our sweet home, our safe haven? It is here. It is within us. The state of Buddhahood that we bring forth in our own lives is our eternal safe haven.

External circumstances do not determine our peace of mind. No matter how wonderful a home we may live in, if we are sad and lonely, we cannot be said to be at ease or leading a happy life. Even if our present circumstances are good, there is no guarantee that they will continue that way forever. Only the "palace" of peace and security that we build within our own life through our Buddhist practice is eternal.

The lay priest and lay nun of Ko practiced Buddhism alongside Abutsu-bo and his wife, the lay nun Sennichi, fellow residents of Sado Island. While warmly observing the two couples' friendship, the Daishonin offered them detailed encouragement so that they could work together in harmonious unity.

There is no doubt that the older one gets, the more one appreciates the good fortune of having supportive and encouraging friends. The members of the Soka Gakkai are extending a network of such treasured friendships throughout their communities and society at large.

Shakyamuni said, "For those who are always courteous and respectful of elders, four things increase: life, beauty, happiness, strength."[8] This certainly makes sense in terms of the law of cause and effect.

A society that respects the elderly is one that respects human life; and such a society will continue to flourish and thrive.

In one of his writings, the Daishonin quotes the Lotus Sutra passage "We may use our long lives to save living beings" (LSOC, 280).[9] "Long life" in this context refers to the immeasurably long life span of the Buddha as presented in the "Life Span of the Thus Come One" (sixteenth) chapter of the Lotus Sutra. The eternal state of Buddhahood wells up within the lives of those who practice the Lotus Sutra.

Also, based on the Buddhist principle of prolonging our lives through faith, we can strengthen our life force and extend our lives.

Moreover, bodhisattvas do not strive to live long solely for their own sake. They do so to serve others to the greatest possible extent, using their experience and their seamless blend of compassion and wisdom to do so. This is a subtle but crucial distinction.

In one of his writings, the Daishonin refers to the leader of the Bodhisattvas of the Earth as "a venerable old man called Bodhisattva Superior Practices"[10] (WND-1, 605). This passage has profound significance from the viewpoint of Buddhism, but what I want to note today is that the expression "old man" here is in no way negative or derogatory. It suggests a venerable majesty, bringing to mind a person possessing qualities indicating a true mastery of life—for instance, firm and unwavering faith; unceasing compassionate action; indomitable courage; superb communication skills; unflagging patience; ineffable nobility and dignity; and a vast, inexhaustible reservoir of wisdom for solving any problem.

We could say that this perfectly describes the Bodhisattvas of the Earth, who are spreading the principles of humanism in the midst of these troubled times.

From a speech at a nationwide representative leaders training course, Shizuoka, Japan, February 1, 1997.

9.6 There Is No Retirement From Faith

Sharing an observation by John Kenneth Galbraith about the importance of living each day to the fullest, no matter how old you are, President Ikeda states that the fundamental means for staying in good health is our daily chanting and Soka Gakkai activities.

Dr. John Kenneth Galbraith, world-renowned economist and professor emeritus of Harvard University, is ninety years old and continues to work at a steady pace. Even now he is writing a new book. We have been friends for twenty years. I have visited him at his home in Boston [in 1993], and we met here in Tokyo [in 1978 and 1990]. He was kind enough to present a commentary when I delivered my second lecture at Harvard ["Mahayana Buddhism and Twenty-First-Century Civilization"].

Something that Dr. Galbraith said during our meeting in Tokyo nine years ago made a very deep impression on me. "I will be eighty-two the week after next [on October 15]," he said, "but I regard each birthday as a fresh start. I believe the older we get, the more there is to learn." This is the philosophy of life of the ever-youthful Dr. Galbraith. He also offered the view that having firm goals or plans for the day when we get up in the morning is important in terms of staying alert and healthy.

We should wake up every morning ready to take on the world. In that regard, doing a vigorous morning gongyo and chanting Nam-myoho-renge-kyo, which enables us to start the day fresh and energetic, is a wonderful way to maintain health and well-being.

Our practice of gongyo and chanting Nam-myoho-renge-kyo represents a sublime ceremony in which we bring the microcosm of our lives into harmony with the fundamental rhythm of the macrocosm, the universe. We join our hands in prayer before the Gohonzon and do gongyo and chant Nam-myoho-renge-kyo. Our voice reaches all Buddhas, bodhisattvas, and heavenly deities—the protective functions of the universe. Though we cannot see them, they gather round us to keep us safe from harm. We are in their midst. How awesome is the power of chanting Nam-myoho-renge-kyo! All of the protective functions become our allies. That is why we have the ability and mission to guide humanity to happiness.

Dr. Galbraith also remarked to me that the biggest mistake the elderly make is to retire from their work, for without having work to do, one ceases to exert physical and mental effort, adding that a decline in mental effort can have a particularly negative impact.

This applies all the more to the realm of faith: there is no retirement from faith. Our Soka Gakkai activities for kosen-rufu represent the greatest mental and spiritual effort. They strengthen our life force and as such are a fundamental means for staying in good health.

From a speech at a Soka Gakkai headquarters leaders meeting, Tokyo, Japan, July 3, 1999.

9.7 Changing Our Attitude Toward Aging

President Ikeda talks about the Buddhist attitude toward aging with reference to Shakyamuni's teaching that to ignore the realities of aging, sickness, and death is a form of arrogance. An excerpt on this topic from his 2013 SGI Day Peace Proposal also appears at the end of this section.

In the Buddhist scriptures, Shakyamuni is said to have meditated on aging, sickness, and death and overcome three types of arrogance or pride.[11] In other words, aversion to the elderly is the arrogance of the young; aversion to the ill is the arrogance of the healthy, and aversion to the dead is the arrogance of the living.

These three types of arrogance indicated by Shakyamuni are by no means things of the past.

In discussing the problems of aging societies today, people often point to changes in society and inadequate institutions as their cause. Those are important factors, but I believe we must focus on the more essential issue of the arrogance in our hearts and work to transform human beings themselves.

People have a strong tendency to scorn or despise whatever is different from themselves. During a lecture I gave at Harvard University ["Mahayana Buddhism and Twenty-First-Century Civilization," in September 1993],

I referred to this as a prejudicial mindset, an unreasoning emphasis on individual differences. Shakyamuni described it as a single, invisible arrow piercing the hearts of the people.

By clinging to this prejudicial mindset, we are narrowing and diminishing ourselves through our own actions. We are limiting ourselves to our present state, refusing to change.

As long as people today try to ignore the realities of aging, sickness, and death, they are rejecting their own possibilities for the future.

We need to change our attitude toward aging. The enormous life experience the elderly possess is a precious treasure—for the elderly themselves, for others around them, and for society and the world as a whole.

In one of his writings, Nichiren Daishonin notes that the long Chou dynasty of ancient China, spanning eight centuries, flourished because its founder King Wen took care of elderly people and respected their wisdom (see WND-1, 916).

The words of the elderly, rich with maturity, have an often startling degree of wisdom and substance. I know many elderly people who glow with great beauty.

Those who have built an indestructible self through engaging in activities for kosen-rufu shine. Please live out your lives with self-confidence and courage.

From Daisan no jinsei o kataru *(A discussion on the third stage of life—Aging in contemporary society), published in Japanese in October 1998.*

Supplementary Reading

In ancient India, Buddhism arose in response to the universal question of how to confront the realities of human suffering and engage with people ensnared in that suffering.

The founder of Buddhism, Gautama Buddha or Shakyamuni, was of royal birth, which guaranteed him a life of earthly comforts. Tradition has it that his determination as a young man to abandon those comforts and seek truth through monastic practice was inspired by the "four encounters" with people afflicted by the pains of aging, sickness, and death.

But his purpose was never simply to reflect passively on life's evanescence and the inevitability of suffering. Later in life, he described his feelings at that time as follows: "In their foolishness, common mortals—even though they themselves will age and cannot avoid aging—when they see others aging and falling into decline, ponder it, are distressed by it, and feel shame and hate—all without ever thinking of it as their own problem,"[12] and he noted that the same holds true in our attitudes toward illness and death as well.

Shakyamuni's concern was always with the inner arrogance that allows us to objectify and isolate people confronting such sufferings as aging and illness. He was thus incapable of turning a blind eye to people suffering alone from illness or the aged cut off from the world.

There is an episode from his life that illustrates this.

One day, Shakyamuni encountered a monk who was stricken by illness. He asked him: "Why are you suffering, and why are you alone?" The monk replied that he was lazy by nature and unable to endure the hardships associated with providing medical care to others. Thus, there was no one to tend to him. At which Shakyamuni responded, "Good man, I will look after you." Shakyamuni took the stricken monk outdoors, changed his soiled bedding, washed him, and dressed him in new clothes. He then firmly encouraged him to always be diligent in his religious practice. The monk was immediately restored to a state of physical and mental well-being and joy.

In my view, it was not just Shakyamuni's unexpected and devoted care that affected the monk in this way. Rather, the fact that Shakyamuni encouraged him using the same strict yet warm language that he used with other disciples in good health revived the flame of dignity that was so close to being extinguished in this man's life.

This story as I have outlined it so far is based on an account in *The Great Tang Dynasty Record of the Western Regions*.[13] However, when we compare this to the version transmitted in other sutras, a further aspect of Shakyamuni's motivation comes to light.

After having tended to the sick monk, Shakyamuni is said to have gathered the other monks and asked them what they knew about his condition. As it turned out, they had been aware of his illness and the gravity of his condition, and yet none among them had made any effort to provide care.

The Buddha's disciples explained themselves in terms almost identical to those of the ailing monk: he had never attended to any of them in their time of illness.

This corresponds to the logic of personal responsibility as it is often used in contemporary settings to negate the need to care for others. For the ailing monk, this attitude fostered feelings of resignation, and for the other disciples it manifested itself as an arrogant justification of their disinterest. This logic atrophied his spirit and clouded theirs.

"Whoever would tend to me, should tend to the sick." With these words, Shakyamuni sought to dispel the delusions clouding the minds of his disciples and spur them to a correct understanding.

In other words, practicing the Buddha's way means to actively share the joys and sufferings of others—never turning one's back on those who are troubled and in distress, being moved by others' experiences as if they were one's own. Through such efforts, not only do those directly afflicted by suffering regain their sense of dignity, but so too do those who empathetically embrace that suffering.

The inherent dignity of life does not manifest in isolation. Rather, it is through our active engagement with others that their unique and irreplaceable nature becomes evident. At the same time, the determination to protect that dignity against all incursions adorns and brings forth the luster of our own lives.

By asserting an essential equality between himself and an ailing monk, the Buddha sought to awaken people to the fact that the value of human life is undiminished by illness or age:

he refused to acknowledge such distinctions and discriminations. In this sense, to regard the sufferings of others due to illness or age as evidence of defeat or failure in life is not only an error in judgment but undermines the dignity of all concerned.

The philosophical foundation of the SGI is the teachings of Nichiren, who emphasized the supremacy of the Lotus Sutra which, he stated, marks the epitome of Shakyamuni's enlightenment. In the Lotus Sutra, a massive jeweled tower arises from within the earth to symbolize the dignity and value of life. Nichiren compared the four sides of the treasure tower to the "four aspects" of birth, aging, sickness, and death (see OTT, 90), asserting that we can confront the stark realities of aging, illness, and even death in such a way that we remain undefeated by the suffering that accompanies them. We can make these experiences—normally only seen in a negative light—the impetus for a more richly dignified and valuable way of living.

The dignity of life is not something separate from the inevitable trials of human existence, and we must engage actively with others, sharing their suffering and exerting ourselves to the last measure of our strength, if we are to open a path toward authentic happiness for both ourselves and others.

From a peace proposal commemorating the thirty-eighth SGI Day, January 26, 2013.

9.8 Making an Art of Life

Referring to the last period of the life of Florence Nightingale, the pioneer of modern nursing, President Ikeda calls on us to live out our lives with passion and commitment.

Florence Nightingale promised her graduates: "I would try to be learning every day to the last hour of my life. . . . When I could no longer learn by nursing others, I would learn by being nursed, by seeing nurses practise upon *me*."[14] And she was true to those words all her life.

At around age forty, when she founded the Nightingale Training School for Nurses, she suffered another serious decline in health. She was constantly afflicted with headaches, nausea, and asthma attacks. Speaking for extended periods exhausted her. Many were worried that she might die too young, and she in fact did face several life-threatening health crises. Still, she never stopped her activities. She dismissed her illnesses, saying, "I am so busy that I have no time to die."[15]

Even though she couldn't move about freely, she could write. For that reason, she always kept a supply of pens and pencils by her bedside. She produced an enormous number of articles and statistical documents, as well as more than twelve thousand letters. Though her doctor advised her to stop writing, this only spurred her on: "They say I must not write letters. Whereupon I do it all the more."[16] She also declared, "Had I lost the Report [i.e., not been able to complete it], what would the health I should have 'saved' have profited me?"¹⁷ These words illustrate the firm conviction that ran through her entire life. Nightingale was fueled by the bright flame of a powerful inner purpose to which she gave herself unstintingly.

Eventually, Nightingale's sight began to fail, yet she declared: "No, no, a thousand times no. I am not growing apathetic."[18] In her early eighties, she went blind. Nevertheless, she did not despair. She kept going with the spirit that she still had ears to hear and a mouth to speak. She astonished her visitors by how well informed she was of current events.

The Buddhist scriptures teach us that even if we lose our hands, we have our feet; even if we lose our feet, we have our eyes; even if we lose our eyes, we have our voice; even if we lose our voice, we have our life.[19] With that resolve, we must spread Buddhism as long as we live. This is the spirit of a true Buddhist.

Even when Shakyamuni Buddha was on his deathbed, he preached the Law to an ascetic who had come to see him; he converted the man and welcomed him as his last disciple in his lifetime.[20]

My mentor, Josei Toda, used to say that whether one's life was happy or unhappy is not decided until one's final years. The last years of Nightingale's life were the most beautiful and rich of all. She described her final years as the best days of her life. No woman was as loved and esteemed as she was at that time. It was said that just hearing her name cheered people up, and many women proclaimed that they wanted to be like her. People came from all over Britain and the world for her guidance and advice. Royalty and political leaders vied to meet her, but she refused to see anyone who did not have an interest in nursing.

She valued young people, saying, "All the more I am eager to see successors."[21] She received hundreds of letters from young girls who wanted to be nurses, and she answered most of them. To the very end, she sought out and challenged things that needed doing, planting the seeds of the future: "To make an art of *Life!* . . . That is the finest art of all the Fine Arts."[22] And that is precisely how Nightingale lived hers.

On August 13, 1910, that "artful life" came quietly to a close. She was ninety years old, and it was in the year marking the fiftieth anniversary of her school's founding. In accord with her wishes, her funeral was simple.

Nightingale viewed death as the beginning of a fresh round of "*immense* activity."[23] Nichiren Daishonin states, "Passing through the round of births and deaths, one makes one's way on the land of the Dharma nature, or enlightenment, that is inherent within oneself" (OTT, 52). Those who have faith in the Mystic Law advance with joy in both life and death on the great earth of their intrinsically enlightened nature—in other words, the earth of Buddhahood.

Life is eternal. That is why it is essential to forge an absolutely indestructible life state of eternity, happiness, true self, and purity in this existence. To do that, we need correct faith, and equally essential are sincere and just actions for the sake of others. Those who devote their lives to kosen-rufu can walk the path of eternal happiness savoring the highest of all joys.

From an essay series On Florence Nightingale—
In Tribute to the Century of Women,
published in Japanese in March 2002.

JOY IN BOTH LIFE AND DEATH

10.1 Consolidating the State of Buddhahood in This Lifetime

In his 1993 lecture at Harvard University, "Mahayana Buddhism and Twenty-First-Century Civilization," President Ikeda, based on the teachings of Nichiren Buddhism, presents the profound Buddhist view of finding joy in both life and death. What is the purpose of life? What is a life of true value? What is death? What happens after death? Nichiren states, "Therefore I should first of all learn about death, and then about other things" (WND-2, 759). By confronting the issue of death head-on, we can build a truly happy life. This chapter features President Ikeda's guidance on how to face and overcome the sufferings of birth and death.

Why do we practice Nichiren Buddhism? So that we may live the most wonderful lives. So that we may serenely overcome the four sufferings of birth, aging, sickness, and death that are an inescapable part of the human condition.

The first of the four sufferings is birth. Having been born, we must live out our lives. It is important that we strive to live on tenaciously to the very end, no matter what happens.

Our Buddhist practice based on the Mystic Law gives us the powerful life force to live each day with strength and confidence, surmounting all kinds of problems and hardships. Why are we born? A life lived without meaning, without knowing the answer to that question, is shallow and empty. To just live, eat, and die without any real sense of purpose surely constitutes a base, animal-like existence.

On the other hand, to do, create, or contribute something that benefits others, society, and also ourselves, and to dedicate ourselves as long as we live to that challenge—that is a life of true satisfaction, a life of value, a life of the loftiest humanity. Our Buddhist practice based on the Mystic Law, moreover, is the driving force that enables us to create the greatest possible value for ourselves and for others.

Aging is the second of the four sufferings. Life passes by in a flash. In the blink of an eye, we are old. Our physical strength wanes, and things start to go wrong with our bodies. Our practice of Nichiren Buddhism enables us to make our old age a time of great richness, like a golden autumn harvest, instead of a time of sad and lonely decline. The setting sun bathes the earth and sky in a magnificent glow. We practice Nichiren Buddhism so we can enjoy just such a vibrant, glowing old age, without regrets.

The third of the four sufferings is sickness. We are mortal beings. All of us experience illness in one form or

JOY IN BOTH LIFE AND DEATH

another. The power of the Mystic Law enables us to bring forth the strength to overcome the suffering of sickness. Nichiren Daishonin writes: "Nam-myoho-renge-kyo is like the roar of a lion. What sickness can therefore be an obstacle?" (WND-1, 412).

Though we may fall ill or experience some other trying situation, if we are devoting ourselves to the realization of kosen-rufu, Nichiren Daishonin will protect us, as will all Buddhas and bodhisattvas and the heavenly deities—the protective functions of the universe.

The Daishonin promises:

> A woman who takes this efficacious medicine [of Myoho-renge-kyo] will be surrounded and protected by these four great bodhisattvas [the leaders of the Bodhisattvas of the Earth] at all times. When she rises to her feet, so too will the bodhisattvas, and when she walks along the road, they will also do the same. She and they will be as inseparable as a body and its shadow, as fish and water, as a voice and its echo, or as the moon and its light. (WND-1, 415)

As this passage indicates, those who embrace faith in the Mystic Law will definitely be protected—not only in this lifetime but throughout eternity.

Death is the last of the four sufferings. Death is uncompromising; we must all face it one day. When that moment comes, those who travel on the path of the Mystic Law will make their way serenely to the pure land of Eagle Peak aboard the "great white ox cart" described in the Lotus Sutra. Their lives will merge with the world of Buddhahood of the universe. The Lotus Sutra describes the "great white ox cart" as being immense in every dimension and adorned with gold, silver, and countless precious gems.[1]

If we attain the state of Buddhahood in this existence, that state will forever pervade our lives. In lifetime after lifetime, we will enjoy lives blessed with health, wealth, intellect, favorable circumstances, and good fortune. We will possess our own unique mission and be born in a form suitable to fulfilling that mission. This state of life is everlasting; it can never be destroyed.

It is precisely so that you may enjoy such eternal happiness that I continually urge you to apply yourself to your Buddhist practice and firmly consolidate the state of Buddhahood in your life in this existence. This is not just a matter of personal sentiment. It is the teaching of Nichiren Daishonin.

It's crucial, therefore, that we do not move off the path leading to Buddhahood but that we keep pressing ever forward with patience and persistence along the path of kosen-rufu and Buddhist practice.

There may well be times when we feel disinclined to do something, or when we would like to take a break. This is only natural since we are ordinary beings. But what matters is that we stay on course, that we continue forging ahead patiently on the path to Buddhahood while encouraging one another along the way.

JOY IN BOTH LIFE AND DEATH

If a plane flies off course or a car veers carelessly off the road, it can easily have an accident or fail to reach its destination. Similarly, if our lives go off course, we, too, can crash, plunging into misfortune and misery. Though it may not be visible to the eye, there is a path or course in life. A path leading to absolute happiness exists without a doubt—and that is the path of the Mystic Law.

If we continue on this path without abandoning our Buddhist practice, we will definitely come to savor a life of complete fulfillment, both materially and spiritually.

From a speech at a meeting at the New York Culture Center, New York City, New York, June 15, 1996.

10.2 Death Gives Greater Meaning to Life

Instead of trying to avoid facing the inevitability of death, properly understanding the crucial issue of life and death with a full awareness of death's weighty significance is an opportunity for elevating our lives.

We all know that we will die someday. But we cling to that idea of "someday," expecting it to be far off in the future. Young people naturally try to brush aside the thought of death, but this is even true of older people, and perhaps increasingly so as we age.

But the reality of life is that it may come to an end at any moment. The possibility of death is always with us—be it from an earthquake, an accident, or a sudden illness. We simply choose to forget this.

As someone once noted: "Death does not lie in wait before us; it creeps up on us from behind."

As we keep procrastinating, telling ourselves, "I'll challenge myself harder someday" or "I'll make greater efforts after I finish doing this," our lives slip by, and before we know it, we are facing death without having achieved anything, without having accumulated any really profound inner treasures of life. Many people live their lives this way. When the final moment comes, it's too late for regrets.

Upon reflection, whether death awaits in three days, three years, or three decades, the reality is essentially the same. That's why it is so important to live fully right now, so that we will have no regret if we die at any moment.

JOY IN BOTH LIFE AND DEATH

From the perspective of eternity, even a century is just an instant. It is genuinely true, as the Daishonin says, that "now is the last moment of one's life" (WND-1, 216). Furthermore, second Soka Gakkai president Josei Toda said, "In truth, we practice Buddhism for the time of our death."

Nothing is more certain than death. That's why it is vital to immediately set ourselves to the task of accumulating the treasures of the heart that will endure for eternity. Yet the great majority of people put off this most crucial of all tasks or leave it for some future time.

There is nothing as important as what Buddhism calls the "one great matter of life and death." Compared to this crucial matter, everything else is minor—a fact that becomes abundantly clear at the moment of death.

Someone who has been at the bedside of many at their last moments has said: "In their final days, it seems that people often recall their lives as if gazing over a vast panorama. What appears to stand out are not things such as having led a company or done well in business but rather how they have lived their lives, who they have loved, who they've been kind to, who they've hurt. All of their deepest emotions—the feeling of having been true to their beliefs and having lived a fulfilled life or painful regrets at having betrayed others—rush upon them as they approach death."

An awareness of death gives greater meaning to our lives. Awakening to death's reality prompts us to seek the eternal and motivates us to make the most of each moment.

What if there were no death? Life would just go on and on and probably become painfully dull.

Death makes us treasure the present. Modern civilization is said to ignore or deny death. It is no coincidence that it is also a civilization characterized by the unfettered pursuit of desires. A society or civilization, just like an individual, that tries to avoid the fundamental question of life and death will fall into spiritual decline as it fails to look beyond living for the moment.

From The Wisdom of the Lotus Sutra, *vol. 4, published in Japanese in December 1998.*

10.3 The Buddhist View of Life That Transcends the Suffering of Death

While confronting the fundamental suffering of death, Shakyamuni established a view of eternal life. Through a consideration of Shakyamuni's enlightenment, President Ikeda explores the essence of the Buddhist conception of life and death.

All living things have an instinctual fear of death. Human beings in particular are afflicted by an indescribable terror when they contemplate what sort of world may await them after departing from the realm of the living. With tremendous courage, Shakyamuni overcame this primal human instinct to fear death, to refuse to countenance or contemplate its reality, and accepted the suffering that is the true nature of human existence. Then, based on that courageous stance, he deeply pondered the essence of life and death.

Buddhism teaches the eternity of life, but not as a simplistic response to people's cherished hopes for immortality. The Buddhist teachings of the impermanence of all phenomena and the four noble truths (clarifying the causes and the resolution of human suffering) directly expose the reality of the suffering inherent in life, a reality that people try to avoid. Shakyamuni did not seek to whitewash the reality of existence by offering some consoling myth or fiction; he looked at it directly, with cool objectivity. All things that are born will die. He affirmed this as the underlying truth of existence.

Why do we die? Are life and death completely separate from one another? Or are they closely interrelated? Is there a continuity underlying life itself? Reflecting on his own life, Shakyamuni sought the answers to those questions with courage, tenacity, and objectivity. And the truth to which he became enlightened is that life is eternal.

Human existence includes both life and death. It flows on eternally, with a powerful force, repeating a cycle of alternating manifest and latent phases. Shakyamuni saw this in the flow of his own life.

His is not a philosophy of the immortality of the soul, arising from a dogged attachment to life, but a solid affirmation of the eternity of life based on a recognition of the law of cause and effect unfolding within each individual life.

The significance of death in such a view of life's eternity is that death exists for the sake of life. It is akin to sleep, which provides us with the rest we need to awaken once again. Death is an "expedient means" for life. Death's purpose is to make life shine brighter, while life is the innate activity of existence. Life and death are not in opposition to one another; death exists for the sake of life. This is the meaning of the Lotus Sutra teaching of "entering nirvana as an expedient means" (see LSOC, 271).[2]

The essential message of Buddhism is not pessimistic or negative; nor is it unfounded optimism. Buddhism looks directly at the suffering of life and offers a philosophy for living with joy by actively engaging with reality rather than trying to escape from it. There is no true joy to be had in fleeing from suffering. An indestructible, everlasting, and inexhaustible joy is achieved only by accurately seeing the true reality of the suffering we would like to escape and courageously rising to its challenge and overcoming it.

From Seimei o kataru *(Dialogue on life), vol. 3, published in Japanese in March 1974.*

10.4 The Oneness of Life and Death

Based on the teachings of the Lotus Sutra, President Ikeda elucidates the eternity of life, that birth and death continue in an endless cycle of latent and active states.

Birth and death are different aspects of life. In other words, life manifests solely through the cycle of birth and death.

In the eyes of ordinary mortals, life begins with birth and ends with death. But the insight of Buddhism sees through this limitation and perceives the essence of life as a whole, manifesting actively as birth or existence and persisting in dormant form as death. From that perspective, how does Buddhism view these two aspects of birth and death?

The "Life Span" chapter of the Lotus Sutra speaks of "ebbing" and "flowing" (see LSOC, 267). "Ebbing" refers to death and "flowing" to life. Based on the standpoint of the eternity of life, the "Life Span" chapter states that life itself does not disappear and emerge, does not undergo birth or death. In *The Record of the Orally Transmitted Teachings*, Nichiren Daishonin reveals an even more profound view of life as the "originally inherent nature of birth and death" (OTT, 127).[3]

According to this principle, living is the state in which our life is actively manifested, and death is the state when it returns to a latent or potential state. These phases of birth and death continue eternally. That is the true nature of life itself.

The supreme teaching of Buddhism that views living as an active state and death as a latent state offers a profound and magnificent view of the eternity of life.

In addition, it teaches the oneness of life and death. Life is activated by a wondrous, underlying power. When life in its latent state comes into contact with the right causes and conditions, it becomes manifest and takes shape as a dynamic living being with a rich individuality. Eventually, that life quietly ebbs and moves toward death. But as it shifts into its potential, dormant phase, it stores a new energy, awaiting the next new phase of life.

Life is an explosion and burning of the stored-up energy that had been in a resting state. Eventually that life brings its story to a close and it drifts back into death. It merges with the universe, is recharged by the power of the life of the universe as a whole, and awaits its next emergence into active life.

This is the nature of life and death inherent in all things, and Nam-myoho-renge-kyo is the foundation of this intrinsic rhythm of the universe.

From a lecture on Nichiren Daishonin's writing
"The Heritage of the Ultimate Law of Life,"
published in Japanese in the Seikyo Shimbun, *April 1977.*

10.5 Savoring Joy in Both Life and Death

Referring to his observations on the Buddhist view of life and death presented in "Mahayana Buddhism and Twenty-First-Century Civilization," the lecture he delivered at Harvard University in 1993, President Ikeda asserts that those who dedicate their lives to kosen-rufu and build a state of absolute happiness can advance along a path in which there is joy in both life and death. Excerpts from the lecture also appear at the end of this section.

I have been invited to speak at Harvard University, one of the most prestigious institutions of higher learning in the United States, on two occasions (in 1991 and 1993). In my second speech, I addressed the Buddhist view of life and death, in which we can experience joy in both life and death.

Dr. Harvey Cox, then chair of the Harvard Divinity School's Department of Applied Theology, commented that I had presented my audience with a completely new perspective on death.

Death is not the end of everything. Birth and death are both aspects of the eternity of life. The cycle of birth and death grounded in the Mystic Law is a drama unfolding on a great stage of life existing eternally. By striving for kosen-rufu, we can firmly establish a state of absolute happiness in this existence. People who achieve that can advance along the path of joy in both life and death.

This planet Earth is not the only place one can be born. In this vast universe, many scientists believe, there are innumerable planets where life exists. The Lotus Sutra presents a grand and expansive view of the universe, teaching that the number of realms in which living beings reside is infinite—a view that is widely supported by contemporary astronomy. There may be some planets where all the inhabitants are good and virtuous, and others, like our Earth, where there are also many who are selfish and devious. There may also be planets where everyone lives happily, in fine health, enjoying long lives, and listening to beautiful music from morning to night.

When the functions of our hearts and minds and the functions of the universe are in sync, we can be born wherever we wish and in any form we desire. The Lotus Sutra speaks of "freely choosing where one will be born" (see LSOC, 202). This is the essence of Buddhism.

President Toda often likened death to sleep. Just as we awake refreshed and energized after a good night's sleep, those who pass away having chanted Nam-myoho-renge-kyo throughout their lives will, after a period of rest, be reborn to once again join the ranks of those striving for kosen-rufu, he used to say.

Nichiren Daishonin repeatedly offers guidance about the moment of death in his writings. For example:

> How can we possibly hold back our tears at the inexpressible joy of knowing that [at the moment of death] not just one or two, not just one hundred or two hundred, but as many as a thousand Buddhas will come to greet us with open arms! (WND-1, 216–17)

JOY IN BOTH LIFE AND DEATH

Without fail, I will be with you at the time of your death and guide you from this life to the next. (WND-1, 965)

When he was alive, he was a Buddha in life, and now he is a Buddha in death. He is a Buddha in both life and death. This is what is meant by that most important doctrine called attaining Buddhahood in one's present form. (WND-1, 456)

A belief in the eternity of life has been shared by many of the world's great writers and thinkers. Their view of life has much in common with the perspective of Buddhism.

Leo Tolstoy was one such individual. In 1907, when he was seventy-nine years old, a few years before he passed away, Tolstoy wrote, "Living is joyous, and death, too, is joyous."[4] These words express the unshakable state of mind that Tolstoy had reached after a life of great vicissitudes.

The eminent British historian Arnold J. Toynbee was also deeply impressed by the Buddhist view of life.

We have faith in, are practicing, and are sharing the supreme teaching of Buddhism, eagerly sought by the world's leading thinkers. There is no life more wonderful.

From a speech at a joint training session,
Nagano, Japan, August 19, 2005.

Supplementary Reading

It was the Greek philosopher Heraclitus who declared that all things are in a state of flux and that change is the essential nature of reality. Indeed, everything, whether it lies in the realm of natural phenomena or of human affairs, changes continuously. Nothing maintains exactly the same state for even the briefest instant; the most solid-seeming rocks and minerals are subject to the erosive effects of time. But during this century of war and revolution, normal change and flux seem to have been accelerated and magnified. We have seen the most extraordinary panorama of social transformations.

The Buddhist term for the ephemeral aspect of reality is "the transience of all phenomena" (Jpn *shogyo mujo*). In the Buddhist cosmology, this concept is described as the repeated cycles of formation, continuance, decline, and disintegration through which all systems must pass.

During our lives as human beings, we experience transience as the four sufferings: the suffering of birth (and of day-to-day existence), that of illness, of aging, and finally, of death. No human being is exempt from these sources of pain. It was, in fact, human distress, in particular the problem of death, that spawned the formation of religious and philosophical systems.

It is said that Shakyamuni was inspired to seek the truth by his accidental encounters with many sorrows at the gates of the palace in which he was raised. Plato stated that true philosophers are always engaged in the practice of dying, while Nichiren, founder of the school of Buddhism followed by members of the SGI, admonishes us to "first of all learn about death, and then about other things" (WND-2, 759).

Death weighs heavily on the human heart as an inescapable reminder of the finite nature of our existence. However seemingly limitless the wealth or power we might attain, the reality of our eventual demise cannot be avoided. From ancient times, humanity has sought to conquer the fear and apprehension surrounding death by finding ways to partake of the eternal. Through this quest, people have learned to overcome control by instinctual modes of survival and have developed the characteristics that we recognize as uniquely human. In that perspective, we can see why the history of religion coincides with the history of humankind.

Modern civilization has attempted to ignore death. We have diverted our gaze from this most fundamental of concerns as we try to drive death into the shadows. For many people living today, death is the mere absence of life; it is blankness; it is the void. Life is identified with all that is good: with being, rationality, and light. In contrast, death is perceived as evil, as nothingness, and as the dark and irrational. Only the negative perception of death prevails.

We cannot, however, ignore death, and the attempt to do so has exacted a heavy price. The horrific and ironic climax of modern civilization has been in our time what

Zbigniew Brzezinski has called the "century of megadeath." Today, a wide range of issues is now forcing a reexamination and reevaluation of the significance of death. They include questions about brain death and death with dignity, the function of hospices, alternative funerary styles and rites, and research into death and dying by writers such as Elisabeth Kübler-Ross.

We finally seem to be ready to recognize the fundamental error in our view of life and death. We are beginning to understand that death is more than the absence of life; that death, together with active life, is necessary for the formation of a larger, more essential, whole. This greater whole reflects the deeper continuity of life and death that we experience as individuals and express as culture. A central challenge for the coming century will be to establish a culture based on an understanding of the relationship of life and death and of life's essential eternity. Such an attitude does not disown death but directly confronts and correctly positions it within the larger context of life.

Buddhism speaks of an intrinsic nature (Jpn *hossho*, sometimes translated as "Dharma nature") existing within the depths of phenomenal reality. This nature depends upon and responds to environmental conditions, and it alternates between states of emergence and latency. All phenomena, including life and death, can be seen as elements within the cycle of emergence and latency, or manifestation and withdrawal.

Cycles of life and death can be likened to the alternating

JOY IN BOTH LIFE AND DEATH

periods of sleep and wakefulness. Just as sleep prepares us for the next day's activity, death can be seen as a state in which we rest and replenish ourselves for new life. In this light, death should be acknowledged, along with life, as a blessing to be appreciated. The Lotus Sutra, the core of Mahayana Buddhism, states that the purpose of existence, the eternal cycles of life and death, is for living beings to "enjoy themselves at ease" (LSOC, 272). It further teaches that sustained faith and practice enable us to know a deep and abiding joy in death as well as in life, to equally "enjoy ourselves at ease" in both. Nichiren describes the attainment of this state as the "greatest of all joys" (OTT, 212).

If the tragedies of this century of war and revolution have taught us anything, it is the folly of believing that reform of external factors, such as social systems, is the linchpin to achieving happiness. I am convinced that in the coming century, the greatest emphasis must be placed on fostering inwardly directed change. In addition, our efforts must be inspired by a new understanding of life and death.

From a lecture at Harvard University, "Mahayana Buddhism and Twenty-First-Century Civilization," Cambridge, Massachusetts, September 24, 1993.

10.6 Advancing on the Path of Buddhahood in Both Life and Death

The aim of Buddhism is to establish a state of indestructible happiness enduring throughout past, present, and future, making it crucial that we strengthen our inner life state of Buddhahood in this lifetime.

Buddhism began from the quest to find a solution to the sufferings of birth, aging, sickness, and death. Life and death are the most important questions of existence, yet many people turn away from looking at them.

Nichiren Daishonin writes:

> The Nirvana Sutra states, "Human life runs its course more swiftly than a mountain stream; the person here today will not likely be here tomorrow." The Maya Sutra reads, "Imagine, for instance, a flock of sheep being driven by a chandala to the slaughterhouse. Human life is exactly the same; step by step one approaches the place of death." The Lotus Sutra states, "There is no safety in the threefold world; it is like a burning house, replete with a multitude of sufferings, truly to be feared."[5]
>
> In these passages from the sutras, our compassionate father, the World-Honored One of Great Enlightenment [Shakyamuni Buddha], admonishes us, the ordinary people of the latter age; it is his warning to us, his ignorant children. Nevertheless,

JOY IN BOTH LIFE AND DEATH

> the people do not awaken for even one instant; nor do they conceive a desire to attain the way for even a single moment. In order to decorate their bodies, which, if abandoned in the fields, would be stripped naked overnight, they spend their time striving to pile up articles of clothing.
>
> When their lives come to an end, within three days their bodies will turn into water that washes away, into dust that mixes with the earth, and into smoke that rises up into the sky, leaving no trace behind. Nevertheless, they seek to nurture these bodies and to amass great wealth. (WND-1, 891)

The Daishonin's description of human foolishness in forgetting the inevitability of death and seeking for meaningless things is just as true today as it was then—perhaps even more so. No matter how we may appear to flourish, as long as we sidestep the fundamental issue of life and death, we remain as rootless as floating weeds or like a castle built on sand.

Life is indeed impermanent—but simply being aware of its impermanence is no solution. Despairing over this reality also serves no purpose. The question is how we can create eternal value in this fleeting existence. The Lotus Sutra holds the answer.

Nichiren Daishonin describes the lives of practitioners of the Lotus Sutra very simply as follows: "Passing through the round of births and deaths, one makes one's way on the land of the Dharma nature, or enlightenment, that is inherent within oneself" (OTT, 52).

In other words, those who practice the Lotus Sutra advance serenely and steadily in both life and death on the boundless land of the Dharma nature, the firm ground of Buddhahood. They press onward in the supreme and magnificent "great white ox cart."

The ground of Buddhahood is a state of indestructible happiness. It is the life state of one's own attainment of Buddhahood, as firm and solid as the earth itself. When that life state is established, it continues throughout the three existences of past, present, and future. That's why we must make our best effort in this present existence.

We advance with joy in both life and death on the earth of the Dharma nature. This means that we make our way through repeated cycles of birth and death. We advance upon the earth of our own lives, not the earth of others. That means that happiness is something we build ourselves. It is not something given to us by others. For, ultimately, things given to us by others do not last.

You may depend on your parents, but the day will come when they are no longer there. You may depend on your spouse or partner, but they may die before you. In addition, we never know what changing times will bring. For example, World War II, and the times preceding and following it, were filled with countless tragedies.

The foundation for true happiness is built through one's own efforts, one's own wisdom, one's own good fortune. The

JOY IN BOTH LIFE AND DEATH

purpose of our Buddhist practice is to solidify that foundation, while our Soka Gakkai activities serve to strengthen and empower us. This is the meaning of the Daishonin's words "one makes one's way on the land of the Dharma nature" (OTT, 52).

The Daishonin also says that wherever we may frolic or play, no harm will come to us; we will move about without fear like the lion king (see WND-1, 412).

We will enjoy such a state eternally—that is the aim of our Buddhist faith and practice.

We advance eternally on our own "land." When we die, we do not go either to heaven or to the depths of hell. We remain on the same land or foundation and continue to enact our drama of mission through the cycle of birth and death. We press forward along the golden path of kosen-rufu for all time.

The Daishonin urges us to keep forging ahead on the firm ground of our Buddhahood, experiencing joy in both life and death, and to continue solidifying that all-important foundation. Such is the profound view of life and death taught in Nichiren Buddhism.

From a speech at a nationwide representatives conference, Tokyo, Japan, March 29, 1996.

10.7 The Death of Someone Close to Us

Referring to Nichiren Daishonin's encouragement to his disciple Nanjo Tokimitsu and his mother, President Ikeda offers the wisdom we need to accept the suffering of separation from those we love.

How can we overcome the inherent human sufferings of birth, aging, sickness, and death? The wisdom of Buddhism provides a sound and illuminating answer to this question.

No one can avoid the suffering of having to part from loved ones. Buddhism offers clear insights on this point.

Nanjo Hyoe Shichiro, Nanjo Tokimitsu's father, died of illness while still quite young. Tokimitsu was only seven at the time. By embracing the Daishonin's teachings, unafraid of the persecution this would invite, Hyoe Shichiro had opened the way for transforming the karma of his entire family.

In a letter of encouragement to the lay nun Ueno, Tokimitsu's mother, the Daishonin writes: "When [your deceased husband] was alive, he was a Buddha in life, and now he is a Buddha in death. He is a Buddha in both life and death" (WND-1, 456).

Life is eternal. Those who dedicate their lives to the Mystic Law are Buddhas in both life and death. Therefore, they will without fail move ahead serenely and confidently in a boundless state of being in which both life and death are filled with joy.

JOY IN BOTH LIFE AND DEATH

Carrying on her late husband's spirit, the lay nun Ueno maintained strong faith. She raised Tokimitsu and her other children to become outstanding successors who followed in their father's footsteps as sincere practitioners of Nichiren Buddhism.

It appears that Tokimitsu must have regretted losing his father at such a young age and thus missing out on receiving instruction and guidance from him.[6] Keenly aware of Tokimitsu's feelings in this regard, the Daishonin encourages and assures him:

> Persons who uphold [the Lotus Sutra], though they may be strangers to one another, will meet on Eagle Peak. And how much more certain is it that you and your late father, because you both have faith in the Lotus Sutra [Nam-myoho-renge-kyo], will be reborn there together! (WND-2, 500)

Ties based on the Mystic Law are eternal. A family whose members dedicate their lives to the Mystic Law can be born together again in the same place—such is the wondrous power of the Mystic Law.

Among the Daishonin's followers was a couple who had been moved to embrace his teachings because of the death of their beloved son, the experience contributing to deepening their faith. This husband and wife earnestly practiced the Mystic Law and sincerely supported the Daishonin. In praise of their faith, the Daishonin writes:

> [The sincerity of your faith] is no ordinary matter. Indeed, Shakyamuni Buddha himself may have taken possession of your body. Or perhaps your deceased son has become a Buddha and, in order to guide his father and mother, has taken possession of your hearts. . . .
>
> If anything should happen to you, just as the moon emerges to shine in the dark night, so the five characters of Myoho-renge-kyo[7] will appear as a moon for you. Be convinced that Shakyamuni Buddha, the Buddhas of the ten directions, and the son who preceded you in death will appear in this moon. (WND-1, 1049–50)

Lives connected by the Mystic Law are always together, transcending the bounds of life and death, encouraging, protecting, and guiding one another as they advance on a course of absolute happiness and victory.

There is no sorrow or gloom in the realm of the Mystic Law. Family members who practice the Mystic Law will always be enveloped in the moonlight of eternity, happiness, true self, and purity—the four noble virtues of Buddhahood. Their lives will impart immeasurable hope and courage to those who follow in their footsteps.

From a speech at a Tokyo No. 2 Area representatives conference,
Tokyo, Japan, February 20, 2006.

10.8 Our Own Attainment of Buddhahood Enables the Deceased to Attain Buddhahood

Referring to Nichiren Daishonin's writings, President Ikeda explains the principle that our efforts toward our own attainment of Buddhahood are the best offering we can make to the deceased.

In *The Record of the Orally Transmitted Teachings*, Nichiren Daishonin states:

> Now when Nichiren and his followers perform ceremonies for the deceased, reciting the Lotus Sutra and chanting Nam-myoho-renge-kyo, the ray of light from the daimoku reaches all the way to the hell of incessant suffering and makes it possible for them to attain Buddhahood then and there. This is the origin of the prayers for transference of merit for the deceased. (OTT, 17)

The power of chanting Nam-myoho-renge-kyo is unfathomable. The "light" of the daimoku we chant reaches every corner of the universe, illuminating even those agonizing in the hell of incessant suffering after death and enabling them to attain Buddhahood directly, says the Daishonin.

In "The Offering of an Unlined Robe," the Daishonin

writes [to the lady of Sajiki], "Be firmly convinced that the benefits from [your sincere offering] will extend to your parents, your grandparents, nay, even to countless living beings" (WND-1, 533). The great benefit of our Buddhist practice dedicated to kosen-rufu also flows on to the deceased as well as to unborn future generations.

Offering prayers based on the Mystic Law—chanting Nam-myoho-renge-kyo—is the best and truest offering we can make for the deceased. Because the Mystic Law has the power to help all people attain Buddhahood, not only those here in the present but throughout the three existences of past, present, and future.

The father of one of the Daishonin's disciples, Joren-bo, was a Nembutsu practitioner. In a letter to Joren-bo after his father's death, the Daishonin writes: "The body that the father and mother leave behind is none other than the physical form and mind of the child. The blessings that you, the Honorable Joren, acquire through your faith in the Lotus Sutra will lend strength to your kind father" (WND-2, 572).

Even if our parents do not practice Nichiren Buddhism, the benefit that we receive as practitioners of the Mystic Law will also become their benefit. We are alive today thanks to our parents. They gave birth to us. As such, our attainment of Buddhahood leads to their attainment of Buddhahood.

The past doesn't matter; it's the present that counts. Our ancestors' actions are not decisive; it is our actions that determine the future. All it takes is one awakened individual to shine like the sun and illuminate all of his or her family members and relations with the light of the Mystic Law.

The Daishonin notes that, without obtaining Buddhahood oneself, it would be difficult to help even one's parents attain Buddhahood, much less help other people to do so (see WND-1, 819). Let us take this insight deeply to heart.

From a speech at a spring memorial service, Tokyo, Japan, March 21, 2006.

10.9 Ties Based on the Mystic Law Are Eternal

President Ikeda encourages a high school division member who asks if she will ever be reunited with her beloved grandmother, who has passed away.

Nichiren Daishonin says that we can be reunited with deceased loved ones. For example, he gently tells a mother who had lost her child[8]:

> There is a way to meet [your deceased child] readily. With Shakyamuni Buddha as your guide, you can go to meet him in the pure land of Eagle Peak. . . . It could never happen that a woman who chants

Nam-myoho-renge-kyo would fail to be reunited with her beloved child. (WND-1, 1092)

By saying that they will "meet in the pure land of Eagle Peak," the Daishonin is in effect saying, "Your child has attained Buddhahood, and you can attain Buddhahood too, with the result that you will both be together in the same realm of Buddhahood."

This could mean that a life that has merged with the universe can feel at one with the life of another, or that two lives can meet in another Buddha land somewhere else in the universe.

Recently, it was estimated there are about 125 billion galaxies in the observable universe [according to observations with the Hubble Space Telescope by the American Astronomical Society in January 1999]. But compared to the Buddhist conception of the universe, that is still far from a large number. The "Life Span" (sixteenth) chapter of the Lotus Sutra that we recite during gongyo offers an even grander view of the universe, on a scale that can be conceived only as infinite. At any rate, Earth is not the only planet inhabited by life; countless others exist.

You may be reborn with your grandmother on one of the Buddha lands among those planets. Or you may be born together on a planet where kosen-rufu is still taking place, like Earth, and work together to aid suffering beings there. The Lotus Sutra teaches that we can be reborn freely just as we desire.

JOY IN BOTH LIFE AND DEATH

Life is eternal. Though you may be separated by death, in actuality, it is as if one of you had just gone off for a time on a trip overseas, and you couldn't meet for a while.

As a young man, Mr. Toda lost an infant daughter. Many years later, when encouraging someone who had lost a child and who had asked him whether it would be possible to forge a parent-child relationship with that child again in this lifetime, he said:

> I lost my infant daughter, Yasuyo, when I was twenty-three. I held my dead child all through the night. At the time, not yet having taken faith in the Gohonzon, I was overcome with grief and fell asleep with her in my arms.
>
> And so we parted, and now I am fifty-eight. Since she was three when she died, she would now be a fine woman had she lived. Have I or have I not met my deceased daughter again in this life? This is a matter of one's own perception arising from faith. I believe that I have met her. Whether one is united with a deceased relative in this life or the next is all a matter of one's perception through faith.[9]

After Mr. Toda lost his daughter, his wife also passed away. He grieved terribly over their deaths, but he said that because he had experienced such personal loss and various other kinds of hardships he was able to encourage many others and to be a leader of the people who could understand their feelings.

Everything that happens in life has meaning. If you press ahead undefeated, through the sadness, the pain, and the feeling you can't go on, the time will come when you see its meaning. That's the power of faith, and the essence of life.

From Discussions on Youth II,
published in Japanese in September 2000.

10.10 Sudden and Untimely Deaths

In this excerpt from The New Human Revolution, *the novel's protagonist Shin'ichi Yamamoto (whose character represents President Ikeda) hastens to a regional area to encourage members after the untimely death of one of their central leaders in a car accident.*

Throughout his writings, Nichiren Daishonin speaks of the three obstacles and four devils, one of which is the hindrance of death. This devilish function serves to arouse doubt and confusion through the death of those striving diligently in Buddhist practice.

We all have our own karma, but as ordinary mortals we cannot grasp its depth. Even should steadfast practitioners of Nichiren Buddhism die young, their death will enable them to actualize the Buddhist principle of lessening karmic retribution.

Those who strive energetically for kosen-rufu as genuine practitioners of the Mystic Law are certain to attain Buddhahood, however their lives may end.

An early Buddhist scripture tells the story of a lay believer named Mahanama. He asked the Buddha where and in what form of existence he would be reborn were he to suddenly meet his end in an accident due to being distracted by the bustle of the town instead of concentrating his thoughts on the three treasures—the Buddha, the Law, and the Buddhist Order.

The Buddha responded, "For instance, Mahanama, if a tree bends to the east, slopes to the east, tends to the east, which way will it fall when its root is cut?"

To which Mahanama replied, "It will fall [in the direction that] it bends, slopes, and tends."[10]

Through this story, the Buddha taught that those who embrace Buddhism and practice assiduously, even if they were to meet with an unexpected, accidental death, will be carried by the Law in the direction of rebirth in good circumstances.

Shin'ichi then began to talk about the death of Isamu Ishizaki [a central leader in Tottori Prefecture]: "There may be some members who are wondering why, given that he practiced Nichiren Buddhism, Mr. Ishizaki met with such an accident. The causes and effects inherent deep in our lives, the workings of our karma, are strict indeed. That is why, even if we practice Nichiren Buddhism, the manner of our death can occur in any number of ways.

"There may be some who die giving their lives in the struggle to uphold Buddhism, like Mr. Makiguchi who died in prison for his beliefs. There may be some who die young as a result of illness or accidents. But when viewed through the eyes of faith, it all has some extremely profound meaning.

"Those who have dedicated their lives to working for kosen-rufu are Bodhisattvas of the Earth. They are followers of the Buddha. Life is eternal. In light of the teaching of the Mystic Law, such people will absolutely attain Buddhahood. Their surviving family members will also definitely be protected. I state unequivocally that, as long as those left behind continue to persevere in faith, the good fortune and benefit accumulated through their loved ones' dedication to kosen-rufu will also pass on to them, and they will, without fail, enjoy unsurpassed happiness."

Hearing Shin'ichi's tremendous conviction, the feelings of doubt that had been clouding the members' minds evaporated, and the sun of hope began to rise in their hearts.

Shin'ichi continued: "Being without a spouse or partner doesn't mean that we will never be happy. Prestige and wealth also do not guarantee happiness. True happiness, absolute happiness, is only found when we awaken to the fact that our lives embody the Mystic Law, carry out our human revolution, and manifest the great life state of Buddhahood through our Buddhist practice. We are born alone and we die alone. Only the Mystic Law has the power to protect us across the three existences of past, present, and future.

"If you continue devoting yourselves earnestly to kosen-rufu, the Buddhas and bodhisattvas throughout the ten directions and three existences will protect you. Therefore, no matter what happens, no matter what others may say or how badly they may treat you, you must never be swayed or shaken. If you become cowardly and distance yourself from faith, you will only end up miserable.

"Life is eternal, but this present lifetime flashes by in an instant. I hope you will be aware of your mission in this existence, devote yourselves to kosen-rufu, and accumulate abundant good fortune."

From The New Human Revolution, *vol. 10,*
"Bastion of the Pen" chapter.

10.11 Clear Proof of Attaining Buddhahood

With reference to the writings of Nichiren Daishonin, President Ikeda describes the final moments of those who have remained fully committed to their faith throughout their lives.

Accompanied by a group of French youth division members, I once visited [in 1993] the château where Leonardo da Vinci's life came to a close.¹¹ These words of the Renaissance giant were engraved on a bronze plaque in the bedroom where he died: "A fulfilling life is long. As a well-spent day brings happy sleep, so a well-spent life brings happy death."

Those who have lived a good life without regrets do not fear death. How much more certain it is, then, that a life spent striving tirelessly for others and for truth and goodness, in accord with the eternal Law pervading life and the universe, will reach the summit of true joy.

Nichiren Daishonin writes:

> Continue your practice without backsliding until the final moment of your life, and when that time comes, behold! When you climb the mountain of perfect enlightenment and gaze around you in all directions, then to your amazement you will see that the entire realm of phenomena is the Land of Tranquil Light. The ground will be of lapis lazuli, and the eight paths¹² will be set apart by golden ropes. Four kinds

of flowers will fall from the heavens, and music will resound in the air. All Buddhas and bodhisattvas will be present in complete joy, caressed by the breezes of eternity, happiness, true self, and purity. The time is fast approaching when we too will count ourselves among their number. (WND-1, 761)

This describes the state of life—brimming with "the greatest of all joys" (OTT, 212)—found in the worlds of Buddhas and bodhisattvas that move in rhythm with the universe.

The Nanjo family made a lasting contribution to kosen-rufu during the Daishonin's lifetime. Nanjo Shichiro Goro, Nanjo Tokimitsu's youngest brother, died suddenly at the young age of sixteen. He was a youth of fine character and handsome appearance, and the Daishonin had high hopes for his future. His mother was pregnant with him when her husband died, and she loved him deeply.

Intensely grieving Shichiro Goro's sudden death, the Daishonin repeatedly assured the Nanjo family that the deceased young man would attain Buddhahood without fail. In the postscript to one of his letters, he writes, "He had devoted himself to Shakyamuni Buddha and the Lotus Sutra, and he died in a fitting manner" (WND-2, 887).

Though someone may seem to have died prematurely or unexpectedly, there will be clear proof that they have attained Buddhahood. One manifestation of this is the fact that they are deeply mourned and missed by so many people. Another is the way in which the surviving family members go on to enjoy protection and prosperity. When a family carries on courageously with their lives after a loved one has passed away, the deceased continues to live on in their hearts.

The Daishonin encourages Shichiro Goro's mother:

> I hope that, if you, his loving mother, are thinking with longing about your son, you will chant Nam-myoho-renge-kyo and pray to be reborn in the same place as the late Shichiro Goro and your husband, the late Nanjo.
>
> The seeds of one kind of plant are all the same; they are different from the seeds of other plants. If all of you nurture the same seeds of Myoho-renge-kyo in your hearts, then you all will be reborn together in the same land of Myoho-renge-kyo. When the three of you are reunited there face to face, how great your joy will be! (WND-1, 1074)

Based on the profound teaching of the Mystic Law, the Daishonin offers a vision of the wondrous realm of happiness stretching out before us.

From an essay series "Thoughts on The New Human Revolution,*" published in Japanese in the* Seikyo Shimbun, *November 3, 2000.*

10.12 Transforming the Sufferings of Birth and Death

Buddhist practice to accumulate the treasures of the heart in this lifetime is crucial to overcoming the sufferings of birth and death and attaining a state of eternal happiness.

According to a Buddhist story, seven elder Brahmans once traveled from afar to visit Shakyamuni. Though they had made the long trip to learn about the Buddhist teachings from him, they spent their days in the lodging where they were staying, engaged in idle conversation, laughing and amusing themselves.

Shakyamuni came to see them and said: "All beings rely on five things. What are the five? One, they rely on their youth. Two, they rely on their upright appearance. Three, they rely on their great strength. Four, they rely on their wealth. Five, they rely on their noble family. While you, seven sirs, are speaking in a low tone or loudly laughing, what do you rely on?"[13]

Shakyamuni then went on to tell them that life is uncertain and fleeting, characterized by the four sufferings of birth, aging, sickness, and death. Hearing Shakyamuni, the seven Brahmans realized for the first time what they should be doing and began to strive seriously in their practice.

"What do you rely on?" Shakyamuni asked. In other words, what sustains you in this life?

Nichiren Daishonin teaches three treasures in life: the treasures of the storehouse, the treasures of the body, and the treasures of the heart (see WND-1, 851).

The five things that all beings rely on in the story all correspond to the treasures of the storehouse or the treasures of the body. Wealth, of course, corresponds to the treasures of the storehouse. Youth, beauty, health, and ability, along with social status, correspond to the treasures of the body. All of these things have value in life, and it may be natural, in that respect, for us to pursue them. But the question is whether they are really genuine treasures in life that can offer eternal sustenance.

Let me give some concrete examples. Some people are harmed or killed for their wealth. Those who are physically attractive may be envied or exploited by others. Fame and power can lead people to become arrogant and ruin their lives, and there are many of high social position who allow themselves to be seduced by the devilish nature of power, to their own undoing. None of these so-called treasures continue forever.

As such, the treasures of the storehouse and the treasures of the body are not genuine sustenance that can provide true happiness. On their own, they cannot enable us to lead a life of real fulfillment.

What do we need to live such a life? The Daishonin tells us, "The treasures of the heart are the most valuable of all" (WND-1, 851).

JOY IN BOTH LIFE AND DEATH

The treasures of the heart refer to faith in the Mystic Law. Faith is the eternal treasure and sustenance of human life. It encompasses immeasurable benefit and boundless good fortune. Its power is as vast as the universe and can transform our entire environment or world. It is the source of inexhaustible joy and immense wisdom and compassion, enabling us to employ the treasures of the storehouse and the treasures of the body to attain eternal happiness.

Each of you already possesses this supreme sustenance of life. All you have to do is tap its limitless power.

Life is brief. Youth passes by in a flash, easily wasted in indecision, complaining, criticizing others, or being defeated by one's own laziness. Every day is precious.

I hope you will spend your youth in a fulfilling manner, leading strong lives in the real world and at the same time contemplating the vast universe, pondering eternity, and making each day worth a thousand years, a thousand eons.

From a speech at an Okinawa Prefecture
youth division representatives training course,
Okinawa, Japan, February 19, 1988.

GLOSSARY

actual three thousand realms in a single moment of life: The doctrine of three thousand realms in a single moment of life, which is the fundamental teaching for attaining enlightenment, is classified into two as the theoretical principle and the actual embodiment of this principle. These are respectively termed "theoretical three thousand realms in a single moment of life" and "actual three thousand realms in a single moment of life." The theoretical principle is based on the theoretical teaching (first half) of the Lotus Sutra, while the actual principle is revealed in the essential teaching (latter half) of the Lotus Sutra. However, in the Latter Day of the Law, these are both theoretical; and the Law of Nam-myoho-renge-kyo that Nichiren Daishonin revealed is the actual teaching of three thousand realms in a single moment of life.

amrita: A legendary, ambrosia-like liquid. In ancient India, it was regarded as the sweet-tasting beverage of the gods. In China, it was thought to rain down from heaven when the world became peaceful. *Amrita* is said to remove sufferings and give immortality. The word *amrita* means immortality and is often translated as sweet dew.

attaining Buddhahood in one's present form: This means attaining Buddhahood in this lifetime just as one is, without undergoing endless eons of Buddhist practice.

attainment of Buddhahood by persons of the two vehicles: In the first half of the Lotus Sutra, persons of the two

GLOSSARY

vehicles—voice-hearers and cause-awakened ones—receive a prophecy from Shakyamuni Buddha that they will attain Buddhahood in future ages. This prophecy refutes the view of the provisional Mahayana teachings, which deny persons of the two vehicles the attainment of Buddhahood, for they seek only personal salvation and do not strive to save others. The Lotus Sutra says that they will practice the bodhisattva way and attain Buddhahood.

Ceremony in the Air: One of the three assemblies described in the Lotus Sutra, in which the entire gathering is suspended in space above the saha world. The heart of this ceremony is the revelation of the Buddha's original enlightenment in the remote past and the transfer of the essence of the sutra to the Bodhisattvas of the Earth, who are led by Bodhisattva Superior Practices.

chandala: A class of untouchables, below the lowest of the four castes in the ancient Indian caste system. People in this class handled corpses, butchered animals, and carried out other tasks associated with death or the killing of living things. Nichiren declared himself to be a member of the chandala class because he was born to a fisherman's family.

countless kalpas of practice: Practice toward enlightenment over a period of countless kalpas (one kalpa being approximately sixteen million years according to one account). In the pre–Lotus Sutra teachings, attaining enlightenment, or Buddhahood, was thought to require countless kalpas of practice over many lifetimes. This idea contrasts with that of attaining Buddhahood in this lifetime or in a single lifetime.

daimoku: The practice of chanting Nam-myoho-renge-kyo with belief in the fundamental Law of the universe expounded by Nichiren.

Eagle Peak: A term that symbolizes the Buddha land or the state of Buddhahood, as in the expression "the pure land of Eagle Peak."

GLOSSARY

embracing the Gohonzon is in itself observing one's own mind: In other words, through faith in the Gohonzon, one can tap the Mystic Law inherent in one's life and attain Buddhahood.

essential nature of phenomena: Also, Dharma nature, or enlightenment.

five components: Also, five components of life. They consist of form, perception, conception, volition, and consciousness. Buddhism holds that these constituent elements unite temporarily to form an individual living being. Together they also constitute one of the three realms of existence, the other two being the realm of living beings and the realm of the environment.

four kinds of flowers: Mandarava, great mandarava, manjushaka, and great manjushaka flowers. Fragrant red and white flowers that, according to Indian tradition, bloom in heaven.

four noble truths: A fundamental doctrine of Buddhism clarifying the cause of suffering and the way of emancipation. The four noble truths are the truth of suffering, the truth of the origin of suffering, the truth of the cessation of suffering, and the truth of the path to the cessation of suffering. Shakyamuni is said to have expounded the four noble truths at Deer Park in Varanasi, India, during his first sermon after attaining enlightenment. They are: (1) all existence is suffering; (2) suffering is caused by selfish craving; (3) the eradication of selfish craving brings about the cessation of suffering and enables one to attain nirvana; and (4) there is a path by which this eradication can be achieved, namely, the discipline of the eightfold path. The eightfold path consists of right views, right thinking, right speech, right action, right way of life, right endeavor, right mindfulness, and right meditation.

fundamental ignorance: The most deeply rooted illusion inherent in life, said to give rise to all other illusions. The inability to see or recognize the truth, particularly, the true nature of one's life.

GLOSSARY

fusion of reality and wisdom: The fusion of the objective reality or truth and the subjective wisdom to realize that truth, which is the Buddha nature inherent within one's life.

great white ox cart: A carriage adorned with jewels and drawn by a great white ox. It appears in the parable of the three carts and the burning house in "Simile and Parable," the third chapter of the Lotus Sutra, where it represents the one Buddha vehicle, or the supreme vehicle of Buddhahood.

heavenly devil: Also, devil king of the sixth heaven. The king of devils, who dwells in the highest or the sixth heaven of the world of desire. He is also named Freely Enjoying Things Conjured by Others, the king who makes free use of the fruits of others' efforts for his own pleasure. Served by innumerable minions, he obstructs Buddhist practice and delights in sapping the life force of other beings, the manifestation of the fundamental ignorance inherent in life. The devil king is a personification of the negative tendency to force others to one's will at any cost.

immediately attaining enlightenment: This means the immediate attainment of Buddhahood based on the doctrine of three thousand realms in a single moment of life. It refers to beings in the nine worlds bringing forth their inherent Buddhahood and attaining enlightenment. The term is used in contrast to attaining Buddhahood through transformation, that is, through devoting oneself ceaselessly to arduous Buddhist practice over countless lifetimes until one gradually ascends to the highest stage of supreme enlightenment.

Land of Eternally Tranquil Light: Also, Land of Tranquil Light. The Buddha land, which is free from impermanence and impurity. In many sutras, the actual saha world in which human beings dwell is described as an impure land filled with delusions and sufferings, while the Buddha land is described as a pure land free from these and far removed from this saha world. In contrast, the Lotus Sutra reveals the saha world to be the Buddha land, or the Land of Eternally Tranquil Light, and explains that the nature of a land is determined by the minds of its inhabitants.

lessening karmic retribution: This term, which literally means, "transforming the heavy and receiving it lightly," appears in the Nirvana Sutra. "Heavy" indicates negative karma accumulated over countless lifetimes in the past. As a benefit of protecting the correct teaching of Buddhism, we can experience relatively light karmic retribution in this lifetime, thereby expiating heavy karma that ordinarily would adversely affect us not only in this lifetime, but over many lifetimes to come.

major world system: Also, thousand-millionfold world. One of the world systems described in ancient Indian cosmology.

Mount Hiei: The site of Enryaku-ji, the main temple of the Tendai (T'ien-t'ai) school and leading center of Buddhist studies in Japan at the time. It is located northeast of Kyoto, which was then the imperial capital.

mutual possession of the Ten Worlds: The principle that each of the Ten Worlds possesses the potential for all ten within itself. "Mutual possession" means that life is not fixed in one or another of the Ten Worlds but can manifest any of the ten—from hell to Buddhahood—at any given moment. The important point of this principle is that all beings in any of the nine worlds possess the Buddha nature. This means that every person has the potential to manifest Buddhahood, while a Buddha also possesses the nine worlds and in this sense is not separate or different from ordinary people.

mystic truth that is originally inherent in all living beings: This refers to the Mystic Law, or Nam-myoho-renge-kyo, which is inherent in all life. By awakening to this Law, we can bring forth the great life state of Buddhahood. The mystic truth also indicates our inherent Buddhahood or Buddha nature.

prolonging one's life through faith: This is based on the passage in the "Life Span" chapter of the Lotus Sutra that reads: "We beg you to cure us and let us live out our lives!" (LSOC, 269). This is in the section that explains the parable of the outstanding physician, who gives "good medicine" to his children who have "drunk poison" (that is, succumbed to delusion), and who implore him to cure their illness. Through taking this good medicine (that is, embracing faith in the wonderful Law of the Lotus Sutra), they are cured and able to enjoy many more years of life.

purification of the six sense organs: Also, purification of the six senses. This refers to the six sense organs of eyes, ears, nose, tongue, body, and mind becoming pure, making it possible to apprehend all things correctly.

reducing the body to ashes and annihilating consciousness: A reference to the doctrine asserted by some Buddhist schools that one can attain nirvana, escaping from the sufferings of the endless cycle of birth and death, only upon extinguishing one's body and mind, which are deemed to be the sources of earthly desires, illusions, and sufferings.

seven kinds of treasures: Also, the seven treasures. Seven precious substances. The list differs among the Buddhist scriptures. In the Lotus Sutra, the seven are gold, silver, lapis lazuli, seashell, agate, pearl, and carnelian.

Sho-bo: Though originally a disciple of Nichiren Daishonin, he abandoned his faith in the Daishonin's teachings around the time of the Izu Exile in 1261 and eventually turned against his mentor. According to one account, he died around 1269.

six stages of practice: Also, six identities. Six stages in the practice of the Lotus Sutra formulated by the Great Teacher T'ien-t'ai in his *Great Concentration and Insight*. They are as follows: (1) the stage of being a Buddha in theory; (2) the stage of hearing the name and words of the truth; (3) the stage of perception and action; (4) the stage of resemblance to enlightenment; (5) the stage of progressive awakening; and (6) the stage of ultimate enlightenment, or the highest stage of practice.

ten demon daughters: The ten female protective deities who appear in "Dharani," the twenty-sixth chapter of the Lotus Sutra as the "daughters of rakshasa demons" or the "ten rakshasa daughters." They vow to the Buddha to guard and protect the sutra's votaries.

Ten Worlds: The realms of hell, hungry spirits, animals, *asuras*, human beings, heavenly beings, voice-hearers, cause-awakened ones, bodhisattvas, and Buddhas. They are also referred to as the ten life states of hell, hunger, animality, anger, humanity, heaven, learning, realization, bodhisattva, and Buddhahood.

three bodies: The three kinds of body a Buddha may possess. The three bodies are the Dharma body, the reward body, and the manifested body. The Dharma body is the fundamental truth, or Law, to which a Buddha is enlightened. The reward body is the wisdom to perceive the Law. And the manifested body is the compassionate actions the Buddha carries out to lead people to happiness.

threefold world: The world of unenlightened beings who transmigrate within the six paths (from hell through the realm of heavenly beings). The threefold world consists of, in ascending order, the world of desire, the world of form, and the world of formlessness. In a general sense, it refers to the saha world in which we dwell.

three obstacles and four devils: Various obstacles and hindrances to the practice of Buddhism. The three obstacles are (1) the obstacle of earthly desires, (2) the obstacle of karma, and (3) the obstacle of retribution. The four devils are (1) the hindrance of the five components, (2) the hindrance of earthly desires, (3) the hindrance of death, and (4) the hindrance of the devil king.

GLOSSARY

three thousand realms in a single moment of life: A philosophical system established by the Great Teacher T'ien-t'ai of China based on the Lotus Sutra. The "three thousand realms" indicates the varying aspects that life assumes at each moment. At each moment, life manifests one of the Ten Worlds. Each of these worlds possesses the potential for all ten within itself, thus making one hundred possible worlds. Each of these hundred worlds possesses the ten factors and operates within each of the three realms of existence, thus making three thousand realms. In other words, all phenomena are contained within a single moment of life, and a single moment of life permeates the three thousand realms of existence, or the entire phenomenal world.

true aspect of all phenomena: The ultimate truth or reality that permeates all phenomena and is in no way separate from them. Through the explanation of the ten factors, "Expedient Means," the second chapter of the Lotus Sutra, teaches that all people are inherently endowed with the potential to become Buddhas, and clarifies the truth that they can tap and manifest this potential.

true cause: Also, mystic principle of the true cause. Nichiren Buddhism directly expounds the true cause for enlightenment as Nam-myoho-renge-kyo, which is the Law of life and the universe. It teaches a way of Buddhist practice of always moving forward from this moment on based on this fundamental Law.

voluntarily assuming the appropriate karma: This refers to bodhisattvas who, though qualified to receive the pure rewards of Buddhist practice, relinquish them and make a vow to be reborn in an impure world in order to save living beings. They spread the Mystic Law while undergoing the same sufferings as those born in the evil world due to karma. This term derives from Miao-lo's interpretation of relevant passages in "The Teacher of the Law," the tenth chapter of the Lotus Sutra.

NOTES

Chapter 1: What Is True Happiness?

1. Anusorn, comp. and ed., *Ngeakhit khamkhom lea khamuayphon* [Thai proverbs and maxims] (Bangkok: Ruamsan, 1993), 207.
2. Translated from Japanese. Josei Toda, *Toda Josei zenshu* [The collected writings of Josei Toda], vol. 4 (Tokyo: Seikyo Shimbun-sha, 1989), 257–59. (Guidance given at the West Japan Joint Chapter General Meeting held in January 1955.)
3. See Robert Burns, "Epistle to Davie, A Brother Poet," *The Complete Poetical Works of Robert Burns, 1759–1796*, ed. James A. Mackay (Darvel, Scotland: Alloway Publishing, 1993), 87.
4. By Japanese author Fumiko Hayashi.
5. Walter Pater, *The Renaissance* (New York: Random House, 1873), 198.

Chapter 2: Developing a Life State of Happiness

1. John Milton, *Paradise Lost*, ed. Christopher Ricks (London: Penguin Books, 1989), 12.
2. This translation of *The Record of the Orally Transmitted Teachings* has been updated to reflect a revised English translation of the Lotus Sutra as it appears in *The Lotus Sutra and Its Opening and Closing Sutras*.
3. Translated from Japanese. Josei Toda, *Toda Josei zenshu* [The collected writings of Josei Toda], vol. 2 (Tokyo: Seikyo Shimbun-sha, 1982), 446–47.

Chapter 3: The Practice for Transforming Our State of Life

1. The word Gohonzon is formed in Japanese by appending the honorific prefix *go* to the word *honzon*, object of fundamental respect or devotion.
2. Translated from Japanese. Josei Toda, *Toda Josei zenshu* [The collected writings of Josei Toda], vol. 6 (Tokyo: Seikyo Shimbun-sha, 1992), 608. (Lecture on "The Real Aspect of the Gohonzon," March 6, 1956.)
3. The Japanese word for faith (*shinjin*) consists of two Chinese characters.

NOTES

4. The full quote from "The Object of Devotion for Observing the Mind" reads: "Showing profound compassion for those unable to comprehend the gem of the doctrine of three thousand realms in a single moment of life, the Buddha wrapped it within the five characters [of Myoho-renge-kyo], with which he then adorned the necks of the ignorant people of the latter age" (WND-1, 376). Myoho-renge-kyo is written with five Chinese characters, while Nam-myoho-renge-kyo is written with seven (*nam*, or *namu*, being comprised of two characters). The Daishonin often uses Myoho-renge-kyo synonymously with Nam-myoho-renge-kyo in his writings.
5. Translated from Japanese. Nichikan, *Kanjin no honzon-sho mondan* [Commentary on "The Object of Devotion for Observing the Mind"], in *Nichikan Shonin mondan-shu* [The commentaries of Nichikan Shonin] (Tokyo: Seikyo Shimbun-sha, 1980), 548.
6. In "The Real Aspect of the Gohonzon," Nichiren Daishonin writes: "Never seek this Gohonzon outside yourself. The Gohonzon exists only within the mortal flesh of us ordinary people who embrace the Lotus Sutra and chant Nam-myoho-renge-kyo. . . . To be endowed with the Ten Worlds means that all ten, without a single exception, exist in one world. Because of this it is called a mandala. Mandala is a Sanskrit word that is translated as 'perfectly endowed' or 'a cluster of blessings.' This Gohonzon also is found only in the two characters for faith. This is what the sutra means when it states that one can 'gain entrance through faith alone' [LSOC, 110]" (WND-1, 832).
7. Translated from Japanese. Nichikan, *Kanjin no honzon-sho mondan* [Commentary on "The Object of Devotion for Observing the Mind"], in *Nichikan Shonin mondan-shu* [The commentaries of Nichikan Shonin] (Tokyo: Seikyo Shimbun-sha, 1980), 472.
8. In "The Entity of the Mystic Law," the Daishonin writes: "This passage of commentary [in T'ien-t'ai's *Profound Meaning of the Lotus Sutra*] means that the supreme principle [that is the Mystic Law] was originally without a name. When the sage was observing the principle and assigning names to all things, he perceived that there is this wonderful single Law [*myoho*] that simultaneously possesses both cause and effect [*renge*], and he named it Myoho-renge. This single Law that is Myoho-renge encompasses within it all the phenomena comprising the Ten Worlds and the three thousand realms, and is lacking in none of them. Anyone who practices this Law will obtain both the cause and the effect of Buddhahood simultaneously" (WND-1, 421).

NOTES

9. In "How Those Initially Aspiring to the Way Can Attain Buddhahood through the Lotus Sutra," the Daishonin writes: "When we revere Myoho-renge-kyo inherent in our own life as the object of devotion, the Buddha nature within us is summoned forth and manifested by our chanting of Nam-myoho-renge-kyo. This is what is meant by 'Buddha'" (WND-1, 887).
10. Myoho-renge-kyo is written with five Chinese characters, while Nam-myoho-renge-kyo is written with seven (*nam*, or *namu*, being comprised of two characters). The Daishonin often uses Myoho-renge-kyo synonymously with Nam-myoho-renge-kyo in his writings.
11. Translated from Japanese. Josei Toda, *Toda Josei zenshu* [The collected writings of Josei Toda], vol. 5 (Tokyo: Seikyo Shimbun-sha, 1985), 298.
12. See note 10.
13. In "The Meaning of the Sacred Teachings of the Buddha's Lifetime," Nichiren Daishonin states: "Now in the teachings of the Lotus Sutra, people are certainly self-empowered, and yet they are not self-empowered. This is because one's own self, or life, at the same time possesses the nature of all living beings in the Ten Worlds. Therefore this self has from the beginning been in possession of one's own realm of Buddhahood and of the realms of Buddhahood possessed by all other living beings. Therefore when one attains Buddhahood one does not take on some new or 'other' Buddha identity.

    "Again, in the teachings of the Lotus Sutra, people are certainly other-empowered, and yet they are not other-empowered. The Buddhas, who are considered separate from us, are actually contained within our own selves, or the lives of us ordinary people. Those Buddhas manifest the realms of Buddhahood of all living beings in the same manner as we do" (WND-2, 62).
14. See note 10.
15. From a commentary by Fu Ta-shih.
16. In his lecture "A New Humanism for the Coming Century," delivered at the Rajiv Gandhi Foundation in 1997, SGI President Ikeda explained this concept of "cosmic humanism" as "a humanism based on an expansive cosmology, a worldview that sees the individual as being one with the entire universe, expanding and growing with it, and therefore meriting the most profound reverence."
17. Vapor condenses on a mirror placed outside at night. It was said that the mirror drew this water down from the moon.

NOTES

Chapter 4: "It Is the Heart That Is Important"

1. A quote from the Six Paramitas Sutra.
2. The phrase translated as "conducted himself fittingly" here suggests a self-congratulatory note of having done a good job and enhancing his reputation as a result.
3. T'ien-t'ai, *The Words and Phrases of the Lotus Sutra*.
4. The four major persecutions are: the Matsubagayatsu Persecution (1260), the Izu Exile (1261), the Komatsubara Persecution (1264), and the Tatsunokuchi Persecution and Sado Exile (1271).
5. Translated from Japanese. Tsunesaburo Makiguchi, *Makiguchi Tsunesaburo zenshu* [The collected writings of Tsunesaburo Makiguchi], vol. 10 (Tokyo: Daisanbunmei-sha, 1987), 282.
6. *Makiguchi Tsunesaburo zenshu*, vol. 10, 285.
7. The Daishonin writes: "All your virtuous acts will implant benefits and roots of goodness in your life. With this your conviction you should strive in faith" (WND-1, 4).
8. The Daishonin writes: "If votaries of the Lotus Sutra . . . practice as the sutra directs, then every one of them without exception will surely attain Buddhahood within his or her present lifetime. To cite an analogy, if one plants the fields in spring and summer, then, whether it be early or late, one is certain to reap a harvest within the year" (WND-2, 88).

Chapter 5: Transforming Suffering Into Joy

1. William Shakespeare, *As You Like It*, in *The Complete Works, Illustrated* (New York: Gramercy Books, 1975), 239. Act 2, scene 7.
2. Maxim Gorky, *The Lower Depths: Unabridged*, trans. Jennie Covan and ed. Julie Nord (Toronto: Dover Publications, 2000), 5.
3. Sir Walter Scott, *Rob Roy*, ed. Ian Duncan (New York: Oxford University Press, 2008), 211.
4. This famous parable about a woman named Kisa Gotami appears in the *Therigatha Atthakatha* [Commentary to the *Therigatha*].
5. Nichiren Daishonin writes: "Shakyamuni's practices and the virtues he consequently attained are all contained within the five characters of Myoho-renge-kyo. If we believe in these five characters, we will naturally be granted the same benefits as he was" (WND-1, 365).
6. Leo Tolstoy, *Tolstoy's Diaries*, ed. and trans. by R. F. Christian, vol. 1 (London: Athlone Press, 1985), 264. In the entry dated September 15, 1889.

NOTES

7. Nichiren Daishonin had been pardoned the previous year, in March 1274, and was residing at Minobu when he wrote this letter, "Winter Always Turns to Spring," dated May 1275.
8. "The blessings obtained by protecting the Law": This phrase from the Parinirvana Sutra is quoted in "Letter to the Brothers" (WND-1, 497).

Chapter 6: The Principle of Cherry, Plum, Peach, and Damson

1. Nichiren Daishonin says, "Each thing—the cherry, the plum, the peach, the damson—in its own entity, without undergoing any change, possesses the eternally endowed three bodies [of the Buddha]" (OTT, 200).
2. Translated from Japanese. Saneatsu Mushanokoji, *Mushanokoji Saneatsu zenshu* [The collected writings of Saneatsu Mushanokoji], vol. 11 (Tokyo: Shogakukan, 1989), 81.
3. Translated from Japanese. Josei Toda, "Mizukara no inochi ni ikiyo" [Taking responsibility for your own life], in *Toda Josei zenshu* [The collected writings of Josei Toda], vol. 1 (Tokyo: Seikyo Shimbun-sha, 1992), 183–84. (An editorial that appeared in the February 1956 issue of the *Daibyakurenge*.)
4. Translated from Japanese. Josei Toda, *Toda Josei zenshu*, [The collected writings of Josei Toda], vol. 4 (Tokyo: Seikyo Shimbun-sha, 1989), 541–43. (A speech delivered at a young men's division leaders meeting in June 1957.)
5. Percy Bysshe Shelley, "Ode to the West Wind," *Shelley—Selected Poetry*, selected by Isabel Quigly (London: Penguin Books, 1956), 162.
6. "Human Education for World Citizenship" (address to the education division of the Soka Gakkai in Osaka, October 22, 1991).

Chapter 7: Happiness for Both Ourselves and Others

1. Translated from Japanese. Josei Toda, *Toda Josei zenshu* [The collected writings of Josei Toda], vol. 4 (Tokyo: Seikyo Shimbun-sha, 1984), 378.
2. Translated from Japanese. *Agonbu* [The Chinese versions of the Agamas], in *Kokuyaku issaikyo* [The Japanese translation of the complete Chinese Buddhist canon], ed. Shin'yu Iwano, vols. 9–10 (Tokyo: Daito Shuppansha, 1969), 152. (Ekottarāgama 38.5.)
3. *Agonbu* in *Kokuyaku issaikyo*, 152.
4. Translated from Japanese. Tatsuo Morimoto, *Ganji to Tagoru* [Gandhi and Tagore] (Tokyo: Daisanbunmei-sha, 1995), 116–17.
5. *Ganji to Tagoru*, 117.

NOTES

Chapter 8: Facing Illness

1. Translated from German. C. Hilty, *Kranke Seelen* [Sick souls] (Leipzig: J. C. Hinrichs'sche Buchhandlung, 1907), 71.
2. Nichiren Daishonin writes: "You also are a practitioner of the Lotus Sutra, and your faith is like the waxing moon or the rising tide. Be deeply convinced, then, that your illness cannot possibly persist, and that your life cannot fail to be extended! Take care of yourself, and do not burden your mind with grief" (WND-1, 656).
3. The Daishonin writes: "Life is the most precious of all treasures. Even one extra day of life is worth more than ten million *ryo* of gold. . . . So you must hasten to accumulate the treasure of faith and quickly conquer your illness" (WND-1, 955). A *ryo* was a unit of weight in ancient Japan. One *ryo* was equivalent to about 37.5 grams (about 1.25 ounces), though the exact weight differed according to the historical period.
4. The Daishonin writes: "And could not this illness of your husband's be the Buddha's design, because the Vimalakirti and Nirvana sutras both teach that sick people will surely attain Buddhahood? Illness gives rise to the resolve to attain the way" (WND-1, 937).
5. The seated meditation referred to here is an ancient Indian practice for ordering the mind and body, later adopted by Buddhism. It involves sitting with correct posture, closing one's eyes, and thinking deeply. The Great Teacher T'ien-t'ai held that this practice, when improperly done or carried to an extreme, could cause illness.

Chapter 9: Creating a Brilliant Final Chapter in Life

1. Henry Wadsworth Longfellow, "Morituri Salutamus," in *The Poetical Works of Henry Wadsworth Longfellow*, vol. 3 (New York: AMS Press, 1966), 196.
2. Margaret England Armbrester, *Samuel Ullman and "Youth": The Life, the Legacy* (Tuscaloosa, AL: University of Alabama Press, 1993), 113.
3. Victor Hugo, *Les Misérables*, trans. Julie Rose (London: Random House, 2008), 1094.
4. I. B. Horner, trans., *Discourse on the Auspicious (Bhaddekarattasutta)*, in *The Collection of the Middle Length Sayings (Majjhima-nikaya)*, vol. 3 (Oxford: Pali Text Society, 1993), 233.
5. Andre Malraux, *Fallen Oaks: Conversations with De Gaulle*, trans. Irene Clephane (London: Hamish Hamilton, 1972), 91.
6. See Immanuel Kant, *Critique of Judgment*, trans. Werner S. Pluhar (Indianapolis, IN: Hackett Publishing, 1987), 203.

NOTES

7. Norman Cousins, *Anatomy of an Illness as Perceived by the Patient: Reflections on Healing and Regeneration* (New York: W. W. Norton, 1979), 89.
8. *The Dhammapada: Sayings of the Buddha*, trans. Thomas Cleary (New York: Bantam Books, 1995), 40.
9. Cited in the writing "*Shaka ichidai goji keizu*" [Outline of the five periods of the Shakyamuni's lifetime teachings]; not translated in WND, vols. 1 or 2.
10. When Shakyamuni declares in the "Emerging from the Earth" chapter of the Lotus Sutra that the vast multitudes of the Bodhisattvas of the Earth who have emerged are his original disciples, bodhisattva Maitreya expresses doubt, saying that it is as though a young man of twenty-five were to point to an old man of one hundred and say, "This is my son!" (LSOC, 261).
11. See F. L. Woodward, trans., "The Book of Threes," in *The Book of the Gradual Sayings (Anguttara-Nikaya) or More-Numbered Suttas*, vol. 1 (Oxford: Pali Text Society, 1995), 129–30.
12. Translated from Japanese. Hajime Nakamura, *Gotama Budda I* [Gautama Buddha Vol. I] (Tokyo: Shunju-sha, 1992), 156.
13. See Xuanzang, *The Great Tang Dynasty Record of the Western Regions*, trans. Li Rongxi, (Berkeley, CA: Numata Center for Buddhist Translation and Research, 1996).
14. Lynn McDonald, *Florence Nightingale: The Nightingale School* (Ontario, Canada: Wilfrid Laurier University Press, 2009), 761–62. From a speech delivered at an SGI- USA Youth Training Session, Malibu Training Center, California, February 20, 1990.
15. Zachary Cope, *Florence Nightingale and the Doctors* (Philadelphia: J. B. Lippincott, 1958), 37.
16. Cecil Woodham-Smith, *Florence Nightingale* (London: Constable, 1951), 387.
17. Woodham-Smith, *Florence Nightingale*, 300.
18. Woodham-Smith, *Florence Nightingale*, 589.
19. See Sutra of Collected Birth Stories concerning the Practice of the Six Paramitas and Nagarjuna's *Treatise on the Great Perfection of Wisdom*.
20. Maha Parinibbana Suttanta [the Pali Nirvana Sutra], in *Dialogues of the Buddha*, trans. T. W. and C. A. F. Rhys Davids, part 2 (Oxford: Pali Text Society, 1995), 149–69.
21. Cecil Woodham-Smith, *Florence Nightingale*, 585–86.
22. Edward Cook, *The Life of Florence Nightingale*, vol. 2 (London: Macmillan, 1913), 430.
23. Cecil Woodham-Smith, *Florence Nightingale*, 591.

NOTES

Chapter 10: Joy in Both Life and Death

1. In a portion of the speech not included in this excerpt, President Ikeda cited the passage from Nichiren Daishonin's writing "On the Large Carriages Drawn by White Oxen": "These large carriages drawn by white oxen [the great white ox carts] are able to fly at will through the sky of the essential nature of phenomena [Dharma nature, or enlightenment]. Those persons who come after me will ride in these carriages and journey to [the pure land of] Eagle Peak. And I, Nichiren, riding in the same kind of carriage, will come out to greet them" (WND-2, 976).
2. In the Lotus Sutra, Shakyamuni declares that his life as a Buddha is eternal, but as a means to help living beings arouse a seeking spirit, he appears to enter nirvana, or extinction.
3. In *The Record of the Orally Transmitted Teachings*, Nichiren Daishonin says, "We may also say that nonexistence (*mu*) and existence (*u*), birth and death, ebbing and flowing, existing in this world and entering extinction, are all, every one of them, actions of the eternally abiding inherent nature" (OTT, 127–28).
4. Translated from Japanese. Leo Tolstoy, *Torusutoi zenshu* [The collected works of Tolstoy], vol. 21 (Tokyo: Iwanami Shoten, 1931), 408.
5. Quoted material from *The Lotus Sutra and Its Opening and Closing Sutras*, trans. Burton Watson, 105.
6. Nichiren Daishonin writes: "You lost your father at a very early age, and hence were deprived of his instruction and guidance. When I think of what this must have meant for you, I cannot restrain my tears" (WND-2, 500).
7. See note 10 in Chapter 3.
8. Written to the lay nun Ueno, the mother of Nanjo Tokimitsu, upon the sudden death of Tokimitsu's youngest brother Shichiro Goro.
9. Translated from Japanese. Josei Toda, *Toda Josei zenshu* [The collected writings of Josei Toda], vol. 2 (Tokyo: Seikyo Shimbun-sha, 1982), 174.
10. Rhys Davids, trans., *The Book of the Kindred Sayings (Sanyutta-Nikāya) or Grouped Suttas*, Part 5 (Oxford: Pali Text Society, 1994), 321.
11. Le Clos-Lucé, formerly the castle of Cloux, near Amboise, France; it is now a Leonardo da Vinci museum.
12. The eight paths lead in eight directions, that is, toward the eight points of the compass.
13. Charles Willeman, trans., *The Scriptural Text: Verses of the Doctrine, with Parables* (Berkeley, CA: Numata Center for Buddhist Translation and Research, 1999), 116.

INDEX

A

ability, 3, 199, 222; to lead others, 304
Abutsu-bo, 78, 300
academic credentials, 151–52
action, 79, 232, 239; based on prayer, 233; for others, 230; source of benefit and, 80; treasuring every, 238
actual proof, of benefit, 25, 274–75; illness as opportunity to demonstrate, 251
advancement, xvi–xvii, 5, 14, 33–34, 39, 49, 114, 125, 143, 170, 175, 183, 196, 202, 205, 248, 299, 318, 337, 346; turning adversity into the energy for, 27, 170–71, 182
adversity, facing, 31; overcoming, 42
alert, staying, 303
Amazon River, 213
American Astronomical Society, 344
Aniruddha, 231–32
apology, prayers of, 102
appreciation, 102, 137, 139, 207, 230, 237–38; chanting before the Gohonzon and, 130; practice of Buddhism and, 138
arrogance, 136–37, 230, 305, 307; confronting, 151; preventing, 119
astronomy, 328
Athayde, Austregésilo de, 239
attaining Buddhahood in one's present form, 91–92, 329
attitude, 16, 32, 136–40, 154–55, 157, 272, 284, 294; in chanting before the Gohonzon, 102
attributes, displaying inherent dignified, 64

B

"before long this person will proceed to the place of enlightenment," "place of enlightenment" in, 38; "this person" in, 37
behavior, 62, 89, 102, 181
benefit, 59, 62, 67, 79–80, 100, 138, 233, 277, 281, 287, 342, 355; chanting Nam-myoho-renge-kyo and, 129–30; kinds of, 128–29
"The Benefits of Responding with Joy" chapter (Lotus Sutra), 17–18
"Benefits of the Teacher of the Law" chapter (Lotus Sutra), 18, 115; purification of six sense organs in the, 116
Bharat [India] Soka Gakkai members, 217
birth and death, metaphor of waves on the ocean and, 84
bodhisattva, spirit of, xvi, 22, 42, 71, 84, 109, 229–30, 239–42, 253, 270, 301–2, 348
Boston, 303
Britain, 313
Brzezinski, Zbigniew, 332
Buddha, 95
Buddha nature, 51, 59, 95, 240–41; metaphor for revealing people's, 73, 96

INDEX

Buddhahood, life state of, xii, 7, 12, 14, 16–17, 29, 34, 38, 40–50, 53, 55, 61, 66–67, 71, 75, 78, 80, 84–85, 89–92, 95, 99, 104, 109, 114, 125, 133, 135, 137, 144–47, 153, 155, 159–60, 175, 183–85, 189–90, 192–94, 207, 228, 233, 247, 251, 257, 285, 289, 299–301, 313–14, 318, 327, 334, 336, 338, 341–44, 347–49, 351; basic life tendency and, 45–46; example of the power of, 265–66; illness as impetus for achieving life state of, 256

Buddhism, xii, 3, 5, 9, 18–19, 24–25, 32, 35–36, 40–42, 44, 47, 53, 59–62, 65–67, 83, 88, 91, 99, 108, 113, 118, 121, 130, 138, 144, 146, 148, 152, 157, 168, 170, 172–73, 175, 179, 183, 190, 193, 197, 207, 212, 218, 224, 227, 237, 242, 247, 253, 268, 283–85, 287, 290, 293, 295–96, 324, 328, 334, 338, 346; analogy of mirrors in, 74–77, 80–81, 116; expressing value of diversity, 219–20, 222; eternity of life and, 323–24; exemplifying the greatness of, 163; final moments of the practice of, 350–51; "freely choosing where one will be born" and, 328; instantly attaining the life state of Buddhahood and, 92–93; "internal way" in, 84–85; leadership and, xiii–xiv; leading value creating lives and, 170–71; life state of Buddhahood and, 43; Lotus Sutra and, 104; new vision of universal religion and, 97–98; object of devotion in, 54–55, 58; open to all, 89–90, 93, 100, 218; practice of, 2–7, 13–14, 18, 23, 30, 34, 39, 41, 58, 79–80, 89, 99, 116, 123, 128–29, 131, 140, 142–43, 160, 162, 172, 184, 186, 192, 204, 217, 231, 240, 255, 259, 289, 300, 316, 318–19, 333, 337, 349, 353; practitioners of, 6, 8, 21–22, 33–34, 37, 57, 104, 154, 157, 177, 191, 232, 312; prayer in, 120–21, 126; promoting, 7, 93, 138, 159, 232, 245, 279–80, 291, 312, 329; reason and, 120, 127; rejection of supernatural power in, 66; sufferings and, 170–71; unseen virtue brings about visible reward in, 77; victory and, 27; voluntarily assuming the appropriate karma example in, 269–70

Burns, Robert, on happiness, 11

C

cause and effect, Buddhist law of, 4, 76–77, 159, 173, 175, 221, 301, 324, 348

Ceremony in the Air, 73

challenge, spirit of, xiii, 6, 101, 131, 140, 168, 192, 210, 213, 215, 233, 248, 284, 324

champions of life, living as, 185, 236

changing poison into medicine, 143, 172–73, 176, 183, 251, 299

Chaplin, Charlie, 31

character, building, 24, 61, 144–45, 153, 157, 161–62, 171, 187, 210, 217, 222, 276

Chikuma River, Nagano, 213

China, 281

circumstances, transforming entire, 355

civilization, decline of, 322

"cluster of blessings," cause for, 67

coexistence, 222, 234

Columbia University Teachers College, xii

commitment, 137; living with, 311

compassion, xii, 2–3, 22, 29, 48, 56, 64, 89, 102, 106, 108, 113, 137,

374

INDEX

144, 151, 162, 195–96, 217, 227, 229, 253–55, 256, 302, 355; expression of, 258–59; two aspects of, 239; wisdom of, 175
community, building better relations with the, xiii, 119, 139, 162, 181, 199, 280–81, 301
confidence, xii, 7, 14, 133, 139, 142, 186, 206, 212, 316; lacking in, 206; living with, 103, 106, 214
conformism, 211
consistency from beginning to end, 19
conviction, xiv, 14, 22–23, 50, 80, 122, 125, 127, 142, 167, 186, 188–90, 196, 205–6, 213, 240, 255, 299, 348; happiness and, 204; living with, 192
cooperation, 222, 287
correct object of devotion [the Gohonzon of Nam-myoho-renge-kyo], 41–42. *See also* Gohonzon
correct teaching, prayer and, 118
courage, 1, 24, 29, 64, 106, 108, 113, 124, 143–44, 162, 175, 213, 232, 251, 255, 267, 269, 274, 306, 323, 340; convictions and, 209
cowardice, 149, 349
Cox, Harvey, 327
criticism, defeating, 185
culture, 222; humanistic, 224

D

Daibyakurenge, xv
daimoku (Nam-myoho-renge-kyo), 254; chanting, 21–22, 100, 124–25, 130, 159, 252, 256, 269; language of, 132; to move the universe, 124–25
Darshan Samiti, 140
death, awareness of, 321; Buddhist perspective of, 57, 157, 293, 318, 320–24, 327, 331–34; encouragement to family members encountering unexpected, 346–48, 351–52;

hindrance of, 346–47; negative perception of, 331–32; valuing the present moment and, 322
defeat, never give into, 29, 31, 119, 161–62, 185, 214, 260, 266, 272, 276
de Gaulle, Charles, on hope, 295
delusion, 83; vanquishing, 50, 84, 118, 144–45
dependent origination, 221
desires, accomplishing, 9, 123–24
destiny, architect of one's, 165–66
determination, 88, 124, 155, 167, 183, 186, 212, 216, 251, 258–60, 267, 273–74; to activate the protective functions of the universe, 96; for change, 154; "heart of a lion king" like, 259; illness gives rise to new, 250, 256; influence of, 78–80; renewed sense of, 45, 106, 145; to win, 102
Devadatta, 55
devil of illness, vanquishing the, 31, 251, 272–75
devilish functions, 51; rebuking the, 266
differences, respecting, 218, 222
dignity, 177, 310; example of regaining a sense of, 308–9
direction, finding your life's, 213
disciple, path of, 147, 190, 289
discussion, having an open, 217
Discussions on Youth, 212
dishonesty, 149
"Distinctions in Benefits" chapter (Lotus Sutra), 17–18
diversity, appreciation for, 220
doubt, succumbing to, 175–76
dynamic transformations, 155

E

Eagle Peak, 132, 318, 339, 344
Earth, 344
earthly desires into enlightenment, 47, 142, 168, 170, 172;

375

INDEX

transforming the energy of, 16, 162
East-West Center, Hawaii, 220
education, humanistic, 222–23, 242
effort, 47, 143, 156, 158, 213, 217, 238, 289, 336; in Buddhism, 266; importance of encouragement and, 211
embracing the Gohonzon is in itself observing one's mind, 92
empathy, feeling, 48, 222, 308–10, 345, empowerment, 50–51, 74–75, 145, 237; life state of Buddhahood and, 337
encouragement, importance of, xii–xiv, xvi–xvii, 28, 106, 137, 141, 167, 180, 253, 256, 258–59, 269, 275, 280, 283, 298, 308, 318, 346; offering documentary proof relevant to situations and, 167
"Encouragements of the Bodhisattva Universal Worthy" chapter (Lotus Sutra), 37
energy, 142, 279, 282–83, 287
"enjoy themselves at ease," 5–6
equality, spirit of, xiv, 222, 309
eternity of life, 61, 110, 168–69, 176, 272, 329, 338, 345, 348–49; hardships from the perspective of, 194; wisdom based on, 169
evil, defeating, 144, 189
"Expedient Means" chapter (Lotus Sutra), 107; attaining the life state of Buddhahood in the, 92; "true aspect of all phenomena" in the, 108
experiences, sharing, 275–76
"experiencing the boundless joy of the Law," 181
expertise, gaining a degree of, 125

F

faith for overcoming hardships, 194–95
family members, chanting Nam-myoho-renge-kyo for the deceased, 341–42; encouragement to, of the deceased, 341–43; reunited with the deceased, 343–45, 352; transforming the destiny of one's, 140
Faust (Goethe), 291
fear, banishing, 106, 109
fighting spirit, 140, 177, 259, 268, 276
five components, 167
Flower Garland Sutra, 167
fostering, capable individuals, xiii, 49, 222
four noble truths, 323
four powers, in Buddhism, 60, 119
four universal sufferings, 5, 65, 83, 161, 176, 247, 258, 297, 305–7, 334; overcoming, 25–27, 84–85, 142, 250, 257–58, 261, 283, 293, 310, 315, 316–19, 338, 353; transience of, 330
four virtues, of life state of Buddhahood, 27, 56, 71, 106, 161, 250, 258, 261, 293, 313, 340, 351
freedom, 106, 124–25; chanting Nam-myoho-renge-kyo and, 16; life state of inner, 16–19
friendship, 186, 282; fostering, 236
fulfillment, 21–22, 114, 125, 133, 157–58, 193, 220, 259–60, 265, 280, 284–86, 319, 354
fusion of reality and wisdom, 42, 70
future, opening a hopeful, 225
future division members, 126–31; hopes for the, 142

G

galaxies, in the universe, 344
Galbraith, John Kenneth, 303
Gandhi, Mahatma, 140–41; government and, 242; politics and, 242; on religion, 242
Gandhi Smriti, 140
global citizenship, 223–24

INDEX

goal, 49, 142, 166, 171, 181, 207, 216, 295, 303; all-out efforts toward the, 215–16
Goethe, Johann Wolfgang von, 291
Gohonzon, 2, 21, 29, 53, 59, 61–62, 66, 73, 75, 99, 102, 111, 113, 116, 125, 132, 155, 185, 199, 269; benefits all people, 62, 66; chanting before the, 59, 73–74, 78–79, 120, 131–33, 304; honesty before the, 122–23; importance of the, 125–26; layout of the, 54, 63–65, 70–72; mirror analogy of the, 78; upholding the, 60–61, 67, 79, 92, 129, 135, 162, 175, 205–6, 252, 264; workings of the, 55–57. *See also* Buddhahood; Nam-myoho-renge-kyo
gongyo (recitation portions of the Lotus Sutra), 21, 47, 55, 73, 79, 107, 109, 111, 113, 129–30, 277–78, 303–4, 344; language of, 132; "spiritual workout" and, 130
good circumstances, creating, 22, 36, 62, 79–80, 114, 128, 137–38, 142, 171–72, 183, 193, 231–33, 237–38, 242, 257, 277, 281, 283, 286, 336, 349, 355
goodness, spirit of human, 64, 350
Gorky, Maksim, 166
government, humanistic, 242
gratitude, xv, 137, 139, 285
greater self, 57, 161–62, 169
"greatest of all joys," 333
grief, overcoming, 346
growth, 120, 143, 171; obstruction to, 201; renewed sense of, 64–65, 183, 186, 214, 251, 257
guidance, 291

H

happiness, xiii, 1–5, 8, 10–14, 18–19, 31–32, 37, 39, 50–51, 56–57, 59, 62, 80, 84, 89, 94, 96, 101, 103, 106–7, 110, 114, 123, 128, 132–33, 135, 142, 154–55, 157, 160–63, 169, 177, 180–81, 187, 193, 198–99, 227, 231–32, 255, 265, 282, 286, 292, 304, 318–19, 334, 340, 348; building inner, 21–25, 158, 181, 315, 336–37; determination and, 10; effort and, 11; inner life state and, 35–36; life state of eternal, 204–5, 353; Mystic Law and, 32; obstruction to, 80, 136, 200–201, 219, 265; prayer and, 126; renewed sense of, 3, 9, 37–39, 47, 61, 139–40, 142–43, 159, 165, 168, 170, 183, 250, 256–57; tailwind to, 160; victory and, 250
happiness of oneself and others, 3, 90, 228–29, 237–39, 286, 310
happiness of others, 22, 24, 48, 89, 169, 227, 231; action for the, 159, 217, 242, 280, 313–14; Buddhist model for benefiting the, 245, 259; closing years as opportunity to promote the, 300; working for the, 211, 235, 239, 241, 243–44, 261, 265, 279, 281, 350
hardships, encountering, 185, 194–95; leading fulfilling lives and, 10; overcoming, xiii, 6, 27–28, 31, 193–95; practice of Buddhism and, 183
harmony, 218, 222
Harvard Divinity School's Department of Applied Theology, 327
Harvard University ["Mahayana Buddhism and Twenty-First-Century Civilization" in September 1993] lecture at the, 303, 305, 315, 327
health, 260–61, 250, 277–78, 304; illness as opportunity to gain, 252

INDEX

hearts of others, opening the, xii, 13, 119, 167
hell, life state of, 55; transforming the life state of, 56, 341
helplessness, vanquishing, 105
Heraclitus, state of flux and, 330
high school division member, 343–46
high school students, hopes for the, 212–16
Hilty, Carl, on illness, 254
Himalayas, 213
Hinayana Buddhist teachings, 104
hope, 1, 3, 23, 28, 31, 39, 45, 49, 127, 140, 142, 155, 160, 165, 167, 187, 218–19, 252, 259, 265, 271, 275–76, 281, 288, 296, 299, 340, 348; creating, 141, 295; living with, 34
Hubble Space Telescope, 344
Hugo, Victor, 292; on death, 26
human beings, greatness of, 157
human life, transforming, 53; value of, 309–10
human revolution, xiii, 45, 140, 201–2, 217, 283; example of, 269–71; happiness and, 348–49; opportunity for, 247, 254
Human Revolution, The, 50
human rights, 219
humanism, xiv, 61, 84; of the Lotus Sutra, 106–7; promoting, 302
humankind, happiness of, 63, 82, 85, 98, 108; transforming the destiny of, 89, 237–38
humor, 140–41, 295–96

I

ideals, 158, 288
ignorance, 81; defeating, 90, 96, 145
Ikegami brothers, 193
illness, 26, 248, 258, 262–64; Buddhist view of, 247–48; encouragement in battling, 259, 272–75; experience of, 254–55, 273; facing, 30, 56, 159, 195, 247, 249, 251, 254, 265, 272, 274, 292, 298, 316–17; happiness in spite of, 253–54; health and, 266; overcoming, 205, 247–54, 257, 259–60, 262, 264, 266, 271–76, 317; susceptibility to, 279; understanding of life and, 249, 253, 256; wisdom to deal with, 248–49
illuminating and manifesting one's true nature, 217
illusion, vanquishing, 96
impasse, breaking through, 59, 90, 101, 114, 183
impatience, transforming into action, 49
impediment, practices as, 99
impulses, winning over negative, 200–202
India, 141; Buddhism in ancient, 307
individual, valuing the, 50, 84–85, 112–13, 179, 235
individuality, 72, 209–11, 219; affirming one's, 218
ingenuity, 74
injustice, 144, 189
inner strength, 10, 128, 139, 143, 181, 202, 214, 245
inner transformation, 32, 106, 119, 135, 204; chanting Nam-myoho-renge-kyo and, 145; happiness based on, 333
inspiration, 23, 179, 275–76, 299
interactions, 309–10
Ishikari River, Hokkaido, 213
Ishizaki, Isamu, 348; death of, 348
"it is the heart that is important," 11, 31–32, 62, 136–39, 141, 143–44, 156–58

J

Japan, conformism in, 209–11
Joren-bo, 342
joy, xii, xv, 2–3, 18, 25, 33, 45, 49, 56, 101, 132–33, 137–38, 144, 161–62, 178, 196, 198, 228, 232, 255, 314, 350–51, 355;

INDEX

living with, 2–3, 23, 32–34, 46, 103, 125, 162, 177–79, 181, 241, 260, 289, 324; renewed sense of, 165, 324
junior high students, 208; hopes for the, 210–11

K

Kansai, 262
Kansai doctors division, 277
Kant, Immanuel, 291, 295
karma, 26, 137, 346; redefining the concept of, 193; transforming, 4, 16–17, 73, 127, 163, 193–94, 202, 252, 257, 264, 268; workings of, 61, 140, 263–64, 268, 348
"karmic reward from the past," 35
knowledge, wisdom compared to, 248
Ko, lay priest of, 300
Ko, lay nun of, 300
kosen-rufu, 33, 110, 136, 139, 142, 145, 159, 191, 194–96, 254, 296, 298, 328, 337, 342, 344; activities for, 14, 16, 79, 306; commitment to, 49, 109, 143, 152, 157–58, 178, 185, 191, 202, 257, 266, 290, 314, 317, 327, 349; living in the realm of, 30; promoting, 183; in rhythm with, 101; vow for, 260–61; working for, 237, 243, 265, 286, 347–48; worldwide, xv
Kübler-Ross, Elisabeth, 332
Kyoto, 148
Kyushu, 291

L

Land of Eternally Tranquil Light, 132, 350; transforming into, 4, 36–38
Latter Day of the Law, xvii, 22, 62, 68, 87, 90, 108
laughter, 295

leaders, 24, 27, 91, 99, 143, 179; arrogance in, 151
Leonardo da Vinci, on life of fulfillment, 350
lesser self, purifying the, 161
lessening karmic retribution, 193, 299, 346–47; examples of, 194
life, Buddhist way of, xi, 2, 7–8, 13, 16, 19–20, 22, 25, 40, 49, 78, 88–89, 105–6, 110–11, 116, 118, 128, 145, 168, 177–79, 181–82, 191–93, 204, 206, 217–18, 254, 260, 285–86, 300, 306, 313, 335, 346; death as expedient means for, 324; living out, 160, 189, 268; unlocking the treasures within, 5; winning in, 38–39, 181–82, 237
life and death, Buddhist perspective on, 293, 325–26, 336–37; joy in both, 313, 327, 336–38; law of, 267
life force, 5–6, 32, 57–58, 61, 64, 101, 109–11, 113–14, 157, 172, 192, 214, 230, 245, 248, 251, 255, 257, 264, 274, 292, 301, 304, 316; happiness and, 204; living with strong, 296
"Life Span" chapter (Lotus Sutra), 17–18, 48, 86–87, 105, 107, 262, 301, 325, 344; "attainment of Buddhahood in the remote past" in the, 108; eternity of life in the, 109; teaching of hope and joy of the, 109–10; three mystic principles of the, 69
life state, 2, 8–9, 13, 30, 34–35, 62, 76–77, 120, 144, 154, 162, 177, 292; determination and, 183; obstacles as springboard for expansive, 57, 60; prosperity of society and, 36; renewed sense of, 250, 255, 320; transforming one's inner, 35–36, 43, 45, 80, 116, 128, 132, 138, 142–43, 153, 163, 169, 193, 230, 248, 257

379

INDEX

living, healthy, 101, 106, 112, 181, 245, 248, 254, 257, 259–62, 266–67, 277–82, 303; to the fullest, 243, 290, 303, 306, 320
living beings, value of, 87, 96
longevity, 260–61, 272, 278, 301; influence on, 294–97
Longfellow, Henry Wadsworth, on older adults, 288
Lotus Sutra, xii, xvi, 5, 18, 58, 65, 74, 85–86, 88, 100, 104, 118, 138, 186, 229, 239, 252, 292, 301, 318, 325, 333–34, 341, 344, 351; Ceremony in the Air of the, 63–64, 68–70, 73; "entering nirvana as an expedient means" in the, 324; practice of the, 240; practitioners of the, 117–18, 335–36; spirit of the, 289; superiority of the, 310; three thousand realms in a single moment of life of the, 95, 153, 155; trust in the, 122–23; view of the universe and the, 328; wisdom of the, 104–8

M

Mahanama (lay believer), 347
Mahayana Buddhist teachings, 83–84, 104, 333; provisional, 104
Makiguchi, Tsunesaburo, xii, xvi, 7–8, 204, 223; death of, 348; humanitarian competition championed by, 225; seeking spirit of, 291–92; life state of, 154; Soka Kyoiku Gakkai (Value-Creating Education Society; forerunner of the Soka Gakkai) of, 291
Many Treasures Buddha, in the Lotus Sutra, 55, 63, 69–71, 122
Many Treasures Group, members of the, 292, 297; as examples for older adults, 299

May 3, Soka Gakkai Mother's Day, 15
Maya Sutra, 334
medical science, 264
members, 191, 201; benefit and, 60; chanting for the, 254; commitment to the, 191; happiness and, 60; as inspiration to others, 269; as manifestation of the Mystic Law, 29–30; respecting the, 52, 231; supporting the, 137, 231; victory for the, 191
memory, left at the close of life, 243, 286
men's division, 262–64
mentor, in Buddhism, 146–47; attaining the life state of Buddhahood and, 147; peace proposal of the, 222; resolve of the, 195–96; seeking the, xi–xii, xiv, 147–48
mentor-disciple relationship, xv
Miao-lo, 68
Milton, John, on the human mind, 35
mission, 38, 52, 57, 125, 156, 191, 197–99, 212, 213–15, 219, 242, 253, 261, 288, 296, 349; place of, 158
Moscow, 243
motion, power of, 279–80
Mount Aso, Kyushu, 213
Mount Hiei, 148
Mount Minobu, 300
Mount Zao, 199
mutual possession of the Ten Worlds, 40–41, 44, 48, 63–65, 95, 204
"My life is none other than Nam-myoho-renge-kyo!" spirit (Toda), 97
myo [of *myoho* or Mystic Law], 4, 72–73, 224, 251
Myoichi, lay nun, 187, 190
Mystic Law, xii, 6, 34, 39, 50, 65, 69, 84–87, 92, 94, 96, 108, 113, 124, 147, 162, 181, 192, 199,

380

INDEX

213, 250, 280, 297–98, 319, 342, 347–50, 352; blessings of the, 71–72, 114, 193–94, 293; bonds based on the, 339–40; chanting the, 135, 198, 283; devotion to the, 3–4, 8, 12, 16–17, 19, 25–27, 29–30, 33–34, 56, 88, 116, 131, 142, 161, 165, 193, 228, 251–53, 255, 258, 262, 292, 313, 317, 338, 355; expressions of the, 54–55, 64, 108–9; manifesting the inherent, 126, 145; as masters of the mind, 146; practitioners of the, 116, 342, 347; promoting the, xvi–xvii, 33, 75, 109, 124, 138, 152, 169, 244, 261; in rhythm with the, 18, 101, 120, 185; universality of the, 95; vitality and, 4; workings of the, 125

N

Nagarjuna, 68
nam, 87
Nam-myoho-renge-kyo, 69–70, 86–87, 93, 135, 145, 155, 175; awareness to the Law of, 91; as the chanting, xii, xiv, 3, 5–6, 12, 17–18, 32, 37–38, 47, 50, 53, 55–56, 58, 60, 63, 73, 75, 82, 87–93, 95–98, 99, 100–103, 108–9, 111, 113–16, 118, 122–24, 127–29, 143, 163, 168, 170–71, 181, 185, 201–2, 207–8, 213–14, 217–18, 233, 243, 251–52, 255, 257, 259–60, 262, 265, 269, 272–73, 277–78, 286, 294, 298, 303–4, 317, 328, 341, 352; entirety of the Lotus Sutra within, 99–100; expression of, 114; our lives as entities of, 298; on joy, 227–28; as object of devotion, 71, 95, 108; promoting, 18, 87, 151, 243; in rhythm with, 36, 100, 326; two aspects of, 70. *See also* prayer

Nanjo Hyoe Shichiro, 338
Nanjo Shichiro Goro, 351
Nanjo Tokimitsu, 266, 338–39, 351
Nara (city), 212–13
negative influences, 263–64; defeating, 264, 267
new age, opening a, 248
New Human Revolution, The, 50, 101, 200, 262, 346
Nichigen-nyo, 296
Nichikan Shonin, *Commentary on "The Object of Devotion for Observing the Mind,"* 60, 78; on Gohonzon, 60
Nichiren Daishonin, xii–xiii, xvi, 2, 4–5, 16-18, 27, 32, 34, 40, 42, 49, 65, 71–72, 87–88, 92, 95, 103–5, 113, 116, 118, 122–23, 125, 129, 132, 155, 159–61, 181, 193, 200, 204, 215, 233, 240, 251, 258, 284, 289, 293, 298, 300, 310, 313, 325, 331, 337, 339, 341, 343–44, 346, 352; allegory by, 99–100; always being with, 103; "On Attaining Buddhahood in This Lifetime," 75, 82, 85–86, 93, 114; on attitude, 11–12, 62, 137–38, 143–44; as Bodhisattva Superior Practices, 69; as Buddha of the Latter Day of the Law, 54–55, 89, 103, 194; on chanting Nam-myoho-renge-kyo, 97, 133; compassion of, 151, 190, 266–67; conviction of, 266–67; on creating good circumstances, 296; on death, 321; on difficulties, 182; disciples betraying, 188; empathy of, 187–90; exemplify the path to kosen-rufu, 151; "The Entity of the Mystic Law," 86; expression to the Law by, 86–89; on four universal sufferings, 258; "On the Four Stages of Faith and the Five Stages of Practice," 99;

381

INDEX

on the Gohonzon, 59, 63–64, 66, 68; on happiness, 352; on human obsession, 334–35; humanism of, 190; on illness, 248–50, 259–60; "Letter from Sado," 179, 194; "Letter to Niike," 133; life state of, 46, 154, 178, 182; on manifesting the life state of Buddhahood, 60–61, 90; on memory of present life, 243; on moment of death, 328–29; on Mystic Law, 145; on Nam-myoho-renge-kyo, 25, 78, 251, 259, 317; "The Object of Devotion for Observing the Mind," 40, 46, 69, 77, 91; "The Offering of an Unlined Robe," 341; "On Offerings for Deceased Ancestors," 133; "The Opening of the Eyes," 23, 46, 194; persecutions faced by, 153–54, 188, 190; "On Prayer," 120; "The Real Aspect of the Gohonzon," 58, 62, 68; "Reply to Sairen-bo," 132; Sado Island exile of, 46, 187, 190, 194; spring of victory for, 188; on studying death, 315; Tatsunokuchi Persecution of, 178, 187; on the three treasures, 354; on treasure of life, 253–54; writings of, 19, 35, 37, 50, 55, 62, 74, 108, 117, 135–36, 143, 153, 167, 180, 182, 186, 188, 202, 220, 224, 242, 252, 256, 265, 281, 285–86, 292, 301–2, 306, 334, 338–39, 350
Nightingale, Florence, 313; artful life of, 311–13; on death, 313; on successors, 313
nine worlds [the realm of ordinary people], 16, 43, 45–47; world of Buddhahood compared to the, 42, 47, 94–95, 175
Nirvana Sutra, 250, 256, 334
Nobel Peace Prize, 296

Norton, David L., on Buddhist model of diversity, 223

O

object of devotion, life's direction and, 53; manifesting the, 60–61
objectivity, 323
"observing the mind," Gohonzon for, 77–8
obstacles, facing, 175, 196, 276; overcoming, 32–33, 96, 125, 180, 205, 259
older adults, 201, 284, 292–93, 304; attitude toward, 305–6; respecting, 287, 301; responsibility to show victory of happiness by, 191
oneness of life and death, the, 326
oneness of life and its environment, the, 13
oneness of life and the universe, the, 328
oneness of mentor and disciple, the, xiv–xvi, 147–48
opinions, 201
optimism, 14, 23–24, 295; leading lives of, 29–31
ordinary people; era of, 65–66
"other power," 97–98
outlook, changing the present, 156

P

"palace of happiness," opening the, 12–14
"palace of oneself," opening the, 12–14
parents, appreciation to, 342; happiness of, 342–43
passion, living with, 311
patience, 212, 252, 274, 318
peace, 4, 106–7, 111
peace and security, achieving inner "palace" of, 300
people, creating a new age of the, 152, 285

INDEX

persecutions, 187
perseverance, 3, 39, 117, 152, 158, 160, 201, 216, 269, 308, 318, 323
Peru, members in, 101–3
philosophy, 22, 330
physics, law of conservation of energy in, 268
Picture of Dorian Gray, The (Wilde), 76–77
planets, existence of life on other, 327–28
Plato, 287, 331
poems, xvi, 19, 107, 272
poison into medicine, transforming, 172–73, 176
Popeye (cartoon), 205
positive forces of the universe, increasing the influence of, 56
possibilities, opening unlimited, 5
potential, developing the full inner, 52, 73, 145, 166, 181, 208, 212, 219, 277, 306
poverty, overcoming, 205
power, within, 118
praise, giving, 207, 298
prayers, 9, 117–19, 120–23, 125–27, 273–74
pre–Lotus Sutra teachings, divide between Buddha and ordinary people in the, 96–98; incomplete truth in the, 94–95
present, living in the, 5, 183, 235, 295, 321, 336, 342, 349, 355
pride, 14, 213
prolonging one's life through faith, 262, 301
prosperity, 154, 228–29
protagonists, people as, 106–7
protective forces, of the universe, 79, 103, 137, 252, 304, 317, 349
psychological disorders, facing, 252–53
psychology, 106, 241

Q

quality, 287

R

reborn just as we desire, 344
Record of the Orally Transmitted Teaching, The, xii, 12, 16–17, 37, 42, 78, 103, 159, 161, 170, 198, 233, 284, 298, 325, 341
regrets, living lives without, 27–28
relationships, 285
religion, 94, 203, 330; serving the people and, 224
resentment, cause of, 51
respect, 219, 222, 234, 236; for the dignity of life, 85, 239–40, 310; for others, 221, 233, 240
responsibility, 48, 121, 137, 282
result, getting the best, 125, 128–29
retirement, illusion of, 304
revitalization, xii, 123, 280–81; inner, 279; rhythm, setting a daily, 6, 130
role model, for others, 147–48, 190, 198, 223, 240
Russia, 274
Russian Orthodox Church, 177

S

Sado Island, 78, 154, 300
saha world, transforming the, 7, 38
Sammi-bo, 148; arrogance of, 149; defeated by devilish functions, 150–51
satisfaction, 39, 123, 206–7, 286
Schweitzer, Albert, 296
Scott, Walter, 166
security, 45–46; sense of, 103
seeking spirit, xv, 291–92
self-centeredness, promoting humanitarian competition and, 225
self-confidence, 49, 51, 167, 306; building, 208–8
self-control, 42, 48, 279
self-development, 232
self-disciple, 101
self-identity, sense of, 198–99, 209

INDEX

self-importance, 137
self-improvement, 6, 101, 130, 202, 207, 210, 218, 233, 255
self-interest, 149, 195
self-mastery, 80, 133; commitment to, 19; lacking, 119
"self-power," activating, 97–98
self-reflection, 48
self-restraint, 222
Sennichi, lay nun (wife of Abutsu-bo), 300
sense organs, purifying the six, 17–18
separation, encouragement to families suffering, 338–40
SGI, aligning with the, 101; human revolution and the, 225; philosophical foundation and, 310
SGI Day, 222
SGI Day Peace Proposal, of 2013, 305
SGI members, 331
SGI-Peru, pioneer members of, 244
Shakespeare, 165
Shakyamuni, 2, 50, 55, 63, 69–70, 85–86, 104, 122, 168–69, 217, 231, 288, 294, 301, 305–6, 310, 340, 343, 351, 353–54; on attitude on aging, 307–8; eternity of life and, 322–23; exemplifying the spirit of equality, 231–33; on happiness, 232; inspiration for, 330–31; Nam-myoho-renge-kyo and, 71; obtaining the same benefits as, 91–92; promoting the Law, 312; "relying on the Law" and, 146–47
Shariputra, 289
Shijo Kingo, 178, 180, 296
Sho-bo, 150
Sholokhov, Mikhail, 243
Silk Road, 54
sincerity, 340; interacting with, 233
six paths, 41–43
slander, 79
sleep, fresh start and, 278–79
smiling, importance of, 140–41

society, building a better, xiii, 13, 43, 162, 169, 279, 285, 301; building a humanistic, 218, 253; creating a peaceful, 110–11; kosen-rufu in, 47
Soka (grassroots movement), new age of, xii–xiv
Soka Gakkai (literally, "Value-Creating Society"), 8, 25, 31–32, 183, 195, 290, 294; living in the realm of the, 30, 296; "object of devotion for kosen-rufu" and, 68; pioneer members of the, 244; religious revolution and, 15, 18; unity of the, 52
Soka Gakkai activities, 79, 281, 296, 303, 337; inner strength and, 238; for kosen-rufu, 304; self-development and, 202
Soka Gakkai discussion meeting, a model for older adults in society, 287
Soka Gakkai members, xv, xvii, 59, 252, 265, 283, 296–97, 301
Soka Gakkai spirit, xv, 50, 121, 195, 289
speech(es), commemorating anniversary of Josei Toda's death, 203–6; at First Nationwide Women's Division Leaders Meeting, 15–19
stagnation, overcoming, 161, 255, 280
strength, 3, 24, 177, 196, 213, 237, 259, 273, 275, 281, 316
stress, relieving, 278
study, of Buddhism, xv
successors, xv–xvi
sufferings, 171–72, 269–71; facing, 168, 174; helping the, 344; joy and, 180, 181; overcoming, 3–4, 16–17, 50, 59–60, 84, 102, 105, 114, 144, 175, 241, 255, 276; source of, 219
sufferings of life and death lead to nirvana, 172
support, xiii, 106, 118, 211, 275

INDEX

T

talent, innate, 213, 215
ten factors of life, 108
Ten Worlds, 37–38, 40, 55, 63, 78, 87; basic life tendency and, 44; increasing the influence of the 56, 64–65
three bodies, 17, 200
three existences, 4, 14, 17, 30, 36, 61, 157, 159, 173, 176, 194, 257, 286, 336, 342, 349
Three Great Secret Laws, 38, 190
three obstacles and four devils, facing the, 34; workings of the 346
three thousand realms in a single moment in life, 35–36, 63, 65, 78, 138, 175, 204; life philosophy in the teaching of, 165
three treasures, 8–9, 242, 354–55
T'ien-t'ai, 2, 68, 281; *Great Concentration and Insight*, 54
time management, 278
Toda, Josei, xvi, 26, 45, 61, 92, 147, 151, 195, 204, 206, 217, 225, 245, 248, 253, 278; awareness of, 15, 97; on closing years of life, 312; on daimoku [Nam-myoho-renge-kyo], 255; and daughter, Yasuyo's, death, 345; on death, 321, 328; on encouragement, 345; on fighting spirit, 299; global family call by, 223; on Gohonzon, 2, 58–59, 113, 255; on happiness, 6–7; on happiness of others, 228; on human body, 251; on illness, 258; on living the Buddhist way, 203–4; as people's leaders, xi–xii; on youth division, 205–6, 216
"Toda University," xii
Toki, lay nun (wife of Toki Jonin), 259, 298; facing illness, 259–60
Toki Jonin, 99, 259
Tokyo, 198–99, 303
tolerance, 24
Tolstoy, Leo, 234; on joy, 177; life state of, 329
Toynbee, Arnold J., 329
"the transience of all phenomena," 330
"Treasure Tower" chapter (Lotus Sutra), 63
treasures of the heart, accumulating the, 321; manifesting the, 8–9
true aspect of all phenomena, 63, 65, 86, 115. *See also* Nam-myoho-renge-kyo
trust, 236
truth, 350; awareness of the, 106, 232
turning point, making effort at the, 210
two vehicles, persons of the, 289
twenty-first century, creating a peaceful, 105–7

U

Ueno, lay nun (Tokimitsu's mother), 338–39
Ullman, Samuel, 289
understanding, 22, 24, 153–55
uniqueness, appreciation of, 220; respect for, 221
United Nations Sustainable Development Goals, xiv
unity, xiii
universe, Buddhist perspective of the, 344; compassion of the, 132–33; law of the, 218; life and, 111–12; life forms and, 4; in rhythm with the, 114, 192, 278

V

value creation, 5, 8, 56, 64, 73, 88, 125, 162, 179, 222, 224–25, 250, 259, 276, 287, 310, 316, 321, 335; difficulties as impetus to lead lives of, 174–75
Vasubandhu, 68

INDEX

victory, 6, 101, 115–17, 140, 160, 165, 172–73, 202, 235, 247, 252, 254–55, 274–75, 268, 282, 296, 340; in the end, 158, 268–69; experiencing spring of, 39, 189, 191; over inner habits, 276; transforming into place of, 39
Vimalakirti Sutra, 250, 256
vitality, 10, 49, 142, 283, 291–92, 296
voice, exercising the, 278; for kosen-rufu, 96, 132
votary of the Lotus Sutra, Nichiren Daishonin as the, 37, 105, 117, 178, 259
vow, xvi, 88

W

weakness, overcoming inner, 49, 146
wealth, spiritual, 287
Wilde, Oscar, 76
"winter always turns to spring," 186, 189
wisdom, xii, xvi, 2–3, 5–6, 13, 24, 29, 54, 56, 58, 61, 64, 84, 86, 88–89, 101, 109, 113–15, 120, 133, 162, 176, 181, 227, 229, 237–38, 256–57, 264, 279, 281, 302, 306, 336, 338, 355; compassion compared to, 228;
for daily life, 224, 261; for happiness, 248; lives with, 242
"The Wisdom for Creating Happiness," xv, xvii
"wonderful workings of one mind," showing proof of, 155, 169
World War II, xi; postwar, 223, 336

Y

Yamagata Prefecture, 197, 199
Yamamoto, Shin'ichi, 101, 200, 262, 346, 348
Yellow River, China, 213
young men's division, hopes for the, 142
young women's division, hopes for the, 142
young women's division nurses group, 277
yourself, living true to, 49, 97, 122, 172, 181, 199, 207, 212, 217, 236; valuing, 52
"Youth" (Ullman poem), 289
youth, happiness viewed by, 38; hopes for, 143, 355; life of, 289–90; third stage of, 284–85, 290; trust and, 206; vigor of, 287
youth division, hopes for the, 158

ABOUT THE AUTHOR

Daisaku Ikeda, born in Tokyo, Japan, on January 2, 1928, is a peacebuilder, Buddhist philosopher, educator, author, and poet. He became the third president of the Soka Gakkai in 1960 and is respected as one of the three founding presidents—along with Tsunesaburo Makiguchi and Josei Toda—in light of his unparalleled leadership and contribution to the organization's development throughout the world. He has also served as president of the Soka Gakkai International (SGI), an international association of the Soka Gakkai, since its foundation in 1975. The Soka Gakkai is a global community-based Buddhist organization that promotes peace, culture, and education centered on respect for the dignity of life.

ABOUT THE AUTHOR

Ikeda has written numerous essays, articles, and books on the Buddhist philosophy of Nichiren Daishonin and the Lotus Sutra and its application to life in the modern world.

Ikeda is also the founder of the Soka (value-creating) school system based on an ideal of fostering each student's unique creative potential and cultivating an ethos of peace, social contribution, and global awareness. The Soka school system runs from kindergarten in several countries to graduate study in Japan and the US. He has also founded a number of international nonprofit peace and cultural institutions.

Since 1983, Ikeda has penned an annual peace proposal addressing themes such as abolition of nuclear weapons, international dialogue and cooperation, environmental conservation, and human rights. In recognition of his efforts to promote peace, he was awarded the United Nations Peace Medal in 1983 and the United Nations High Commissioner for Refugees Humanitarian Award in 1989.

Ikeda's various works have been translated into fifty languages. In particular, he has published dialogues with more than seventy prominent individuals including Arnold Toynbee, Joseph Rotblat, Mikhail Gorbachev, Abdurrahman Wahid, Adolfo Pérez Esquivel, Elise Boulding, and Linus Pauling.

Ikeda has been awarded around four hundred honorary degrees and academic honors from universities and institutions of higher learning around the world.